Also by Betty Rohde:

So Fat, Low Fat, No Fat

More So Fat, Low Fat, No Fat

Italian So Fat, Low Fat, No Fat

Mexican So Fat, Low Fat, No Fat

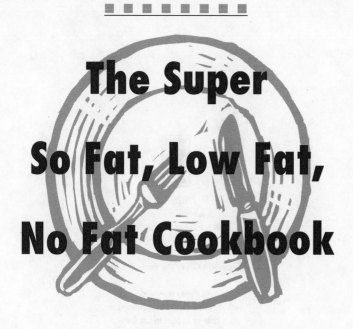

The Super
So Fat, Low Fat,
No Fat Cookbook

Betty Rohde

A FIRESIDE BOOK
Published by Simon & Schuster

FIRESIDE
Rockefeller Center
1230 Avenue of the Americas
New York, NY 10020

Manufactured in the United States of America

1   3   5   7   9   10   8   6   4   2

Library of Congress Cataloging-in-Publication Data
Rohde, Betty.
The super so fat, low fat, no fat cookbook / Betty Rohde.
p.   cm.
"A Fireside book."
Includes index.
1. Low fat diet—Recipes.   I. Title.
RM237.7.R629   1997
641.5'638—dc21   97-31848
CIP

ISBN 0-684-84998-4

This book incorporates materials previously published in
So Fat, Low Fat, No Fat copyright © 1993 by Betty Rohde and
More So Fat, Low Fat, No Fat copyright © 1996 by Bette Rohde

Dedication of this book is again to Bob, as he is still my guinea pig, official taster, and critical critiquer, and he is still alive. He certainly has been an asset to each and every one of you, as well as to me. You don't have any idea how many rejects get produced along with the accepted. He is just about to get a little concerned with what is on his plate in the evening. Seems like it doesn't matter—he eats it and does his critiquing and believe me he does express his opinion, for which I am very grateful, even if I don't agree. You know what Billy Graham said about a married couple: "If you both agreed on everything, one of you would be unnecessary." Well, I wouldn't ever want him to think I am unnecessary, so I see to it that I remain necessary.

Thank you, Bob, for being such a caring and concerned companion. Most of all, thank you for your taste buds and for some of your opinions. Lifetime love surrounds you.

Contents

Introduction

HOW I LOST 40 POUNDS
IN 6 MONTHS
WITHOUT EVER BEING HUNGRY,
WAS STABLE FOR 3 MONTHS,
LOST 20 MORE POUNDS
IN THE NEXT 3 MONTHS,
LOWERED MY CHOLESTEROL
FROM 274 TO 210
IN THE FIRST 6 MONTHS, AND
LOWERED MY TRIGLYCERIDES
FROM 678 TO 240
IN THE FIRST 6 MONTHS

I had been having health problems for some time and was feeling very depressed. I finally made a visit to the doctor for a checkup, and what I found was not at all a pretty picture. My doctor told me, "Lady, you're a walking time bomb." I was sitting on my porch when I got the phone call from him advising me of my terribly high counts. After our conversation, I sat there looking at the spring that was coming alive. We live in the country in a big Victorian-style house that is just a few years old, with all the beauty surrounding us that many dream of in fairytale books.

My family is close, my town is clean, my church is alive and growing, my friends are fun, my husband is supportive—what more could a person ask? I believe that was the moment I decided that I and I alone had to do something to improve my health and just maybe I better listen to Mr. Doctor Man.

I knew that I had to completely change my life and the way I ate, the way I shopped, the way I cooked, even the way I thought. That may just have been the real challenge.

I made dinner that night, cooking the old standby for dieters: broiled chicken breast and steamed vegetables. I sat there eating that tasteless meal knowing that this would be it for some time. I made up my mind that I was going to do something about my eating and health, but that I also was going to have something that was fit to eat, that tasted as good as the things I was used to eating and was at the same time helping me to improve my health.

This book will show you how I changed, rearranged, and developed my techniques. The book came to be after the first six months and I had lost forty pounds, was never hungry, never felt deprived or that I was missing anything except the fat that I had lost and I was glad to be missing that. Think of this: I was a tight size 16, now I am a 10. This was the most fun: all new clothes, plus the fun of people not knowing me. I stood and talked to a former neighbor at a Christmas party that I had not seen for over a year and she did not know me. Of course I did get a new hairdo, contacts, the works. Now, ladies, this is fun—try it. It was the easiest thing I have ever done to lose weight, and believe me I have been on *all* the diets, have lost more than I weigh three times over. The nicest thing is that I have *never* even gained one pound back. Taking it off this way keeps it off, unlike so many fad diets, where the weight comes back as soon as you get it off. You get used to eating and cooking fat-free and the weight stays off.

I had full balanced meals, entertained, ate out, baked and snacked along with our daily routines, with only a little effort and thought as to how and what I was doing with my food. It has become an effortless way of life. I don't even look for the oil in the kitchen but I do still use my skillet, as explained in this book.

I have learned moderation and balance rather than deprivation and starvation. I eat as much as I want of anything that I want as long as it is fat-free. I have never limited my portion sizes. I would have lost faster probably if I had, but well enough should be left alone. I wish you could have seen my doctor's face when he saw me—I had lost the first forty pounds without seeing him. He is so proud of me, he now uses my book and recommends it to his patients. I have learned and am enjoying the skills, techniques, and resources for healthy eating.

I love food, preparing it, experimenting with it, tasting it, talking about it, and entertaining with it. The meals I serve certainly do not skimp on the flavor or the portions. We entertain a lot, and after the first six months my friends kept saying I should write these recipes down, put some of these ideas in a book—it was working for me and why should it not be working for other people? I am grateful for the encouragement and support that led to the publication of *So Fat Low Fat No Fat*. I have met so many new friends, which is as much of an asset as anyone could ask. The moral is: Ladies, it is never too late; all you have to do is to make up your mind. I have started a complete new life and career. You never know what lies around the corner.

I never dreamed this would happen to me when I wrote my book. I made my first order for just two hundred books. It was such a hit because it is good basic down-home easy recipes. Ladies, take heed! It is *never* too late. Start *today*!!!

I started by going to the grocery store the first day for about a two-hour visit. You have to read the labels. I read everything in that store, I thought. Soon it became a challenge to see what I could find fat-free, then it became a game. It is fun. Every day since I started it seems there has been some new product on the market. When this first started for me there was very little out, but for you starting now this is going to be really easy: the market is full of fat-free products.

One day I explored in the candy counter. I read every label on that counter and came home with a basketful of candy. I was so happy, because I am a sugar freak! I know it is bad for me and if you can you should try to limit your sugar intake. This is what I told my doctor when he said to me that if I had limited my sugar and exercised I would have lost more, faster. My reply was this: "If I had cut out the fat, cut out the sugar, limited my portion sizes, and exercised myself weak, I would have lasted about two weeks." He said I was probably right, and whatever I was doing or not doing, to keep it up.

If you are wondering just what *would* I eat, here are some ideas:

Breakfast is easy. You can have an English muffin (1 gram of fat) with jelly (jelly has no fat grams). Leave *off* the butter; you'll never miss the butter after a couple of weeks. (There is a fat-free margarine on the market now; you be the judge.) I use fat-free cream cheese on the toasted muffin or bagel, or on toast—fat-free bread of course. There are so many cereals out now that are fat-free. Try them with skim milk (read your labels; just because they say "skim" does not mean they are fat-free), juice, and if you are an egg person, try scrambling some egg substitute—after about the second time you won't know the difference. We even make sandwiches in the evening with egg substitute. This is a pretty healthy breakfast, and if you had eaten everything I named you would have only had 1 gram of fat.

Lunch is just as easy—use your thinker! Brown-bag it. We do. It is economical, convenient, and healthy. And it leaves you more time to do something else, like shopping or visiting. Example: bread (fat-free), mayonnaise (fat-free), lettuce, tomato, pickle, mustard (all fat-free). Use 98 percent fat-free turkey, ham, or whatever lunch meat you like that is low in fat and you have a wonderful sandwich. You may prefer to take soup (there are plenty of fat-free soups), and a salad with fat-free dressing. You can even have fat-free cookies, cake, or candy. So far today you have had about 4 grams of fat. You're doing good!

Dinner: If you go out, choose your restaurants carefully. Beware of the places that are greasy: *keep away.* You are usually better off with a buffet-style dinner, but ordering from the menu is also easy. Order fish baked (I don't like fish so I choose something else), broiled, or poached; chicken baked, broiled, or stir-fried. Order steamed vegetables, which is what most restaurants do anyway because of the preparation time—just ask them to leave off the butter. Take your own dressing for the salad (and you should try it on a baked potato—pretty good). Be sure you always ask at every restaurant, "Do you have fat-free?" More and more establishments are starting to have low-fat and/or no-fat entries. The more we ask, the more we will be able to get them to carry. Most cafeterias will give you a vegetable plate, with three vegetables. I order mashed potatoes with no gravy or a baked potato, and a couple of veggies that look lower in seasoning—usually the broccoli without the cheese sauce and a bean of some sort.

Dessert: Forget it until you get home: this will take care of the late-night snackies anyway. I keep fat-free yogurt or ice cream on hand and fat-free cookies—that is, if I haven't had time to bake or don't have any cake around. You can stop at some ice cream establishments and get fat-free cones if you are making a night of it.

So far this one day you have had about 10 grams of fat at the most. This is what I kept my intake to, but then my doctor told me I would lose weight on 30 to 50 grams a day. I was so mad at me that I had cut to 10—but it was so easy I was surprised. I am sure that I sometimes ate more than 10 grams because I have to rely on the manufacturers' labels entirely.

I have given you an example of a day away from home. Now you can choose your meals from this book and have just as low a count. Plus sometimes you can have leftovers for your lunch next day. Everything that you could possibly need is included: entertaining, Mexican, Italian, Greek, American, and most of all, good basic down-home old-fashioned cooking without having to go to a specialty shop for your ingredients. I use everyday staples; you won't have to buy a $3.00 bottle of special seasoning for one dish and have it for the rest of your life. How many of you have that jar of weird seasoning that you have had ever since you can remember and it is starting to crystallize around the lid? I think that we all have one of those souvenirs. I live in Gore, America, with one *small* grocery store here and if I can find the ingredients here you can find them *any*where.

My recipes will help you to continue with or to start your fat-free or low-fat eating habits as well as trim your figure. I wish I had kept a log of the number of people who have come to me and said, "I have been just cooking strictly out of this book and I have lost X number of pounds in the last so many weeks or months." I have many women come to me and say, "My husband just had open heart surgery and we are now on the fat-free and he is really loving the recipes I make from your book because they taste just like normal."

After you have been on the fat-free for a couple of weeks and get used to not eating the fat, when you do eat something that is fat, your mouth will feel greasy. You will say, "*Yuck!*" One bite is all that it takes. I have numerous people ask me, "Don't you ever binge, or pig out on something that you are not supposed to eat?" My feeling is that it is not worth it. It sometimes makes me sick if I do eat even a small amount of grease, and that makes me happy, as it is like alcohol. I am happy to have the "fat habit" broken. I want it to make me sick so that I will know if I do eat it what will happen, and it is easier to just say, "No, thank you."

Include lots of fresh fruit in your daily eating. I am one of the unlucky ones who do not like fruit, so this is another hardship when trying to diet. Three things that I hate: fruit, fish, exercise. This is why I feel that I have found the secret, I have lost all this weight without those three demons. I have cut out red meat; it is said to have the largest percentage of fat of anything in our diets. I will have a filet on special occasions, but when I do, I have a baked potato and salad and skip the bread. I take my own salad dressing, don't eat the bacon around the steak, and I am OK. Just don't do it every day. Moderation. I must admit I have not had a hamburger in two years, nor a french fry. You know what? I don't even miss them. In the summer we make chicken patties, grill them on the barbie, and use our burger just as if it were beef. They are pretty good, and look at all the grams I saved!

"Eating at her house is not what it used to be, but it's not bad," said my brother.

I can guarantee you will lose weight if you do exactly as I tell you: Eat one page a day out of this book with 8 ounces of water and you will lose weight. Ha! Now try the recipes and you *will* lose weight.

Successful Entertaining

Entertaining can be very rewarding without being taxing on the hostess. The main thing is to use your head. My dad always told me, "Girl, if you don't use your head, you might as well have two rear ends." Now that I am older I must say that I agree with him. One moment to plot a plan will save you many hours of grief.

Decide how many guests you are going to have. Don't overload yourself, or first thing you know you'll have turned a fun affair into a frantic work project.

Decide what type of entertaining—casual, formal, theme, holiday, etc. You can have lots of fun with little effort. We have these friends—there are eight of us—and somehow we got the nickname "the Mangy Gang." We do all kinds of fun things, including theme-type parties. For instance, my friend Jean once had a Roadkill party. She made up menus that had all kinds of entrees like Chunk of Skunk, Snake Steak, Possum Pie, Owl Stew, and Guess This Mess. She wrote one out and copied it on a copy machine, and she and her husband dressed really neat in vests, jeans, chef hats, etc. They stood at each table and took orders as if we were at a restaurant. Of course everyone was getting the same thing (it was a New Year's party and we were having black-eyed peas and so on) but it was really fun ordering. She served on (tin) pie plates, with one spoon to eat with, fruit jars for glasses, weeds in the center of the tables, and so forth. This was a wonderful party, but there was one thing that surprised her, so all the planning in the world won't keep the unexpected from happening. What happened was we all found out the party theme, secretly talked, and every one of us wore something we dug out of the depths of our past to do with fur. I have an old rabbit coat, twenty-five years old. Bob wore overalls, tied a couple of our grandchildren's stuffed toys by the leg with a rope, and threw these over his shoulder like he had picked them up off the road. One of our group wore an old fur hat. You can really have a lot of fun doing simple inexpensive things like this. We all arrived at her house at the same time. You should have seen her face! We do have pictures.

Try your recipes ahead of time. Never advertise your menu in advance. Last-minute disasters can cause many changes that they never need to know about.

Always save time for yourself to get dressed. Look as if you haven't been doing a thing.

When entertaining special guests, like the boss or the husband's boss, don't be afraid of the menu. Don't think just because they are the boss that you have to spend a lot of money or knock yourself out with your menu. I will never forget one time I was taking on a major entertaining project. My first husband's boss was in town for an oil show, along with reps from all over the country. I did my head work—when they all arrived for a sit-down dinner I think that I was most popular. I served in the kitchen and had a regular old-fashioned beans and corn bread, ham, and potatoes dinner. I thought the men were going to kill themselves eating. The boss made the comment, "I get so tired of being served steaks everywhere I go, I am really enjoying this wonderful real food." Steaks are nice, but—everyone likes good, down-home country cooking. Try it! Doesn't have to be beans and corn bread; whatever is your specialty, your environment, your lifestyle, if it be New England lobster or Louisiana crawfish. Just be yourself, be comfortable, be friends, have fun, enjoy life. It is snuffed out too quick and too soon. Smile at everyone you meet. It makes them think you're up to no good, and wonder what's *she* been eating.

Remember Kahlúa and Cool Whip. You can cover up a multitude of sins and mistakes as well as enhance the simplest little effort with the two of these.

You may try a Road Crawl party. This is where you go from one house to another for your dinner. Some call it a Progressive party. We call it Road Crawl. One person has the before-dinner drinks, next house has hors d'oeuvres, next house has soup, next salad, next main course, next dessert. The number of courses depends on the size of the group.

If you are looking for an extraordinary way to entertain without the hassle of the menu and all the decisions, why not try a Tasting Party?

Make out your guest list and ask each person to bring something to do with the theme you are planning, such as a *So Fat, Low Fat, No Fat* party. Have each one make a recipe from their cookbook or provide them with recipes, or just see what each person can come up with in the low-no fat category. You're in for a lot of fun and a healthy party as well.

Keep the party casual—food, dress, decor, buffet-style service all casual. Eat and drink as you please, visit, discuss the recipes, enjoy the food and friends.

Parties can be so much fun and so easy. I feel people don't entertain enough these days. I think we have gotten so formal that we have neglected entertaining because of the dreaded work and worry. Forget it, be comfortable, enjoy your life.

I have also had very successful wine-tasting parties. On the invitation to the wine tasting, add the letters B.Y.O.B. and make sure the guests are told that the last B stands for Not Tried Before Bottle of wine, or their favorite wine. Everyone who comes will bring a different kind of wine. Provide small glasses for a taste of each one, as well as the snacks—fat-free, of course. We have found out about some of the nicest wines this way. In the summer you can also do this with beer if you're planning a patio party or cookout.

Serve food that complements either the wine or beer theme, whichever the case may be.

You may even want to have a judging. Give small pieces of paper and pencils for your guests to make their choice and vote on the "Best of the Bash."

My most fearful nightmare is that on the night of the party, only two people show up, or that my food and drinks run out after the first ten minutes. I don't know which one I fear the most. To avoid these fears, I try to plan ahead with the following steps:

- Guest list: Decide whom you are inviting and write down the names to avoid forgetting someone.
- Invitations: They can be as informal as a phone call or a quick chat with someone in the hall or at church. Just be sure the communication is clear. Poor communication is the root of all evil. Be it a party or a marriage, good communication is the key. The time, place, kind of party—formal, informal, birthday, whatever the occasion—be sure everyone gets all the statistics. Wouldn't you hate to show up in that cute devil suit grinning from ear to ear at the company party instead of the costume party?

  It is also appropriate to limit the time of a cocktail party. The invitation may say "4 to 7" or "Stop by any time between 4 and 8 P.M." for an open house.

- SCHEDULE

Two to three weeks in advance
Plan menu and cooking schedule.
Check nonfood supplies.
Begin purchase of nonperishables; arrange for rentals.

One to two weeks in advance
Begin purchasing beverages.
Begin preparing foods that can be made in advance and stored (frozen).
Start making extra ice—maybe an ice mold if you're planning to use one.
Discuss extra parking with neighbors if necessary.

Three to six days in advance
Begin decorating.
Make sure all is in order with your glassware, dishes, utensils.
(If large ones are needed, borrow or rent.)

One to two days in advance
Buy perishables.
Purchase flowers and other fresh decorations.
Make extra room in the refrigerator by removing nonperishables to store elsewhere.
Make sure there is a place for guests' coats.
Check your tapes or CDs for appropriate music; you may need to borrow some.
Wash, clean, and cut vegetables and salad greens; store in individual plastic bags.
Make dips and/or salsa.

Day of party
Chill beverages early.
Finish food preparations.
Set out garbage cans.
Make sure all is in order in the bathroom.
Make sure there is a place for guests to put used dishes and glasses.
Set out some kind of outdoor decoration to identify your place for guests who have not been there before.
Time for your beauty treatment.
Welcome guests, make introductions, mingle, and enjoy.

Cooking for a Crowd

ITEM	12 SERVINGS	24 SERVINGS	48 SERVINGS
Punch	1½ quarts	3 quarts	1½ gallons
Iced tea	3 quarts	1½ gallons	3 gallons
Coffee			
(brewed)	9 cups	18 cups	36 cups
Cookies	2 dozen	4 dozen	8 dozen
Cakes			
9 x 13	1 cake	2 cakes	3 cakes
10-inch tube			
9-inch layer			
Tossed salad	4½ quarts	9 quarts	4½ gallons
Rolls	2 dozen	3 dozen	6 dozen
Meats			
(boneless)	3 pounds	6 pounds	12 pounds
Meats			
(bone in)	9 pounds	18 pounds	35 pounds
Cold cuts	2 pounds	4 pounds	8 pounds
Casseroles			
9 x 13	1 casserole	2 casseroles	4 casseroles
8-inch square	2 casseroles	4 casseroles	8 casseroles
Potato salad,			
coleslaw, or			
baked beans	1½ quarts	3 quarts	1½ gallons
Chicken salad	3 quarts	1½ gallons	3 gallons

The number of servings doesn't necessarily mean the number of guests served. Plan on one drink per hour per guest.

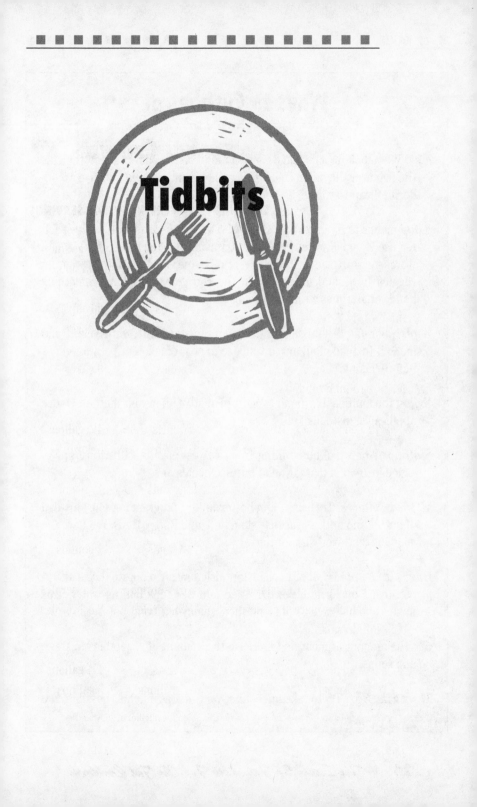

Tidbits

Ways to Cut the Fat

Fish: When baking fish, place rings of onion on the baking sheet, then lay the fish over the onion rings. This will prevent sticking and give a wonderful flavor to your fish.

Sauté means to fry quickly. Instead of sautéing in oil as most recipes call for, use ¼ cup of water instead, or try using chicken broth, rice vinegar, Worcestershire sauce, lime juice, or red wine vinegar. I save broth from veggies in a small container in the refrigerator to have something handy at all times without the expense.

Yogurt, non-fat: Try mixing a little Dijon mustard with some yogurt and using it instead of oil or mayonnaise to coat chicken or potato wedges before baking.

Yogurt the muffins. Use nonfat yogurt instead of oil in your muffins. Or use applesauce instead of oil.

Stuffing: When making stuffing from a two-step mix, substitute applesauce instead of margarine or butter. Nice flavor.

Mashed Potatoes: Try using skim buttermilk (1 fat gram per cup) instead of butter and milk, or just use skim milk and Butter Buds. You have the good butter flavor without the fat.

Hurry-up Potatoes: Mix 2 cups instant dried mashed potato flakes and ⅓ cup dried buttermilk powder, then add 2¾ cups boiling water. This makes about 4 cups of quick mashed, somewhat tangy potatoes.

Cut the amount of meat and increase the amount of vegetables in stews and soups.

There's the Beef: Try to take beef out of your diet as much as possible. You can substitute chicken or turkey in almost every recipe and never be unhappy with the flavor.

Sugar: You can reduce the amount of sugar in your baked goods by at least ⅓ and never know the difference. In all dishes except baked goods, you can use undiluted frozen apple juice, pears, bananas, or honey. Honey is sweeter and you will need less of it than you will of sugar.

Chocolate: Use 3 tablespoons of unsweetened cocoa powder and 1 tablespoon of polyunsaturated oil in place of each ounce of baking chocolate.

Cornstarch Trick: When using yogurt in hot dishes, add 1 teaspoon cornstarch for every cup of yogurt to keep it from separating on heating. If you are out of yogurt and in a hurry, blend 1 cup nonfat cottage cheese and 1 tablespoon of lemon juice with 2 tablespoons of skim milk. Try the cornstarch trick when using nonfat cream cheese also.

Fry Habit: Break the fry habit with broiling, roasting, baking, steaming, poaching, and stir-frying as your main cooking habit. Use the skillet for dry frying and sautéing but forget the oil.

Boil your stew meat or meat for your beans the day before and refrigerate the broth. The fat will congeal on the top. Next day, lift it off and go on with your recipe. You've still got the taste, and you've left the fat behind.

Trim any and all the fat you can possibly see from anything you are cooking. Saves you having to trim it from *you* later.

Eggs: I never use an egg anymore. You can use egg substitute—¼ cup per 1 egg—in any recipe. You will never know the difference.

Salsa: Serving salsa is a good way to cut the fat. Use it instead of salad dressings to marinate chicken or fish, or serve it as a spicy side dish to curb the use of fatty sauces. Try it on your baked potato.

Extra: Cook a little extra of your fat-free meal and put into a divided microwave plate with a cover. Freeze, then take this to work instead of going out for lunch.

Switch to fat-free everything you can find on the market shelves. If you watch your fat intake you don't need to worry about counting your calories.

Water: Start every meal with a glass of water; this helps prevent overeating. Water is the best lubricant there is for your skin. It makes you pretty in more ways than one. Helps your complexion, helps your figure.

Weekends: Be good on weekends. Two days of overindulging can ruin five days of discipline. Make this low-fat eating a way of life, every day, all the time. Think low-fat. See what you can find and what you can eat— the markets are getting loaded with good low-fat products. There were none when I started; now it is a snap.

KEYS TO LIFELONG WEIGHT CONTROL

1. *Avoid fat foods.*
2. *Eat lots of whole grains, whole fruits, beans, and most vegetables,* which are good sources of high-fiber foods. Dietary fiber has a bulking effect that can aid in appetite control.
3. *Exercise.* The calories burned during exercise boost your metabolic rate and increase your body's capacity to burn fat.

"The single most influential dietary change one can make to lower the risk of these diseases is to reduce intake of foods high in fat and to increase the intake of foods high in complex carbohydrates and fiber."
—The Surgeon General's Report on Nutrition and Health (1988)

"It is calculated that, if intake of dietary fat were reduced from the present 40 percent of total calorie intake to 25 percent, about 9,000 lives would be saved annually."
—National Cancer Institute, Annual Review of Public Health

"Eating less fat can reduce the risk of colon, prostate, and breast cancer."
—National Research Council, "Diet and Health" (1989)

Seasonings

Adding a dash of this and a pinch of that is expensive. I try not to use any spices and/or herbs that are not the commonly used regular-on-the-shelf type. Can't find those fancy out-of-the-ordinary spices in Gore, America, anyway.

SHOPPING

Look for bottles or jars with screw-top lids or tins with tight-fitting lids. These types are more airtight.

Shop at large stores that continually restock the shelves. "Old" seasonings with a dull color are safe to use but don't have much flavor.

Purchase dried herbs and spices in small amounts. Once opened, they begin to deteriorate after three months if not stored properly.

For maximum flavor, purchase whole spices and crush small amounts with a mortar and pestle, meat mallet, or rolling pin, or even the bottom of a cast-iron skillet. Grind larger amounts in a pepper mill, coffee grinder, or blender.

STORAGE

Store dried seasonings in a cool, dry, dark place. Protection from heat, moisture, and strong light is essential.

Don't display seasonings on open racks above or near stovetops, ovens, or dishwashers. Heat speeds their deterioration.

Store dried whole spices and herbs in the freezer for up to three years. Store ground seasonings in the freezer for up to six months.

Record the date of purchase with a permanent marker on the container.

Check for a change in color, a musty odor, or a faint aroma. These indicate a spice that is past its prime. Doubling the amount will not make up the difference or loss in flavor.

GARLIC

Select firm heads with plump outside cloves and no noticeable sprouting or dark spots. The flavor of sprouted garlic is harsh. If it must be used, cut the clove in half and remove the center green-colored sprout.

Crushed, minced, or pressed garlic is more intense than garlic cloves that are halved, sliced, or left whole.

Press a clove through a garlic press with the peel left on in order to produce maximum flavor and leave hands odor free. To remove garlic odor from hands, rub them first with lemon juice, then salt; rinse and wash next with soap.

To peel, place the flat side of a chef's knife blade on top of the garlic clove and hit it with your fist. The blow separates the papery skin from the clove for easy removal.

Store whole heads of garlic in a cool, dark, well-ventilated place up to eight weeks. Once broken from the head, individual cloves will keep up to about ten days.

Garlic yields: 1 medium clove garlic equals ½ teaspoon minced fresh or ½ teaspoon minced from a jar or ⅛ teaspoon garlic powder or instant minced garlic.

Source: *America's Best Recipes*

For Working Women

THINGS TO KEEP ON HAND FOR QUICK, EASY COOKING IN MINUTES

Breaded chicken tenders
Oriental frozen stir-fry vegetables
Frozen chopped onions
Frozen chopped green peppers
Fat-free chicken broth
Canned tomatoes—stewed
Dried macaroni
Frozen breaded fish fillets
Frozen chicken patties for burgers

SNACKS

Keep snacks in your purse, briefcase, gym bag, car, etc. Eating a fat-free snack several times a day is better than one burger or candy bar. I eat as much and as often as I want as long as it is fat-free.

Bagels
Breadsticks
Dry cereal—fat-free
Fig bars—fat-free
Granola bars—fat-free
Popcorn cakes
Rice cakes
Pretzels—fat-free
Raw vegetables
Vegetable juice
Fresh fruit

Dried fruit
Frozen juice bars
Fat-free ice cream
Fat-free frozen yogurt
Nonfat yogurt
String cheese—fat-free
Skim chocolate milk
Lunch meat (95% to 98% fat-free)
Water-packed tuna
Turkey breast meat

Hints and Tips

1. Keep a jar of whole nutmegs and a small grater on your spice shelf. Just a sprinkle or two will perk up the flavor on steamed vegetables, mashed potatoes, and rice, for example.
2. Try "cutting" experimenting while in the kitchen. When baking, *cut* back on the amount of butter, margarine, and shortening, or *cut* them out. Often, low-fat yogurt or buttermilk can substitute for the missing fats without noticeable difference. (How do you think we write cookbooks? Everything we eat is an experiment and sometimes an experience.)
3. Marinate your boneless skinless chicken breast in fruit juices flavored with light low-sodium soy sauce, flavored with spices or herbs instead of the oil-based marinades. Try: orange juice with tarragon, pineapple juice with rosemary, or apple juice with ground or fresh ginger.
4. The next time you bake a cake from a mix, try substituting an equal amount of applesauce for the shortening called for on the package and an equal amount of egg substitute for the number of eggs called for ($\frac{1}{4}$ cup = 1 egg). You'll trim a good-sized amount of fat grams just by doing this. Don't tell—no one will know the difference.
5. Try using balsamic vinegar, which has almost no trace at all of fat or calories, sprinkled on a baked potato. More restaurants will probably have this than fat-free dressing, although some are starting to carry fat-free dressing as well as many other items. *Ask* every time you eat out. The more we ask, the more they will help us out. Balsamic vinegar, used sparingly, will also add a special touch to your salad dressings, marinades, pastas, and meats. The best has a sweet-tart, oak-aged blend of flavors and a syrupy consistency.
6. Keep a shaker of confectioners' sugar mixed with ground cinnamon and cloves handy. Use it instead of butter or margarine to dust pancakes, waffles, oatmeal, acorn squash, steamed squash, toast. Again, I say, experiment!

7. Grate the zest (peel) of your citrus fruits after squeezing; store in a zipper-lock plastic bag and freeze to spark up fish, chicken, salads, vegetables, and desserts.

8. Try out some of the prepared mustards. Many are fat-free and will spice up everything from salad dressing to dips.

9. Shake butter-flavored granules over hot moist foods to get the butter flavor that so many of us desire. There are many flavors to choose from—garlic, sour cream, cheese, regular, and no telling what by the time this book gets published. The market has something new every day. I found fat-free wieners yesterday.

10. Use crunchy nugget-type cereals as stand-ins for nuts in batters and for toppings also.

11. If you want to thicken your gravy, sauces, and soups, try puréed vegetables instead of fat and flour; use potatoes, dried peas, winter squash, beans, etc. If you are making a stew, just take some of the vegetables out, place in the blender, purée, and return to the stew to thicken the remaining liquid.

12. Think you are going to die without whipped cream during the holidays? Try whipping evaporated skim milk, and add a touch of vanilla extract or confectioners' sugar for added richness. The secret is get the milk, bowl, and beaters very cold before starting to whip, and it will whip just like cream. Remember, don't tell.

13. Try a little jelly or marmalade thinned with fruit juice as a glaze for meat. Hot pepper jelly is also a nice spicy touch.

14. Use commercial fat-free salad dressings for more than just your salad. Try them on your baked potato, on steamed vegetables, or as a dip. They are great and quick for parties. You may even decide to experiment and add a little more fat-free mayonnaise or Miracle Whip, a little balsamic vinegar, a spicy mustard—or just use them straight out of the bottle.

15. As you will notice after reading some of the recipes, my nonstick skillet is indispensable. *Break* the fry habit but keep out the skillet; you can do wonders with a nonstick pan. Without the stick of butter, you can do wonders getting into last year's jeans.

16. If you hate vegetables like my friend Shirley, you can get your daily dose in a concealed way. (This is also good for fooling kids into getting

their needed amount of veggies.) Dice or shred zucchini, carrots, bell peppers, eggplant, onions, mushrooms, or just about any vegetable and add to your spaghetti sauce. This is one thing almost all kids will eat and so will Shirley. What she doesn't know won't hurt her. (Ha ha, Shirley. Be careful what you think you're eating at my house.)

17. Keep a roll of heavy aluminum foil handy in the summer. Place a few vegetables of your choice, such as onion, carrots, peppers, whatever is in season, on top of a chicken cutlet or chicken tender or a piece of fish. Sprinkle some wine over all, or some fat-free chicken broth. (Keep a can in your pantry for quick fixings.) Fold and crimp the foil edges to form a packet, place on the grill, and cook your entire meal in one. You can also do this on a cookie sheet in a hot oven, about 400 degrees.

18. Keep a bag of sun-dried tomatoes on hand. Choose the ones you simply soak in water instead of the ones packed in oil. Cut them into slivers or dice fine and add to pasta dishes, chicken, and vegetable dishes. They will also add a very nice flavor to pasta salads. Remember where I live—Gore, America—so I can only get these when I go to town. That is what we say down here in the South when we go into the city. But I do have fun going to the grocery stores in the city, as much fun as to the clothing department stores (I lied), oops!

19. Fresh herbs make a world of difference in the taste of your dish. You can plant small pots of basil, oregano, sage, rosemary, parsley, and other fragrant varieties and keep them on your kitchen windowsill. You get much enjoyment out of having your own home-grown herbs. I guess being a farmer's daughter shows I do like to grow things myself (although it's much easier to filch off brother).

20. If you desire bacon crumbles on salads or on your sandwich, cook turkey bacon crisp, crumble it, and use instead of regular bacon. Much less fat, same flavor.

21. Eat beans at least twice a week. They are great heart food, are rich in protein and fiber but lean in fat. Red meat, on the other hand, is one of the highest sources of fat and contains no fiber. It is fine to eat meat in moderation—that's your choice—but you can fill up on beans (legumes) such as white, pinto, (brown) navy, chick-peas, lentils, butter, lima, whatever kind you choose. This brings me to another story.

My escort in one of the cities I toured in with Simon & Schuster last year had never heard of eating a bowl of beans. This young lady is in for a real surprise. She asked me if it took a while to acquire a taste for them and how could anyone sit down and eat a whole bowl of just beans. I couldn't believe my ears. Poor girl, I just think of how much gas she has missed out on during her lifetime. Why, I can't imagine. I felt so sorry for her, I just think I will Fed-Ex her a quart of good home-cooked brown beans. She may move to Oklahoma, or the involuntary gastric explosion may move her out here before she is quite ready. Bless her heart, I love her anyway, even if she doesn't know "beans."

22. Eat a carrot and an orange every day. Researchers are convinced that eating foods high in antioxidant nutrients—including vitamins C and E and beta-carotene—may help prevent heart disease, cancer, and other chronic diseases associated with aging. (I think I will eat two a day.) Carrots are loaded with beta-carotene, oranges with vitamin C. Other foods rich in antioxidants are broccoli, cantaloupe, apricots, spinach, sweet potatoes, and winter squash.

23. You know I hate three things: fruit, fish, and exercise. Even so, I am encouraging you to do all three. Do as I say, not as I do. You should also try to eat fresh fruit instead of just drinking the fruit juice. Juice is a breakfast favorite, but if you eat the whole fruit not only do you get a fiber boost when choosing fruit over juice but eating a piece of fruit takes longer to consume—which tricks you into feeling as if you've eaten more. I will eat an orange, a grapefruit, or an apple on occasion but the other fruits I can't handle. Then again, do as I say. (I do make myself drink orange juice in the morning, so I do practice what I preach. Just had you fooled, didn't I?)

24. Try to include pasta in your diet at least three times a week. It is low in fat as well as filling. Try a cold pasta salad for lunch. Pasta contains any needed B-complex vitamins, iron, and calcium. It is cholesterol-free with the exception of egg noodles—stay away from those—remember eggs are a no-no. Pasta contains little sodium. Use skim milk instead of cream when making white sauces for pasta; use cheese sparingly as a flavor accent, and make it a low-fat or fat-free cheese. Look for prepared tomato sauce that is made without oil, such as

Healthy Choice. If you count calories, a serving of 2 ounces of pasta will contain only 210 calories. I don't count calories, but if you care to do this it is fine. There again, let me say you have to make up *your* mind what you are going to do and then the rest is easy. *Making up your mind* is the key to success in anything you do. If you don't, you are wasting your time.

25. Butter Buds: I use lots of liquid-form Butter Buds in my recipes, and I guess that the most asked question I have heard is "What are liquid-form Butter Buds and where do you get them?" These are granules or sprinkles, and are in a shaker-top container, but they also are in box mix form, and can be used either way. They are in envelopes that have instructions on how much water to add to each. A number you can call if you cannot find them or have questions is (800) 231-1123.

ABCs of Healthy Living

ALTERNATIVES: Save fat and calories by switching from regularly used cheese, sour cream, etc., to fat-free.

BALANCE: Balance your food choices. If you eat a meal that is higher in fat than you know you should be eating, make the next one low-fat or no-fat. If you have something moderately high in fat, balance it with steamed veggies or items with no fat.

CELEBRATIONS: Don't fall victim; choose low-fat or no-fat dips, tortilla chips, angel food cakes. There are so many chips, etc., on the market you can really just about have everything you would normally but *fat-free*.

DRESSINGS: Fat-free bottled dressings taste just as good as their heavyweight brothers and sisters. Carry them with you in your purse—they can be used on everything. (Well, maybe not ice cream.)

EXERCISE: Exercise is as important as a good diet (I hate it!!). Walking will do just as well, but walk briskly for 30 minutes three or four times a week.

FAST FOOD: Forget it, folks. If you find yourself in this position, choose the salad bar with caution. Remember to take your own dressing.

GUILT: Don't be too hard on yourself. Food is meant to be enjoyed—just be careful how good a time you have. And be more careful how you prepare it. If you go overboard one day, ease up the next.

HALF: If you can't resist something illegal, halve it or share with a skinny friend. (We all have *one* of those!)

ICE: Try fruit ices, sorbet, or sherbets.

JUNK FOOD: Keep healthy nibbles on hand. Try low-fat and no-fat pretzels, baked tortilla chips, etc.

KICK THE HABIT: Once you kick the fry habit, you've got it made. A few minutes more to prepare, a lot less fat grams to wear.

LABELS: Read *all* labels before buying. The 0 fat labels are what you're looking for. If it says "zero fat grams" it is in my basket, I don't care what it is! My husband just warned me, "Stay out of the dog food section. Please."

MIDMORNING: If a midmorning snack is a part of your day, pass up the pastry; go for fruit or an English muffin.

NONSTICK: These pans greatly reduce and/or eliminate fat when cooking.

OIL: Oil gets 100 percent of its calories from fat. Use with caution and care, and choose canola, olive, and/or safflower. Better yet—*omit!*

PORTIONS: Reduce your portion size to help reduce your own size.

QUESTIONS: Ask lots—about "Do you have fat-free?" at restaurants and/or grocery stores or "Will you get fat-free?" The more we ask, the more they will carry or have at restaurants.

REFRIGERATE: Broths, stews, and soups, to collect any sneaky fats that are hiding from you.

STEAM: Change to steamed vegetables. Steaming saves vitamins and nutrients and uses no fat.

TRIM: Remove all visible fat and skin before cooking meats.

UNADORNED: You'll really be amazed at how much flavor you're missing by drowning vegetables in butter, sauces, and dressings. Let the real flavor shine through. Eat them steamed or raw.

VARIETY: Don't get into a slump and think you can only eat special or limited foods on a healthy diet. Shop wise and eat many varieties.

WHITES: Substitute 2 egg whites for 1 egg in any recipe. It works, and you'll never know the difference but your heart will.

XXXX SUGAR: Confectioners' or powdered sugar is labeled XXXX sugar. Keep it on hand to sprinkle on cakes or to make a little light sauce for angel food cakes or fresh fruit. (Also means kisses when you send hugs OOOO.)

YOGURT: Frozen fat-free now comes in many flavors. It's great. Look for fat-free yogurt and ice cream; some is fat-free and sugar-free, and is delicious to say the least.

ZIPPER BAGS: Cut up veggies to have on hand and store in zipper bags.

Substitutions

Living in Gore, Oklahoma, sometimes you find yourself short of an ingredient, but there are many substitutions you can make without ruining your dish.

Food Item	Substitute
2 tablespoons amaretto	1/4–1/2 teaspoon almond extract
2 tablespoons Kahlúa or other coffee- or chocolate-flavored liqueur	1/2–1 teaspoon chocolate extract plus 1/2–1 teaspoon instant coffee in 2 tablespoons water
1/4 cup or more red wine	Equal amount of red grape juice or cranberry juice
2 tablespoons rum or brandy	1/2–1 teaspoon rum or brandy extract, plus enough grape or apple juice to get correct amount of liquid needed for recipe
2 tablespoons sherry or bourbon	1–2 teaspoons vanilla extract
1/4 cup or more port wine, sweet sherry, rum, brandy, or fruit-flavored liqueur	Equal amount of unsweetened orange or apple juice plus 1 teaspoon corresponding extract or vanilla extract
1 cup plain yogurt	1 cup low-fat buttermilk (1 gram per cup)
1 cup sour cream	1 cup fat-free yogurt plus 1 tablespoon cornstarch
1 cup buttermilk	1 cup skim milk plus 1 tablespoon white vinegar or lemon juice

1 cup milk	½ cup evaporated skim milk plus ½ cup water
1 pound mushrooms	1 (8-ounce) can sliced mushrooms, drained
1 small onion, chopped	1 tablespoon instant minced onion or 1 teaspoon onion powder
1 clove garlic, minced	⅛ teaspoon instant minced garlic or garlic powder
1 tablespoon chopped chives	1 tablespoon minced scallion tops
1 tablespoon grated fresh ginger	⅛ teaspoon ground ginger
1 tablespoon chopped dried orange peel	1½ teaspoons orange extract or 1 tablespoon grated fresh orange peel
1 (1-inch) piece vanilla bean	1 teaspoon vanilla extract
1 teaspoon ground allspice	½ teaspoon each ground cinnamon and ground cloves, mixed
1 teaspoon dry mustard	1 tablespoon prepared mustard
1 cup powdered sugar	1 cup granulated sugar plus 1 tablespoon cornstarch processed in food processor or blender
1 cup honey	1¼ cups sugar plus ⅓ cup water
1 cup pecans	1 cup regular oats, toasted (can use in baked products)
1 cup light corn syrup	1¼ cups sugar plus ⅓ cup water
1 cup tomato juice	½ cup tomato sauce plus ½ cup water
2 cups tomato sauce	¾ cup tomato paste plus 1 cup water

"THE TWENTY-THIRD DIET"

PROVERBS 17:22 SAYS: "A MERRY HEART DOETH GOOD LIKE A MEDICINE."

My appetite is my shepherd.

I shall always want.

It maketh me to sit down and stuff myself.

It leadeth me to the refrigerator repeatedly.

It destroyeth my shape and my health.

It leadeth me in the paths of fast food, for burgers and fries.

Yea, though I know that I gaineth,

I will not stop eating for the food tasteth so good.

The ice cream and the cookies, they comfort me.

When the table is spread before me, it exciteth me, for I know that soon

I will indulge in food that is good for me and tastes normal.

As I fill my plate continually, my heart and waistline grow stronger and smaller.

For I have found *So Fat, Low Fat, No Fat.*

Surely bulges and excess weight shall leave me all the days of my life,

And I shall eat good food and live healthier forever.

Amen.

MARRIAGE STEW

2 concerned persons
2 cups love
2 pinches understanding
2 teaspoons patience
2 cans trust
2 well-rounded measures of sex
Plenty of honest friendship

Combine the 2 concerned persons and 2 cups of love. Blend with understanding and patience. Beat lightly with a spoonful of laughter. Now add the 2 cans of trust and pour the mixture into the casserole of life. This is also the time to add tears, dreams, touching, and remembering. As the mixture is simmering, sauté sex in tenderness. Cook to taste, garnish with a kiss or two, and serve with honest friendship.

Author unknown

Appetizers

CREAMY DIP

MAKES
ABOUT 1
CUP

0 GRAMS FAT

Prep :05
Cook :00
Stand 2:00
Total 2:05

½ cup fat-free sour cream
½ cup fat-free mayonnaise
1 tablespoon chopped chives
1½ tablespoons Worcestershire sauce
½ teaspoon seasoned salt

In a mixing bowl, combine all ingredients and blend thoroughly. Cover the mixture and chill for a couple of hours before serving, letting flavors blend.

Serve the dip with assorted fresh vegetables and chips.

WHITE BEAN DIP

SERVES 4

0 GRAMS FAT

Prep :10
Cook :00
Stand :1:00
Total 1:10

2 (16-ounce) cans Great Northern beans
1 (4-ounce) can chopped green chiles
¼ cup salsa
2 tablespoons lemon juice
½ clove garlic, minced
Pinch of dried basil
2 scallions, chopped fine
4 to 6 drops hot pepper sauce (careful—add 1 drop at a time)

Drain the beans and chiles. Place in a food processor or blender, add the salsa, lemon juice, garlic, and basil. Blend until smooth.

Remove from the container into a mixing bowl. Stir in the scallions—this will give a little body and crunch to your dip. Add hot pepper sauce a couple drops at a time, tasting frequently. Chill about an hour before serving.

SALSA DIP

1 (8-ounce) package fat-free cream cheese, at room temperature
½ cup spicy salsa
2 to 3 drops hot pepper sauce

In a small mixing bowl, stir all the above ingredients together with a wire whisk. Be gentle with the stirring of the cream cheese; fat-free cheese gets thin very easily. Add only one drop of hot sauce at a time until the temperature suits your taste.

SERVES 4

0 GRAMS FAT

Prep :05
Cook :00
Stand :00
Total :05

SALSA VERDE

2 cups chopped fresh or canned tomatoes
½ cup chopped onion
½ cup chopped cilantro or parsley
1 jalapeño pepper, canned or fresh, chopped
1 clove garlic, minced
½ teaspoon lemon pepper
½ teaspoon crushed oregano
½ teaspoon adobo seasoning or garlic powder
2 to 3 tablespoons lime juice

Combine all the ingredients in a medium bowl; mix well. Refrigerate at least 30 minutes to blend flavors. Serve with White Chicken Chili (page 143) or as a dip with tortilla chips.

SERVES 4

0 GRAMS FAT

Prep :20
Cook :00
Stand :30
Total :50

ONION SALSA

SERVES 4

1 GRAM FAT
PER SERVING

Prep :10
Cook :00
Stand 2:00
Total 2:10

2 cups finely chopped red onion
1 tomato, chopped fine
¼ cup chopped green onions
¼ cup lemon juice
2 tablespoons chopped cilantro leaves
2 tablespoons wine vinegar
1 tablespoon canola oil
1 teaspoon reduced-sodium soy sauce
3 cloves garlic, chopped
¼ teaspoon cayenne pepper

Mix all ingredients in a glass bowl, cover, and refrigerate at least 2 hours.

CHUNKY VEGETABLE SALSA

SERVES 8

0 GRAMS FAT

Prep :15
Cook :03
Stand 1:00
Total 1:18

1 (8-ounce) can tomato juice
1 dash oregano
1 clove garlic, chopped fine, or dash of garlic seasoning
2 tablespoons vinegar
2 teaspoons lemon juice
2 teaspoons lime juice
2 rings jalapeño pepper, chopped fine
1 tablespoon cornstarch (optional)
2 (8-ounce) cans black-eyed peas, drained
2 large tomatoes, chopped
1 cup chopped celery
1 red onion, chopped
1 cup chopped green pepper
1 cup commercial salsa

Combine the tomato juice, oregano, garlic, vinegar, lemon and lime juice, and jalapeño pepper in a small saucepan. Heat to boiling; thicken with a little cornstarch in cold water if desired. Pour over the peas, tomatoes, celery, onions, and pepper. Stir in the salsa. Refrigerate and let stand to blend at least 1 hour before serving.

Serve with chips or fat-free crackers.

VEGETABLE DIP

1 head cauliflower
1 bunch broccoli
1 (16-ounce) bag carrots
2 (8-ounce) packages fat-free cream cheese, at room temperature
½ cup minced onion
½ teaspoon ground cumin
¼ teaspoon chili powder
Dash of salt
8 to 10 drops hot pepper sauce
Dippers: broccoli, cauliflower florets, carrots, celery, cucumber sticks, low-fat chips

SERVES 8

0 GRAMS FAT

Prep :20
Cook :00
Stand 3:00
Total 3:20

Break cauliflower and broccoli into florets. Mince 1 cup of each and reserve remainder for dippers. Mince ½ cup carrots very tiny; cut remainder into small sticks for dippers.

In a medium mixing bowl, blend cream cheese (stir very gently—fat-free cream cheese breaks down easily) with onion and seasonings. Add the hot pepper sauce one drop at a time, tasting after each addition. Stir in the minced cauliflower, broccoli, and carrots. Refrigerate in a covered bowl at least 3 hours or overnight before serving. Crackers are also nice dippers.

ZIPPY DIP

SERVES 8

0 GRAMS FAT

Prep :15
Cook :00
Stand 3:00
Total 3:15

2 (8-ounce) packages fat-free cream cheese, at room temperature
½ cup spicy V-8 vegetable juice
1 (4-ounce) can chopped green chiles, drained
¼ cup chopped bell pepper
¼ cup minced onion
4 drops hot pepper sauce
Fresh vegetables for dippers

In a medium bowl with a wire whisk, gently stir the cream cheese until smooth. (Careful—fat-free cream cheese can break down and get runny.) Gradually add V-8 juice until smooth and well blended.

Stir in chiles, pepper, onion, and pepper sauce one drop at a time, tasting after each, to be sure you don't get it too hot. Cover and refrigerate at least 3 hours.

This is a good make-ahead dip.

DILLED GARDEN DIP

MAKES
ABOUT 1¾
CUPS

0 GRAMS FAT

Prep :10
Cook :05
Stand :00
Total :15

1½ cups no-fat cottage cheese
1 tablespoon lemon juice
1 tablespoon shredded carrot
1 tablespoon sliced green onion
1 tablespoon chopped fresh parsley
1½ teaspoons minced fresh dill weed, or ½ teaspoon dried
½ teaspoon sugar
Dash of pepper

In a blender, combine the cottage cheese and lemon juice and blend 3 to 5 minutes, or until smooth.

Spoon into a bowl and stir in the remaining ingredients.

Serve with raw vegetable sticks or Easy Tortilla Chips (see recipe on page 64).

SPINACH DIP

1 (10-ounce) package frozen chopped spinach, thawed
1 (8-ounce) can water chestnuts, drained and chopped
1 (16-ounce) carton fat-free sour cream
½ cup fat-free salad dressing
1 (8-ounce) envelope vegetable soup mix
½ teaspoon lemon juice

Drain thawed spinach on paper towels, squeezing out liquid. Combine spinach, water chestnuts, and remaining ingredients; cover and chill for 1 hour. Serve with assorted fresh vegetables.

MAKES ABOUT 3 CUPS

0 GRAMS FAT

Prep :15
Cook :00
Stand 1:00
Total 1:15

GUACAMOLE

1 small ripe avocado, peeled and pitted
2 medium tomatoes, chopped into small pieces
½ small red onion, chopped fine
4 teaspoons lime juice
1 clove garlic, chopped fine
½ small jalapeño pepper, seeded and chopped fine, or ¼ cup salsa (see Note)

Place the avocado in a large bowl and mash, not too fine—leave a little lumpy for texture. Add the remaining ingredients.

Note: These may be omitted if you do not desire the spicy Southwest bit.

Tip: Save the avocado pit. If you push it into the center of your guacamole until ready to serve it will keep it from discoloring.

MAKES ABOUT 2 CUPS

1 GRAM FAT PER TABLESPOON

Prep :10
Cook :00
Stand :00
Total :10

GUACAMOLE THE SLIM WAY

SERVES 6

0 GRAMS FAT

Prep :15
Cook :00
Stand :00
Total :15

1 (20-ounce) bag frozen green peas, thawed and drained
¼ cup lime juice
2 tablespoons chopped fresh cilantro or 1 teaspoon dried
½ small onion, quartered
2 tablespoons chopped green chiles
¼ cup picante sauce or salsa
Salt and pepper to taste
1 small fresh tomato, chopped into tiny pieces

In a blender or food processor, process peas, lime juice, cilantro, onion, and chiles until smooth. Transfer to a mixing bowl and stir in picante sauce, salt and pepper, and chopped tomato. Stir together. Serve with Easy Tortilla Chips (page 64).

LAYERED TEX MEX DIP

SERVES 6

1 GRAM FAT

Prep :25
Cook :00
Stand :00
Total :25

1 (14-ounce) can chili beans, extra spicy, drained
1 (8-ounce) carton nonfat sour cream (1 cup)
1 tablespoon taco seasoning mix
2 (4-ounce) cans green chiles, drained
1 (16-ounce) package frozen peas, cooked
3 tablespoons lime juice
1 teaspoon minced garlic
4 ounces fat-free Cheddar cheese, shredded (1 cup)
1 teaspoon sliced green onion
1 cup finely chopped tomato
Easy Tortilla Chips (page 64)

In a blender, process the beans until smooth. Spread the bean mixture thinly on a large shallow platter.

In a small bowl, combine the sour cream and taco seasoning; blend well. Spread over the bean mixture; sprinkle with chiles.

In the blender combine the cooked peas, lime juice, and garlic. Process until smooth. Spread over the chiles.

Sprinkle with the cheese, green onion, and tomatoes. Serve with tortilla chips.

BAKED SOUTHERN DIP

This is pretty to serve for the holidays.

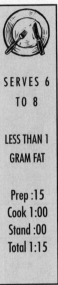

1 round loaf pumpernickel bread, unsliced
1 (8-ounce) package fat-free cream cheese, softened
½ cup fat-free sour cream
1 teaspoon cornstarch
¼ cup salsa (hot)
1½ cups shredded fat-free Cheddar cheese
Fresh vegetable sticks

SERVES 6
TO 8

LESS THAN 1
GRAM FAT

Prep :15
Cook 1:00
Stand :00
Total 1:15

Preheat the oven to 350 degrees. Cut a ¼-inch slice off the top of the bread. Set aside.

Hollow out the bread, leaving a ½-inch-thick shell. (Cut the center into 1-inch cubes. Bake until toasted.)

With an electric mixer, beat the cream cheese, sour cream, cornstarch, and salsa together until smooth. Stir in the Cheddar cheese.

Spoon into the bread shell. Place the top of the bread back on. Wrap with foil.

Bake about 1 hour.

Serve with bread cubes and veggie sticks for dipping.

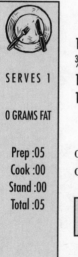

FRUIT DIP

MAKES ABOUT 2 CUPS

0 GRAMS FAT, WITHOUT NUTS

Prep :05
Cook :00
Stand :00
Total :05

1 (8-ounce) package fat-free cream cheese, softened
¾ cup firmly packed brown sugar
½ cup granulated sugar
1 tablespoon vanilla extract
½ cup chopped nuts (optional)

Stir the cream cheese with the sugars and vanilla until creamy. Fold in the nuts if using. Serve with apple wedges or any kind of fruit desired.

PINEAPPLE ALMOND FRUIT DIP

SERVES 1

0 GRAMS FAT

Prep :05
Cook :00
Stand :00
Total :05

1 (8-ounce) carton fat-free cream cheese
¾ cup crushed and drained canned pineapple
1 tablespoon firmly packed brown sugar
1½ teaspoons almond extract

Blend all the above only until smooth. Serve with sliced apples or any fresh fruit; also good with celery and crackers (fat-free of course).

> *Note:* Be careful blending fat-free cream cheese and sour cream—they will break down to liquid very easily.

HAM APPETILLAS

1 package flour tortillas
1 (8-ounce) package fat-free cream cheese, softened
⅓ cup fat-free mayonnaise
2 tablespoons chopped green onions
¼ cup black olive pieces
4 to 5 slices ham, 98 percent fat-free

SERVES 4

VERY LOW-FAT

Prep :15
Cook :00
Stand 3:00
Total 3:15

Let the tortillas sit at room temperature for a short while. Combine the cream cheese, mayonnaise, onions, and olives until well mixed.

Spread a thin layer of the cheese mixture over each tortilla. Arrange a slice of ham over the cheese. Roll up the tortillas and wrap individually in plastic wrap.

Refrigerate at least 3 hours or overnight. To serve, cut into ¾-inch slices.

SKINNY PINWHEELS

1 (8-ounce) package fat-free cream cheese, softened
1 (1-ounce) package ranch dressing mix
2 green onions, sliced
4 flour tortillas (each has 1 gram of fat)
1 (4-ounce) jar diced pimientos
1 (4-ounce) can chopped green chiles
1 (2-ounce) jar sliced black olives

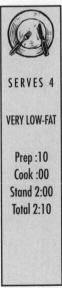

SERVES 4

VERY LOW-FAT

Prep :10
Cook :00
Stand 2:00
Total 2:10

Mix the cream cheese, ranch dressing mix, and green onions. Spread on the tortillas. Drain the pimientos, chiles, and olives and blot dry on a paper towel. Sprinkle in equal amounts on top of the cream cheese. Roll the tortillas tightly. Place seam side down in a dish and chill at least 2 hours.

Cut rolls into 1-inch pieces. Discard end pieces. (I eat them.) Serve with spiral side up.

STUFFED VEGETABLES WITH HERBED CREAM CHEESE

LESS THAN 1 GRAM FAT

Prep :10
Cook :10
Stand :00
Total :20

Vegetables for stuffing (cherry tomatoes, celery stalks, hollowed-out cucumber chunks, mushroom caps, etc.)
1 (8-ounce) package fat-free cream cheese, softened
⅓ cup grated fat-free Parmesan cheese
1 teaspoon skim milk
½ teaspoon Italian herb seasoning
⅛ teaspoon black pepper

Prepare veggies of your choice.
In a small bowl mix the cream cheese, Parmesan, milk, seasoning, and pepper. With a pastry bag, fill vegetables.
(You can put the filling into a zipper bag and cut the corner off to use as a pastry bag.)
Serve chilled.

CHICKEN-STUFFED MUSHROOMS

SERVES 12

1 GRAM FAT EACH

Prep :15
Cook :10
Stand :00
Total :25

1 small onion, chopped
2 tablespoons cilantro leaves
2 tablespoons egg substitute
1 tablespoon Dijon mustard
1½ teaspoons finely chopped fresh ginger root
2 tablespoons reduced-sodium soy sauce
1 clove garlic, chopped fine
½ pound ground raw chicken
12 large mushrooms, stems removed

Preheat the oven to 350 degrees. Spray a cookie sheet with vegetable oil cooking spray. Mix all ingredients except mushrooms. Fill mushrooms with the chicken mixture. Place the mushrooms, filled sides up, on the cookie sheet and bake for 10 to 15 minutes, or until chicken mixture is done. Serve hot.

Broiled Mushroom Caps: Brush stuffed mushrooms with Butter Buds or spray with vegetable oil cooking spray, and bake at 400 degrees for 5 to 10 minutes.

COUNTRY CAVIAR

In the country, we use cornmeal for everything. What you have is what you use, so make something with what you have.

1¼ cups fat-free self-rising cornmeal mix
¼ cup egg substitute
½ cup fat-free sour cream
½ teaspoon chopped chives (fresh or dried)
24 pitted ripe or pimento-stuffed olives

SERVES 12

VERY LOW-FAT

Prep :10
Cook :15
Stand :00
Total :25

Preheat the oven to 400 degrees. Lightly spray two miniature (1¾-inch) muffin pans with vegetable oil cooking spray.

In a heavy zipper-lock plastic bag, combine cornmeal mix, egg substitute, sour cream, and chives. Close the bag and use tips of fingers to mix batter well. Keep walking your fingers around and over the batter until well blended. Shake to one side of the bag and snip off the corner of the bag to make a ¾-inch opening. Squeeze the batter into the prepared muffin pans, filling each about ¾ full.

Press an olive into the center of each cup of batter. Bake for about 15 minutes or until done.

Variations: Use cocktail onions or a ring of jalapeño pepper in place of the olives.

Make a thumbprint in the top of each cup of batter and spoon in about ½ teaspoon of minced fresh jalapeño pepper, or jalapeño pepper jelly.

Add a ½-inch chunk of fat-free cheese, your choice.

Add a ½-inch chunk of 98% fat-free ham.

Add ¼ teaspoon of hot pepper sauce.

HOT AND SPICY PEPPER SQUARES

MAKES 48
SQUARES

0 GRAMS FAT

Prep :10
Cook :40
Stand :10
Total 1:00

½ cup flour
1 teaspoon baking powder
Dash salt
2 cups egg substitute
3 cups grated fat-free Monterey Jack cheese
1½ cups fat-free cottage cheese
2 tablespoons chopped pickled jalapeño pepper
2 tablespoons chopped pimento
2 tablespoons sliced pitted ripe olives

Preheat the oven to 350 degrees. Lightly spray a 13 x 9-inch baking dish with vegetable oil cooking spray.

In a bowl stir together the flour, baking powder, and salt. Set aside.

In a large mixing bowl, beat the egg substitute slightly with an electric mixer, then stir in the flour mixture. Fold in the cheeses, pepper, pimento, and olives.

Pour into the prepared baking dish. Bake uncovered for about 40 minutes, or until set and golden brown. Let stand 10 minutes; cut into 1½-inch squares. Serve warm or with low-fat tortilla chips if desired.

FROZEN GRAPES

SERVES 6

0 GRAMS FAT

Prep :50
Cook :00
Stand :02
Total :52

1½ pounds green or red seedless grapes

Stem and wash the grapes and pat dry. Place in the freezer for about 45 minutes. Remove from the freezer and let stand 2 minutes before serving.

Very good with a hot spicy meal on a hot spicy summer evening.

BEAN TASTIES

½ cup chopped onion
1 (16-ounce) can fat-free refried beans
½ cup salsa
1 teaspoon chili powder
⅛ teaspoon garlic powder
Dash salt (optional)
Dash pepper
¼ cup fat-free cream cheese, at room temperature
½ cup cubed avocado
1 teaspoon lime juice
1 teaspoon lemon juice
10 (6-inch) flour tortillas
½ cup finely chopped green peppers (or red or mixed for holidays)
Salsa and fat-free sour cream

MAKES 40
TASTIES

2.3 GRAMS FAT
PER SERVING
(4 PIECES)

Prep :20
Cook :10
Stand :00
Total :30

In a nonstick skillet lightly sprayed with vegetable oil cooking spray, cook the onion, stirring constantly, until tender. Stir in the refried beans, salsa, chili powder, garlic powder, salt, if desired, and pepper. Set aside.

Combine the cream cheese, avocado, and lime and lemon juice and mash together thoroughly. Spread about 2 tablespoons over each tortilla, leaving about ½-inch border around edge. Spread about 2 tablespoons of the bean mixture over the avocado mixture. Top with a chopped pepper and roll each tortilla up.

Cut the tortilla rolls into fourths; insert a toothpick or wooden pick into each tastie. Serve with salsa and fat-free sour cream.

HAM SWIRLS

SERVES 8

1 GRAM FAT
PER SERVING

Prep :15
Cook :08
Stand 1:00
Total 1:15

8 slices 98% fat-free deli-style ham
1 (8-ounce) package fat-free cream cheese, at room temperature
8 medium whole dill pickles

Spread one side of each ham slice with about 2 tablespoons of cream cheese.

Lay one pickle on each at one side; roll the ham slice around the pickle. Press the edges together. Cover and refrigerate 1 hour. To serve, cut each pickle into six slices. Place on a serving tray, flat side down. Have picks by the tray.

PIZZA APPETIZERS

SERVES 12

2 GRAMS FAT
PER SERVING

Prep :15
Cook :08
Stand :00
Total :23

1 long loaf Italian bread, cut in half lengthwise
¾ cup shredded fat-free Monterey Jack cheese
¾ cup shredded fat-free Cheddar Cheese
¾ cup fat-free pasta sauce
1½ tablespoons dried Italian seasoning
6 thin slices 98% fat-free ham
12 to 15 bell pepper rings
½ cup chopped onion
Parsley for garnish

Preheat the broiler. Place the bread, cut side up, on a baking sheet; toast 4 to 5 inches from the heat source until lightly browned.

Combine the cheeses and sprinkle ¼ of the mixture on each bread half; broil again until the cheese melts, about 1 to 2 minutes.

In a small saucepan, combine the pasta sauce and seasoning. Place over medium heat until thoroughly heated. Spoon evenly over bread halves; top with ham, pepper rings, and chopped onion. Sprinkle each half with the remaining cheeses.

Broil 4 to 5 minutes or until the cheese is melted. Cut each half into 6 pieces. Garnish with a little parsley if desired.

TORTILLA CHEESECAKE

1½ cups crushed baked tortilla chips
¼ cup Butter Buds, liquid form
2 (8-ounce) packages plus 1 (3-ounce) package fat-free cream cheese, at room
    temperature
½ cup egg substitute
2½ cups shredded fat-free Monterey Jack cheese
1 (4-ounce) can chopped green chiles, drained
¼ teaspoon ground red pepper (cayenne)
1 (8-ounce) carton fat-free sour cream
1½ cups chopped bell peppers
½ cup chopped scallions
1 medium tomato, chopped

SERVES 12

**2 GRAMS FAT
ENTIRE DISH**

Prep :35
Cook :45
Stand 3:00
Total 4:20

Preheat the oven to 325 degrees. Lightly spray the bottom of a 9-inch springform pan with vegetable oil cooking spray.

Process the crushed tortilla chips into fine crumbs in a blender or food processor. Or place the chips in a zipper-lock plastic bag and roll into crumbs with a rolling pin or bottle.

Combine the crushed tortilla chips with the Butter Buds and mix well. Press onto the bottom of the springform pan. Bake for 15 minutes and let cool on a wire rack.

Stir the cream cheese gently with a wire whisk. Add the egg substitute slowly, mixing after each addition. Stir in the shredded cheeses, chiles, and ground red pepper. Pour into the prepared pan, and bake at 325 degrees for 30 minutes. Cool 10 minutes on a wire rack. Gently run a knife around the edge of the pan to release the sides, and let cool completely.

Spread the sour cream evenly over the top; cover and chill. Arrange the chopped peppers and chopped scallions over the top and the tomatoes around the edge of top as desired. During the holidays I make mine in the shape of a tree.

Serve with tortilla chips.

CHILES RELLENOS

SERVES 4

LOW-FAT

Prep :25
Cook :40
Stand :00
Total 1:05

6 ounces fat-free Monterey Jack cheese
3 (4-ounce) cans whole green chiles, drained and seeded
½ cup all-purpose flour
⅛ teaspoon salt
⅛ teaspoon pepper
¼ cup egg substitute
1 (14-ounce) can stewed tomatoes, undrained and chopped

Preheat the oven to 350 degrees. Lightly spray a 13 x 9-inch baking dish with vegetable oil cooking spray.

Cut the cheese into pieces; place one piece inside each chile. (You may use shredded cheese.) Set the cheese-filled chiles aside.

Combine the flour, salt, and pepper in a small mixing bowl. Place the egg substitute in another small bowl. Dredge each chile in the flour, then dip in the egg substitute. In a nonstick skillet lightly sprayed with vegetable oil cooking spray, brown the chiles.

Transfer the browned chiles to the prepared baking dish. Pour undrained chopped tomatoes over chiles. Bake for 30 minutes.

Serve with Mexican meals.

PITA PIZZA SNACKS

SERVES 2

0 GRAMS FAT

Prep :10
Cook :12
Stand :00
Total :22

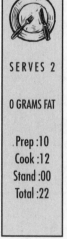

1 fat-free pita bread, split into 2 rounds
2 tablespoons fat-free Italian dressing
2 slices fat-free cheese
Pizza toppings: chopped onions, peppers, sliced mushrooms

Preheat the oven to 375 degrees. Lightly brush the pita bread with dressing, place on a baking sheet, and bake for 8 to 10 minutes or until lightly browned. Brush bread with half of the remaining dressing; top with cheese and desired toppings. Drizzle the remaining dressing over the top. Return to the oven and bake for an additional 1 or 2 minutes, or until cheese begins to melt. Cut each round into 8 wedges.

MINI BAGEL BITS

8 mini bagels, sliced in half
Fat-free pizza sauce
½ cup chopped onion
½ cup chopped bell pepper
1 cup shredded fat-free mozzarella or Cheddar cheese or both

Preheat the oven to 400 degrees. Place the bagels cut side up on a baking sheet. Spread the desired amount of pizza sauce on each bagel half. Top with onion, pepper, and cheese. Bake for about 7 to 8 minutes, until the bagels are hot and the cheese is melted.

SERVES 4

0.5 GRAM FAT
PER BAGEL (2
HALVES)

Prep :10
Cook :08
Stand :00
Total :18

HOLIDAY POPCORN SPECIAL

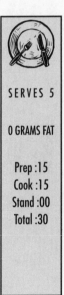

1 egg white
2 tablespoons packed brown sugar or Brown Sugar Twin
⅛ teaspoon cinnamon
3 quarts (12 cups) air-popped popcorn

Preheat the oven to 325 degrees. Lightly spray a 15 x 10-inch baking pan with vegetable oil cooking spray.

In a small bowl, beat the egg white until soft peaks form. Add the brown sugar or Sugar Twin and cinnamon, beating until stiff peaks form (usually about 1 minute). Place popcorn in a large bowl. Fold the egg white mixture into the popcorn. Spread in prepared baking sheet. Bake for 15 minutes, stirring twice during baking. Cool completely. Store in an airtight container.

SERVES 5

0 GRAMS FAT

Prep :15
Cook :15
Stand :00
Total :30

Variations: Substitute 2 tablespoons barbecue seasoning for the sugar and cinnamon. If you like spicy snacks, substitute Cajun seasoning for the sugar and cinnamon.

POTATO SKINS

Fat-free sour cream or sour cream dip or salsa makes a nice dip for these.

SERVES 12

0.06 GRAMS
FAT PER
SERVING

Prep :15
Cook :20
Stand :00
Total :35

6 medium baking potatoes, scrubbed, baked, and cooled (may be leftovers or extras baked the day before)
4 to 6 tablespoons Butter Buds, liquid form
½ teaspoon garlic powder
Black pepper to taste

Preheat the oven to 450 degrees.

Cut each potato in half. Scoop out the centers, leaving about ¼ inch of potato on the inside of each skin. Save the centers for another recipe another day. Cut the skins into quarters. Brush Butter Buds over the inside and sprinkle with garlic powder and pepper. Place skin side down on a baking sheet.

Bake 15 minutes, or until lightly browned. Turn skins over and bake another 5 minutes. Serve immediately.

Variations: Instead of garlic powder, use Cajun seasoning, onion flakes, onion soup mix, or your choice of seasoning.

SWEET POTATO CHIPS

SERVES 4

TRACE OF FAT
SERVING

Prep :10
Cook :25
Stand :00
Total :35

2 large sweet potatoes, peeled
¼ teaspoon salt (optional)

Preheat the oven to 325 degrees. Lightly spray two baking sheets with vegetable oil cooking spray.

Using a very sharp knife or vegetable cutter, slice the sweet potatoes crosswise into ⅛-inch slices. Arrange in a single layer on the prepared baking sheets. Lightly coat the slices with cooking spray.

Bake for 15 to 25 minutes or until crisp. Remove the chips from baking sheets as they begin to brown. Cool; sprinkle with salt if desired. Store in an airtight container.

TATER DIPPERS

4 to 5 cups raw vegetables (mushrooms, bell peppers, broccoli, carrots; see below)
1 cup instant potato flakes
⅓ cup grated fat-free Parmesan cheese
½ teaspoon celery salt
¼ teaspoon garlic powder
½ cup egg substitute
Fat-free ranch salad dressing (fat-free) or dip (optional)

SERVES 6

0 GRAMS FAT

Prep :10
Cook :25
Stand :00
Total :35

Preheat the oven to 400 degrees. Lightly spray two baking sheets with vegetable oil cooking spray.

Prepare the vegetables: Wipe the mushrooms and leave them whole. Core the peppers and cut into rings. Separate the broccoli into florets. Peel the carrots and cut into thin strips.

In a small bowl, combine the potato flakes, Parmesan cheese, celery salt, and garlic powder. In another bowl, beat the egg substitute slightly. Dip the vegetables, one at a time, in the egg substitute, then in the potato mixture. Arrange them on the prepared baking sheets and spray lightly with vegetable oil cooking spray. Bake for 20 to 25 minutes, until tender. Serve with dressing or dip if desired, or you can just use as your vegetable side dish.

EASY TORTILLA CHIPS

MAKES ABOUT 96 CHIPS (16 SERVINGS)

1 GRAM FAT EACH TORTILLA (BEFORE CUTTING)

Prep :05
Cook :15
Stand :00
Total :20

12 (8-inch) flour tortillas

Heat the oven to 350 degrees. Cut each tortilla into 8 to 10 pie-shaped wedges. Place on an ungreased baking sheet in a single layer. Bake 10 to 15 minutes, or until golden brown. (Watch closely—they burn quickly.)

> *Variations:* You can sprinkle the pieces with sugar and cinnamon before baking and eat as cookies. Try cocoa and sugar. Or try spicy chips—bar-b-q seasoning sprinkled over chips before baking, or garlic salt or Cajun seasoning.

PITA CHIPS

Fat-free.

MAKES 64 CHIPS (4 SERVINGS)

0 GRAMS FAT PER SERVING

Prep :05
Cook :12
Stand :00
Total :17

4 (6-inch) whole wheat fat-free pita breads

Heat the oven to 400 degrees. Cut around the outside edges of the pitas to separate them, or slice them open to lay flat, so that you have 8 rounds. Cut each round into 8 pie-shaped wedges. Place in a single layer on a cookie sheet and bake until light brown and crispy.

Soups and Salads

Soups

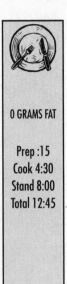

BEEF VEGETABLE SOUP

0 GRAMS FAT

Prep :15
Cook 4:30
Stand 8:00
Total 12:45

Cook beef the day before. Any cut will do but trim all the fat possible off. Put beef and soup bones in a large pot and cover with cold water. Simmer 3 to 4 hours. Defat broth. Refrigerate overnight to collect any excess fat missed. Dip the fat off the top before starting the soup. Save the beef for another dish another day.

Bring broth to a boil. Add 2 medium onions, chopped; 1 clove of garlic, minced; celery, carrots, potatoes, peas (as much as your family prefers), 2 cans tomatoes, spices as you desire. Cabbage may also be added. Simmer all the ingredients slowly for about $1\frac{1}{2}$ to 2 hours. Pasta may also be added if desired.

Season with Herbs to Add Flavor
Fat is flavor. When you take out the fat, you need to add more herbs to enhance the flavor.
Caraway—tangy and slightly sweet
Cardamom—spicy
Celery—strong—be careful
Cumin—a little bitter and sometimes hot
Dill—strong—use sparingly
Fennel—licorice flavor
Mustard—spicy
Sesame—sweet nutty flavor

Be very careful to serve your hot soup *hot* and your cold soup *cold*. A quick way to ruin the taste of an effort-filled soup is to serve it warm.

GARDEN SOUP

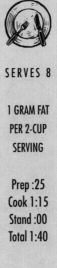

8 boneless, skinless chicken tenders
1 bell pepper, seeded and chopped
2 banana peppers, seeded and chopped
1 large onion, chopped
4 ears corn, kernels cut off the cob (about 2 cups)
1½ cups frozen peas and carrots
1 cup chopped celery
4 medium potatoes, peeled and cubed
Salt and pepper to taste
½ teaspoon oregano
½ teaspoon basil
2 drops Tabasco
¼ teaspoon adobo seasoning (optional)
2 cups sliced okra (½-inch pieces)
1 tablespoon vinegar
1½ cups uncooked rigatoni
1½ cups chopped cabbage

SERVES 8

1 GRAM FAT
PER 2-CUP
SERVING

Prep :25
Cook 1:15
Stand :00
Total 1:40

Bring 2 quarts of water to a boil in a large saucepan or soup kettle. Add the chicken tenders, lower the heat, and simmer until
cooked through, 15 to 20 minutes. Remove the chicken with a slotted spoon. When cool enough to handle, cut into bite-size pieces
and set aside.

Meantime, to the boiling chicken stock add the chopped peppers, onion, corn, peas and carrots, celery, and potatoes. Add a little more water to replace what has boiled away. Season with salt,
pepper, oregano, basil, and Tabasco, and the adobo if desired.
Bring to a boil over high heat, lower the heat to medium, and simmer until tender, about 20 minutes.

In a small saucepan, cover the okra with water, add 1 tablespoon
vinegar (this keeps it from being slimy), and boil until tender, 3 to
4 minutes. Drain and rinse; set aside. In a separate saucepan, boil
rigatoni according to package directions, drain, and rinse; set aside.

When the veggies are almost tender, add the okra, rigatoni, cab-

(continued)

bage, and chicken. Continue cooking until done to desired tenderness.

Serve with Dry-Fried Corn Bread Cakes (page 318).

CREAMY CORN CHOWDER

Corn holds a special place in our family, as it was always Dad's favorite. He would say, "This must be Sloan corn." My brother grows sweet corn and field corn. Best in the world, bar none.

SERVES 4

LESS THAN 1 GRAM FAT PER SERVING

Prep :20
Cook :15
Stand :00
Total :35

4 ears fresh corn or 1 (10-ounce) package frozen whole-kernel corn
¾ to 1 cup peeled and cubed potatoes (small cubes)
½ cup chopped onion
½ cup thinly sliced celery
1 teaspoon instant chicken bouillon granules
Dash pepper (white looks better but black is fine)
1¾ cups skim milk
2 tablespoons flour
2 tablespoons nonfat dry milk powder

If using fresh corn, cut the kernels off with a sharp knife; you should have about 2 cups of corn. In a large saucepan, combine the corn, potatoes, onion, celery, bouillon granules, pepper, and ⅓ cup water. Bring to a boil, lower the heat, and simmer for about 10 minutes or until the corn and potatoes are just tender. Stir often. Stir in 1½ cups of the milk. Continue to cook on low heat until the milk has become hot.

In a separate bowl, combine the flour and dry milk powder. Stir in the remaining ¼ cup of skim milk with a wire whisk, stirring until smooth. Gradually add to the corn mixture, stirring carefully so as not to mash your vegetables, until thickened. Cook about 1 minute more on low heat, being careful not to burn.

Serve in soup bowls, garnished with bacon bits if desired. Makes 4 servings, or 2 servings if this is your main dish; serve with a nice salad.

Cast Iron
Some of you still use cast iron, as I do. Did you know that using cast iron will boost your iron intake? Soup made in cast iron will have about 30 times more iron than if cooked in any other pan. (If it's simmered for a period of time.)

POTATO SOUP

3 or 4 large potatoes
1 medium onion
3 cups skim milk
¼ cup Butter Buds
Salt and pepper to taste

SERVES 4

0 GRAMS FAT

Prep :10
Cook :50
Stand :00
Total 1:00

    Peel and dice potatoes and onion, cover with water, and bring to a boil. Lower the heat and cook until tender, about 35 minutes.

    Drain three quarters of the water off and add the milk. Simmer over low heat for 15 to 20 minutes. Mash the potatoes with a hand masher to make the soup thicken. Add the Butter Buds, salt, and pepper.

    Serve with fat-free soda crackers.

If you get your soup too salty, add a raw potato and simmer for a while, then discard the potato. It will absorb the salt. You should be very careful with your salt—it is as bad for you as the fat.

Testing Freshness of Dried Herbs Rub them between your hands. The oil from your hands will extract the essence of the herb. If there is no smell they are no good.

HEALTHY HEARTY POTATO SOUP

SERVES 8

LESS THAN 1
GRAM FAT PER
SERVING

Prep :10
Cook :45
Stand :00
Total :55

6 medium potatoes
2 carrots
6 stalks celery
2 quarts water
1 onion, chopped
6 tablespoons light margarine
6 tablespoons flour
1 teaspoon salt
½ teaspoon pepper
1½ cups skim milk

Peel and slice the potatoes, dice the carrots and celery, cover with 2 quarts or so of water, and cook until tender, 30 to 40 minutes. Drain, reserving the liquid and setting the vegetables aside.

In the same kettle, sauté the onion in margarine until soft. Stir in the flour, salt, and pepper. Gradually add milk and cook until thickened, about 5 minutes. Stir in the cooked vegetables carefully so as not to smash them. Add 1 cup or more of reserved cooking liquid until soup is desired consistency.

CREAMY POTATO CABBAGE SOUP

SERVES 5

0 GRAMS FAT

Prep :10
Cook :45
Stand :00
Total :55

3 medium potatoes, peeled and cubed
1 (14-ounce) can fat-free chicken broth
½ cup skim milk
2 cups shredded cabbage
½ cup diced carrots
½ teaspoon dried dill weed

Combine the potatoes with the broth in a saucepan. Bring to a boil. Reduce the heat and cook until the potatoes are tender, about 40 minutes. Cool slightly.

Place 1 cup of the hot potato mixture in a blender or food processor. Add the milk, mix until smooth, return to the saucepan, and stir in remaining ingredients. Cook for 5 to 7 minutes, or until the carrots and cabbage are crisp-tender.

Thicken your soup with flour, cornstarch, or mashed potatoes. It's better to remove the pan from the heat before adding your thickeners to avoid the danger of lumping. Cornstarch (dissolved in cold water) is better for soups to be served cold and flour for hot soups. Leftover mashed potatoes thicken bean, potato, or any cream-type soup nicely.

BEAN SOUP

2 cups dried navy or pea beans
Defatted ham broth or water
1 small onion, chopped fine
½ cup chopped celery
Salt and pepper to taste

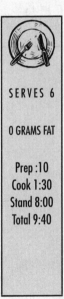

SERVES 6

0 GRAMS FAT

Prep :10
Cook 1:30
Stand 8:00
Total 9:40

Soak the beans overnight in 6 cups of water in a large kettle. Drain, cover with defatted ham broth, and bring to a boil. Lower the heat and simmer, partially covered, for about 1 hour, or until almost tender.

Add the onion, celery, salt, and pepper, and continue cooking until beans are tender and liquid is thick. Mash about ¾ of the beans with a potato masher and continue to simmer for a short while until very thick. (Careful, or they will scorch!) Taste the soup and add additional salt and pepper if needed.

WHITE BEAN SOUP

SERVES 6

0.5 GRAMS
FAT PER 1½-
CUP SERVING

Prep :15
Cook 2:15
Stand :00
Total 2:30

2 cups dried Great Northern beans
2 tablespoons instant chicken bouillon granules
½ teaspoon salt (optional)
1 medium onion, chopped
1 clove garlic, minced
1 medium carrot, sliced
1 stalk celery, sliced
1 medium potato, peeled and diced
1 tablespoon chopped fresh parsley

Look over and wash the beans thoroughly. Place in a deep stock-pot, add 6 cups of water, and bring to a boil. Boil for about 5 minutes, then reduce heat to a simmer. Add the bouillon, salt, if desired, onion, and garlic. Simmer for 1 to 1½ hours, until the beans are tender. Remove 2 cups of bean mixture, purée in a food processor, and return the puréed beans to the stockpot. Add the carrot, celery, and potato.

Cover and simmer an additional 30 to 45 minutes, or until the vegetables are tender. Just before serving, stir in the parsley.

AFTER-THE-HOLIDAYS
TURKEY AND BEAN SOUP

2 cups chopped cooked turkey (left over from the holidays)
1 (16-ounce) can stewed tomatoes
1 (14-ounce) can pinto beans, drained
1 (12-ounce) can Great Northern beans, drained
1 (14-ounce) can whole-kernel corn
1 cup chopped onion
6 rings jalapeño peppers, chopped
2 cloves garlic, minced
2 (16-ounce) cans fat-free chicken broth
1 (12-ounce) can light beer
3 tablespoons chili powder
1 teaspoon dried basil
1 teaspoon thyme leaves
¼ teaspoon pepper

SERVES 6

2–3 GRAMS
FAT PER 1½-
CUP SERVING

Prep :25
Cook 2:00
Stand :00
Total 2:25

In a large dutch oven (I use a cast-iron dutch oven on my wood stove), combine all ingredients. Bring to a boil over medium heat. Reduce the heat and simmer, uncovered, for about 2 hours. Stir occasionally.

This is very nice after the holidays to just dump all in one cookpot, using up some of that leftover turkey, and set it on the wood stove to simmer as you spend a long winter day undecorating, sewing, or whatever you like. Serve with a pone of corn bread (page 318). The aroma of this cooking all day will drive you crazy.

BROCCOLI SOUP

SERVES 6

0 GRAMS FAT

Prep :20
Cook :40
Stand :00
Total 1:00

4 cups chopped fresh broccoli (about 1½ pounds)
1 cup chopped celery
1 cup chopped carrots
¾ cup chopped onion
2¼ cups skim milk
¼ cup flour
4 cups fat-free chicken broth
½ teaspoon minced fresh parsley
1 teaspoon onion salt
Dash garlic powder
Salt and pepper to taste
2 teaspoons cornstarch (optional)
¼ cup cold skim milk (optional)

In your favorite soup kettle or deep dutch oven, bring 4 cups of water to a boil. Drop in the broccoli, celery, carrots, and half the onions. Boil for 3 to 4 minutes, drain in a colander in the sink, and set aside.

In the same pan, sauté the remaining onions in ¼ cup water until tender (watch closely—you may need to add a little more water if it cooks dry). Add ¼ cup of the skim milk, bring to a simmer, and stir in the flour to form a smooth paste. Gradually add the chicken broth and the remaining 2 cups milk, stirring constantly. Bring to a boil over medium heat and stir for 1 minute.

Add the vegetables, parsley, and seasonings. Reduce the heat to low and simmer for 30 to 40 minutes or until the vegetables are tender. Be careful not to burn; keep the heat regulated to low.

When vegetables have reached the desired degree of doneness, cover the pan and turn the heat off. Just before serving you may want to thicken your soup a little with the cornstarch and ¼ cup *cold* skim milk. Mix these together, return the soup to boiling, and stir in the cornstarch mixture a little at a time until soup thickens.

Salads

DAD'S GARDEN

I have many harrowing as well as happy memories of Dad's gardens. My earliest memory of the garden was when I was five years old. All four of us—Dad, Mom, Brother, and I—were down in the garden picking English peas (you may call them green peas). I had a very loose front tooth. I was pestering my dad, flitting around wiggling this terrible-looking loose tooth, all the while being warned by him that he was getting a little weary of my snaggle tooth and he was just about to pull it out.

My grandmother, his mother, lived just down the way, and you know how little girls are about their grandmothers. She was just the berries. I smart-mouthed one time too many as he warned me about pulling this tooth. I remember saying, "No you won't. I'll tell Ma Sloan on you!"

Too late! I was flat on my back in the middle of the pea row and my tooth was gone! I can still remember running down the road, yelling, "Ma! Ma!," blood just trickling but it seemed to me that it was gushing. "Daddy pulled my tooth! Daddy pulled my tooth! Ma! Ma!"

I remember the warmth of those old wrinkled arms wrapped around me to comfort my disbelief that a smart remark could have this result. I can still see that old apron she always wore—she carried vegetables in it cupped up like a basket. There is real magic in a grandma's arms, especially when you need protection from a parent.

He never followed me, or said another word about the tooth. None needed. I never smart-mouthed my dad or threatened him with a grandparent again, ever. Lesson well learned, quick.

Dad, being a farmer, with large fields, never believed in just planting a regular-size garden, like 30 by 50 or so. He always planted a garden about an acre or sometimes 1½ acres. He wanted to be sure everyone had veggies out of his wonderful gardens. He did have the best one in town. My brother and I always got on the end of the long rows, helping to plant sixty, eighty, a hundred tomato plants, planting 200 pounds of potatoes—four to six rows—all the way through the garden of okra. Do you have any idea how much okra was ready to be picked off those long rows every other day? Bob and I would go and pick five or six 5-gallon buckets full of okra. Good grief! What do you do with that much okra? There weren't enough people in the little town of Gore to eat that much okra. I always felt like the Little Red Hen. I would ask if anyone at church wanted any okra. No one, unless you picked it and brought it to them. To say yes, we will come and pick it, was just out of the question.

Dad's gardens were wonderful, but work! Oh, the heat, sweat, dust, bugs . . . and when it was picked, that was just the beginning for me. Dad would get his feelings hurt if you didn't want vegetables, and if no one put them up. Mom used to, but in her later years—the past ten—she didn't, so guess who that left. You got it: me! Sometimes I would go home with five or six 5-gallon buckets of tomatoes to can, five or six 5-gallon buckets of okra to freeze, squash by the basketsful, peppers to freeze—all with Dad to please.

I have a golf cart with a red wagon that we pull behind it for gardening and yard work. Sometimes the cart wouldn't hardly make it over the pond bank between Dad's house and our house. This pond is the fish pond, but I'll make that another story.

This year is the second time I have had my own garden since I have moved back to the country. The first one was the year the house was finished, but we still lived in Tulsa, just coming on the weekends. It was laid out just the way Dad would do it—big. I think maybe he might have had a hand in doing that. Needless to say, we couldn't keep up with it, and not being here every day, with just weekends to work on it, it wasn't enough. We wound up mowing it with an 11-horsepower tractor. That was the end of our gardening on our own for a few years. It was enough just to keep up a five-acre yard.

This spring my brother came over one Sunday afternoon—late, just about five. Bob and I had been working outside, and we'd showered and retired for the evening. *Not!* He said, I think I'll make you a raised bed garden like mine, okay? Well, you don't look a gift horse in the mouth, even though the thoughts were going through my head: I don't want a garden. (I find it too easy to go to Sarge's, a local vegetable stand). What in the world will I do with a garden. Oh, my.

"Oh, that will be nice, thank you."

He said, "I'm going to get my tractor. I'll be back in a minute."

"Okay."

He lived just up the way from me, about half a mile. I commented to Bob, "Guess what? I'm getting a garden." About 15 minutes went by. I thought he was going over to get my nephew's little John Deere that he uses to mow the pasture with, etc. Faint I almost did when he turned into our drive with this tractor that he does his farm with. It is so big, you just can't imagine. It is a long piece of machinery that you cut out dirt with and haul it off. He made a long cut down through my beautiful green lawn, over by the little house and shed. For a raised bed garden, you build up the dirt and build a frame around it. He took out three loads of my poor soil and brought some good soil from some land we have a short ways off. Five loads. It sure looks like a big pile of dirt.

Well, you guessed it, now poor Bob gets to go to work. The next day he had me go over to the lumber yard and order up treated lumber for him to frame it up with—12 inches wide, so the garden is raised 12 inches. I got lumber, $236; nails, $3.45; black soil cloth (cloth you put on top of your flower bed, for instance to keep grass from growing), $23; 50 bags of cedar chips, $185.76; bedding plants, $27.48; fertilizer, $12; a proper tool, $10.95—so far, my little 12-foot-wide and 55-foot-long garden has cost me $498.64 and the frame is not even around it yet.

For the next three days, Bob came home and went straight to the garden to work, driving stakes into the ground to nail the frame with—oops, we didn't get enough lumber, another $137 ($635.64 update). Now, you can't appreciate this man I am married to unless I elaborate to you just a little. He drives for 1 hour and 15 minutes, about 75 miles, to work each day—leaves home at 6:00 A.M. and returns around 6:30 P.M. With Daylight Saving Time, he could put in some pretty good licks on that pile of lumber. Bless his heart. He doesn't mess around once I get him started. In just about four days, it was finished. All this time, from the time he left until he returned, I would be working on the top of this little vegetable patch. Leveling the dirt, putting down the black cloth, spreading the chips—oops, we didn't get enough 40-pound bags of cedar chips. Another $58 ($693.64 update).

After about seven days of continuous work, we had a pretty good-looking garden. I almost had it full with nice pretty little plants—tomatoes, peppers, squash, okra, and oh, yes, no lady should have a garden without flowers. I put flowers across the end and all down both sides at the end of each row. My brother asked me how I was going to cook those red things, and I simply said, "Stir-fry."

I was walking down the back of the yard, where we have an area that we store things in—you know those kinds of things: leftover lumber, leftover bricks . . . Look. Bricks. I know what, I could build myself a little wall around the garden, which would make it a foot larger. I could plant my peppers and things there. Yes! I will build myself a brick wall and it will look nice from the drive as you come in.

I have this man, Carey, who has worked for me for years. His mother worked for my mother. He has moved these bricks from one place to another at least six times. I will call Carey to come and help me. "Hello, Carey, I have this little chore I would like for you to come to help me do." "Okay." He arrives. What is the job? Oh, would you please move the brick from down in the draw up to the garden. I thought he was just going to go get into that old blue Jeep truck he has and run over me, but he laughed and said, "Okay." Bless you, Carey. Fifty-five dollars for Carey. Update: $748.64.

For the next three days, I mixed cement and laid my brick wall, three bricks high. Cement, $4.36. Update: $753. By this time it is beginning to look like the Great Wall of China. I think I'll stop with the end next to the drive and the side next to the drive. Looks pretty sharp. Now all I need is just the right flowers: $36. Update: $789 for this little garden with the brick wall. Did just that: I put the brick holes up and put some potting soil, $16 ($805 update), in the holes, planted little plants in the holes. Wish you could see this lady-looking beautiful garden, and so far the pleasure has been all mine.

I must say, I was really starting to enjoy my little garden. I would spend just about every day out there. I did *not* have one weed in it. I fertilized, watered, planted, and was so proud. It was really growing. I was amazed, most of all at the pleasure I was getting out of this. I thanked my brother several times, even though I was reluctant at first.

My garden was very productive. I definitely am looking forward to planting another one next year. After all, how many vegetables could I have bought for $805? Ha! Not on your life. Today I had to pay Carey to clean out the garden, haul off all the dead vines, pull the tomato stakes out, etc. Next season will be here before we know it, and the cycle starts all over, except the building part is done and paid for, so it won't be so bad again.

I could not believe how many vegetables I did get out of this garden. I gave veggies to everyone. I have retired my canning days— eat it, freeze it, or give it away.

Garden-day memories will never leave me. Every time I do anything out there it reminds me of the days I spent with Dad in his gardens. I can still see him walking from the back of the house down to the garden.

Amen!

Dad died August 10, 1995.

GREEN SALAD

SERVES 4

1 GRAM FAT PER SERVING

Prep :15
Cook :00
Stand :00
Total :15

1 head lettuce, cleaned and torn into bite-size pieces
1 tomato, chopped
1 small green bell pepper, seeded and chopped
2 stalks celery, chopped
2 cups white seedless grapes
1 avocado, peeled, seeded, and diced
Fat-free ranch dressing

Put the lettuce in a bowl and top with the tomato, bell pepper, celery, grapes, and avocado. Toss lightly with the dressing just before serving.

SPINACH-ORANGE SALAD

SERVES 2

1 GRAM FAT PER SERVING

Prep :15
Cook :00
Stand 3:00
Total 3:15

2 teaspoons canola oil
½ teaspoon crumbled marjoram
Pinch of black pepper
Pinch of nutmeg
2 cups coarsely chopped orange sections
2 medium-size radishes, trimmed and sliced thin
1 green onion, top and all, chopped
½ pound fresh spinach, trimmed
1¼ teaspoons rice vinegar or white wine vinegar

Combine the oil, marjoram, pepper, and nutmeg in a serving bowl. Add the orange sections, radishes, and green onion. Toss well. Cover and chill in refrigerator for 2 to 3 hours, tossing occasionally.

Wash and pat dry the spinach. Tear into bite-size pieces. Just before serving, add the spinach and vinegar to the chilled ingredients and toss well.

COLESLAW

SERVES 2

0 GRAMS FAT

Prep :15
Cook :00
Stand 3:00
Total 3:15

Dressing:
3 tablespoons plain nonfat yogurt
2 tablespoons nonfat sour cream
¾ teaspoon prepared yellow mustard
½ teaspoon sugar
½ teaspoon cider vinegar
¼ teaspoon celery seed
⅛ teaspoon salt
⅛ teaspoon pepper

1¾ cups shredded cabbage

Mix dressing ingredients and add to cabbage. Toss well. Cover and refrigerate 2 to 3 hours, stirring occasionally.

To make your cabbage crisp, soak the cabbage head, cut in half, in salted water for about 1 hour. Drain well before chopping.

MARINATED COLESLAW

SERVES 8

2 GRAMS FAT PER SERVING

Prep :15
Cook :00
Stand 6:00
Total 6:15

6 cups shredded cabbage
1 large onion, sliced thin and separated into rings
½ cup sugar
½ cup cider vinegar
1 tablespoon canola oil
¼ teaspoon garlic salt
¼ teaspoon pepper
¼ teaspoon celery seed

In a large container with a cover (Tupperware-type bowl) place the shredded cabbage and onion rings. Toss to mix. In a small bowl stir together the sugar, vinegar, oil, garlic salt, pepper, and celery seed. Pour the dressing over the cabbage mixture; toss to coat.

Cover and chill at least 6 hours, stirring occasionally. Store, covered, in the refrigerator for up to 1 week. Use a slotted spoon to serve.

MAKE-AHEAD COLESLAW

4 to 5 cups shredded cabbage (see Note)
1 medium onion, sliced thin
¾ cup sugar
¾ cup white vinegar
½ cup water
1 teaspoon celery seed
½ teaspoon dry mustard
½ teaspoon lemon pepper

SERVES 4

0 GRAMS FAT

Prep :15
Cook :04
Stand 8:00
Total 8:19

Mix the cabbage and onion together in a large bowl with a lid that will seal, such as a Tupperware container.

In a saucepan, combine the remaining ingredients and boil for 3 to 4 minutes. Pour the hot dressing over the cabbage and onion and mix well. Cover and refrigerate for at least 8 hours, stirring two or three times. Use a slotted spoon for serving.

> *Note:* I use an old-fashioned kraut cutter to process my cabbage and onion, because when I make this it is usually for our church bean dinners and I make about three or four times this amount, so it takes a lot more shredding. It works great, but you need the kind with the sliding box on the top. This should keep some of you wondering. Check them out in the antique shops.

OVERNIGHT SLAW

SERVES 4

0 GRAMS FAT

Prep :20
Cook :00
Stand 8:00
Total 8:20

4 cups shredded cabbage
¼ cup thinly sliced purple onion rings
¾ cup sugar
¾ cup white vinegar
¾ cup water
2 teaspoons salt

Combine the cabbage and onion in a large bowl. Mix the sugar, vinegar, water, and salt, stirring until the sugar dissolves. Pour over the cabbage mixture and toss gently. Cover and chill 8 hours or overnight. Serve with a slotted spoon.

APPLE-CARROT SLAW

SERVES 6

0.3 GRAMS FAT

Prep :20
Cook :00
Stand :40
Total 1:05

1 medium cabbage, shredded (about 4 cups)
1¾ cups shredded carrots
1¾ cups chopped unpeeled red apple
⅔ cup fat-free mayonnaise
2 tablespoons sugar
⅓ cup white vinegar
1 teaspoon celery seed

Combine the cabbage, carrots, and apple in a large bowl. Mix the mayonnaise with the sugar, vinegar, and celery seed. Pour over the cabbage. Toss gently to coat. Cover and chill 45 minutes or longer before serving.

FESTIVE CORN SALAD

1 (12-ounce) can white whole-kernel corn, drained and rinsed
1 medium green pepper, seeded and chopped
1 medium tomato, chopped
1 medium purple onion, chopped
¼ teaspoon pepper
½ cup commercial fat-free Italian salad dressing
Lettuce leaves

Combine all ingredients. Toss lightly. Serve on lettuce leaves.

Variation: Fat-free mayonnaise may be substituted for Italian dressing.

SERVES 2

0 GRAMS FAT

Prep :15
Cook :00
Stand :00
Total :15

CORN AND TOMATO SALAD

¼ cup plain nonfat yogurt
2 tablespoons ketchup
1 teaspoon prepared mustard
2 green onions, including tops, chopped
2 tablespoons snipped fresh dill or ½ teaspoon dried dill weed
2 cups fresh or frozen whole-kernel corn
10 cherry tomatoes, halved
1 small green pepper, chopped
Lettuce leaves

SERVES 1

0 GRAMS FAT

Prep :10
Cook :01
Stand :00
Total :11

Combine the yogurt, ketchup, and mustard in a serving bowl; stir in the green onions and dill. Set the dressing aside.

Bring 2 cups of water to a boil, add the corn, and cook 1 minute, or just until tender. Drain in a colander. Rinse with cold water to stop the cooking and drain again.

Add the corn to the yogurt dressing along with the tomatoes and green pepper. Mix well. Serve on lettuce leaves.

CRANBERRY SALAD

SERVES 6

0 GRAMS FAT
IF NUTS
OMITTED

Prep :25
Cook :00
Stand 4:00
Total 4:25

4 cups cranberries
1 cup sugar
1 (3-ounce) package red gelatin dessert mix
1 cup boiling water
1 cup cold water
¾ cup orange juice
1 (6-ounce) can crushed pineapple, drained
1 medium apple (not peeled), grated
½ cup finely chopped nuts (optional)

In a grinder or food processor, grind the cranberries. Transfer them to a medium-size bowl, add the sugar, and let stand until the sugar is dissolved.

Mix the gelatin with the hot and cold water and the orange juice. Let cool. Mix in the cranberries and add the drained pineapple and grated apple. Add nuts if using.

Stir, pour into your favorite mold or dish, and chill until firm.

Tip: Lovely for the holidays molded and set on a bed of shredded lettuce with green grapes arranged around the dish.

VEGETABLE SALAD

A good do-ahead recipe for entertaining.

2 cups broccoli florets
2 cups cauliflower florets
6 large mushrooms, sliced
1 small onion, sliced
¼ cup sliced celery
½ cup fat-free honey mustard salad dressing
¼ cup white vinegar
1 tablespoon poppy seeds
½ teaspoon salt (optional)

SERVES 6

0 GRAMS FAT

Prep :10
Cook :00
Stand 3:00
Total 3:10

In a large mixing bowl, combine the broccoli, cauliflower, mushrooms, onion, and celery. In a small mixing bowl, combine the salad dressing, vinegar, poppy seeds, and salt if using. Mix with a wire whisk. Pour over the vegetables and toss to coat evenly.

Cover and chill for 3 hours, stirring occasionally. Serve with a slotted spoon.

TASTY TOMATO SLICES

3 medium tomatoes, cut into ¼-inch slices
¼ cup wine vinegar (use tarragon if available)
1 teaspoon canola oil
1 tablespoon chopped fresh tarragon leaves or 1 teaspoon dried
Fresh ground pepper

SERVES 6

1 GRAM FAT
PER SERVING

Prep :10
Cook :00
Stand 2:00
Total 2:10

Place the tomatoes in a glass or plastic container, or a serving dish. Shake the vinegar, oil, and tarragon in a jar to mix well. Pour over tomatoes. Sprinkle with pepper and cover. Refrigerate for at least 2 hours.

This serves as a quick salad and can be made ahead.

CUCUMBER STORY

I live in farm country, am a farmer's daughter, farmer's sister, farmer's aunt. You think that you know a little about farming after so many years, *but* . . . A couple years ago there was a nice man who came into this area wanting some of the farmers to put in cucumbers. Cucumbers had never been grown here on a large scale before, so a challenge was in the air.

After many meetings, much planning, and several months, the cucumber crop was planted. My brother was one of the experimenting farmers.

The nice man and his wife were in this area just at planting, cultivating, and harvest times. They needed a place to stay; we have a little guest house that we rent; so they rented it. He is the type of man who has a contagious smile, an apple-pie boy-next-door face, and a sweet personality, so I nicknamed him "Sweetie." Being the type of man he is, he was rather embarrassed by this name, which just made it much more fun for me as I am rather ornery. He has a car phone in his pickup truck, and when I needed to phone him I always said, "Sweetie," so that all of the farmers in the bottom would become acquainted with his name. Ha. He wanted to kill me! OK, we became the best of friends.

He was referred to in the area by all of the farmers as the Pickle Man. They were even introduced in church as Mr. and Mrs. Pickle Man. That makes him even more special—he is a good Christian man.

The story of the cucumbers is very interesting. Did you know that when they start to bloom you have to have hives of bees brought in and placed all around the field so they can pollinate them? I thought that was very interesting. The pickers are big machines like harvesters that pick them vine and all. They separate the cukes from the vines and dump them in a hopper.

These people did not bother to tell all of us in this area about the bees. We went over to pick some cukes one day and guess what? Bees all over us—in the truck, on our clothes, in our hair. One guy got his truck used as a hive and had to leave it there until they moved. We soon learned not to leave the window down on your truck.

The cucumbers were not too successful in this area—too many weather difficulties, I suppose. But that was quite a summer, having the cukes, bees, and Sweetie around for a few months. Sweetie and I are still the best of friends, as are he and my husband. They really liked to go fishing together. They live in Missouri but we all still keep in touch. You meet some of the nicest people in some of the strangest situations at the oddest times. Meet all of the nice people you can. You never know when there is a Sweetie just around the corner.

I made every kind of pickle I could think of that summer, and made up all kinds of dishes using cucumbers. Whatever is on hand is what you try to use. Try the Creamy Cucumbers. I did *not* try cucumber pie; I will leave that to you to do.

CREAMY CUCUMBERS

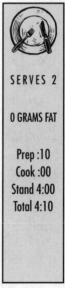

½ cup plain nonfat yogurt
½ teaspoon salt
¼ teaspoon dill weed
2 cups thinly sliced cucumbers
1 small onion, sliced thin and separated into rings
Lettuce Leaves

SERVES 2

0 GRAMS FAT

Prep :10
Cook :00
Stand 4:00
Total 4:10

Mix all ingredients, cover, and refrigerate at least 4 hours.

CORN BREAD SALAD

SERVES 6

0 GRAMS FAT

Prep :15
Cook :00
Stand 1:00
Total 1:15

2 cups crumbled leftover corn bread—fat-free, of course
2 medium tomatoes, chopped
½ cup chopped scallions, tops and all
1 medium bell pepper, chopped
1 teaspoon seasoned salt
Dash of pepper
1 tablespoon sugar or Fructose
½ to ¾ cup fat-free mayonnaise (such as Miracle Whip)

In a mixing bowl, combine the corn bread, tomatoes, scallions, and bell pepper.

In a separate small bowl, mix the seasoned salt, pepper, and sugar with the mayonnaise. Pour this dressing over the corn bread mixture and toss to combine. Let stand about 1 hour before serving.

POTATO SALAD

SERVES 6

0 GRAMS FAT

Prep :25
Cook :30
Stand 1:00
Total 1:55

Salad:
4 to 5 large potatoes
1 cup chopped celery
1 cup chopped onion
¾ cup chopped green pepper
¾ cup chopped dill or sweet pickles

Dressing:
1 cup fat-free mayonnaise (or more, depending on amount of potatoes)
2 to 3 tablespoons mustard
3 tablespoons pickle juice
Touch of salt
Pepper to taste

Boil the potatoes in their skins in water to cover for 30 minutes or until tender. When they are cool enough to handle, peel them and cut into cubes. Mix with the celery, onion, green pepper, and pickles and place in a large bowl.

Mix the dressing ingredients, pour over the salad, and toss gently. Refrigerate at least 1 hour before serving.

> *Variation:* To do a day ahead: Layer vegetables in the bowl, potatoes on top. Do *not* stir. Cover and refrigerate. Mix the dressing, cover, and store. Combine the salad and dressing at least 1 hour before serving.

HOT POTATO SALAD

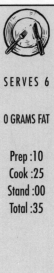

4 to 5 cups thinly sliced potatoes
¾ cup chopped onion
1 tablespoon fat-free margarine or Butter Buds
½ cup fat-free mayonnaise
⅓ cup apple cider vinegar
1 tablespoon sugar
Salt and pepper to taste
Chopped parsley (optional)

SERVES 6

0 GRAMS FAT

Prep :10
Cook :25
Stand :00
Total :35

Cover potatoes with cold water, bring to a boil, and cook 15 to 20 minutes, until just tender—do *not* overcook. Drain and set aside. Sauté the onion in ¼ cup water in a nonstick skillet 3 to 5 minutes, until tender-crisp. Add the margarine, and stir until melted. Combine the mayonnaise, vinegar, sugar, salt, and pepper with the onion mixture. Add potatoes and place the skillet over low heat, stirring constantly until heated. Sprinkle with parsley if desired.

GERMAN POTATO SALAD

SERVES 4

LESS THAN 1 GRAM FAT

Prep :25
Cook :35
Stand :10
Total 1:10

4 medium potatoes
⅓ cup vinegar
1 tablespoon sugar
2 teaspoons flour
¼ teaspoon pepper
1 onion, chopped
¾ cup chopped celery
1 green pepper, seeded and chopped
2 hard-cooked eggs (discard yolks—bad!), chopped
2 tablespoons low-fat bacon bits

Boil the potatoes in water to cover for 30 to 35 minutes, or until tender. Drain. When cool enough to handle, peel them and cut into small cubes. Set aside.

In a heavy saucepan combine the vinegar, sugar, flour, and pepper with ½ cup of water. Whisk over medium heat until the dressing just comes to a boil (2 to 3 minutes).

Combine the potatoes, onion, celery, and green pepper in a serving bowl. Pour the hot dressing over and toss well. Cool to room temperature. When ready to serve, garnish with the chopped egg whites and bacon bits.

WARM GERMAN POTATO SALAD

10 cups cubed potatoes (about 3 pounds), peeled if desired ($1/4$-inch cubes)
$3/4$ cup chopped onion
1 (4-ounce) jar pimentos, drained and chopped
4 slices bacon

Dressing:
1 cup fat-free chicken broth
$3/4$ cup vinegar
2 tablespoons canola oil
2 tablespoons flour
2 tablespoons sugar
$1/2$ teaspoon salt
$1/2$ teaspoon celery seed
$1/4$ teaspoon pepper

SERVES 8

4 GRAMS FAT PER SERVING

Prep :10
Cook :20
Stand: 00
Total :30

Cover the potatoes with water and boil until tender, about 12 to 15 minutes. Drain and place in a large bowl. Add the onion and pimentos.

Meanwhile, in a large nonstick skillet, cook the bacon until crisp (I cook it in the microwave on a paper towel so it's less greasy). If using a regular skillet, when the bacon is crispy, remove and pat with a paper towel. Discard the bacon fat and wipe the skillet to remove any mean old grams hiding in there. Matter of fact, you'd better wash it with soap and water.

In the skillet, combine all the dressing ingredients. Whisk until blended and bring to a boil, whisking often. Reduce the heat and simmer 2 to 3 minutes, or until thickened. Pour over the potatoes and toss gently to coat. Crumble bacon over the top and serve immediately.

If you are being as careful as I had to be at first about the number of grams I consumed a day, you may desire to substitute bacon chips such as Baco or some such product for the bacon. Read your label to find the lowest in fat grams. You can still have the flavor without the 4 grams.

POTATO-GREEN PEA SALAD

SERVES 6

0 GRAMS FAT

Prep :25
Cook :40
Stand 1:00
Total 2:05

Salad:
4 to 5 medium potatoes
2 cups frozen green peas, thawed
1 cup chopped celery
¼ cup sliced green onions
¼ cup chopped green pepper

Dressing:
½ cup fat-free mayonnaise
½ cup plain nonfat yogurt
1 to 2 tablespoons prepared mustard
1 teaspoon vinegar
Salt and pepper to taste

Boil the potatoes in water to cover for 30 to 40 minutes, or until tender. When cool enough to handle, peel them and cut into cubes. You should have about 7 cups.

Combine the potatoes with the rest of the salad ingredients in a serving bowl.

Mix the dressing ingredients and pour over the salad mixture. Toss lightly. Refrigerate at least 1 hour before serving.

> *Variation:* A good do-ahead recipe. Layer the salad ingredients, peas on bottom and potatoes on top. Cover and refrigerate. Combine the dressing ingredients, cover, and refrigerate. Toss together lightly at least 1 hour before serving.

LAYERED MEXICAN GARDEN SALAD

*The amount of ingredients depends on
how many salads you want to make.
This is for two.*

Shredded lettuce
1 (16-ounce) can pinto beans in Mexican-style sauce, drained
1 cup chopped zucchini
1 cup chopped tomato
¼ cup chopped onion
½ cup thick and chunky salsa, or as needed
4 ounces shredded fat-free Cheddar cheese
Red or green chile peppers

SERVES 2

LESS THAN 1
GRAM FAT PER
SERVING

Prep :10
Cook :00
Stand :00
Total :10

Line individual salad plates with lettuce. Cover with a layer of beans, then with layers of zucchini, tomato, and onion. Spoon salsa evenly over the vegetables (more may be added if desired). Sprinkle with cheese. Garnish with red or green chile peppers if desired.

COTTAGE CHEESE SALAD

2 Roma tomatoes, or 1 large tomato, chopped
2 green onions, chopped
2 cups fat-free cottage cheese
Salt and pepper

SERVES 2

0 GRAMS FAT

Prep :10
Cook :00
Stand 1:00
Total 1:10

Mix the chopped tomatoes and onions with the cottage cheese. Let stand about 1 hour to blend flavors. Salt and pepper to taste before serving.

TABBOULEH

SERVES 2

1 GRAM FAT
PER ¾-CUP
SERVING

Prep :20
Cook :00
Stand :30
Total :50

1 cup bulgur or cracked wheat
2 cups boiling water
4 teaspoons lemon juice
2 teaspoons olive oil
2 medium ripe tomatoes, chopped
3 tablespoons minced parsley
½ small red onion, chopped
2 green onions, including tops, chopped fine
¼ teaspoon ground coriander
¼ teaspoon ground cumin
⅛ teaspoon hot pepper sauce
Lettuce leaves

Place bulgur in a large bowl and pour boiling water over. Cover and let stand for 30 minutes. Drain off any liquid that remains.

In another bowl mix the lemon juice, olive oil, tomatoes, parsley, red and green onions, and seasonings. Add the bulgur and toss well to mix. Serve on lettuce leaves.

QUICK PASTA SALAD

SERVES 6

0 GRAMS FAT

Prep :05
Cook :00
Stand :00
Total :05

Salad:
2 cups pasta, cooked and drained
1 cup frozen green peas, rinsed in hot water and drained
2 cups frozen stir-fry vegetables, rinsed in hot water and drained

Dressing:
¾ cup fat-free mayonnaise
¼ cup fat-free Italian salad dressing

Put the salad ingredients in a serving bowl. Combine the dressing ingredients, mix well, and add to the salad. Toss until combined.

MACARONI SALAD

1 (8-ounce) package of macaroni, any style or shape desired
1 large tomato, diced
¾ cup chopped onion
¾ cup chopped green pepper
¾ cup pimiento-stuffed green olives, sliced
1 cup fat-free mayonnaise (approximately)
Salt and pepper

SERVES 6 TO 8

0 GRAMS FAT

Prep :30
Cook :25
Stand :30
Total 1:25

Cook the macaroni in a large pot of boiling water until tender but still firm. Drain in a colander; rinse with cold water and drain thoroughly.

In a large bowl, combine the macaroni with the tomato, onion, green pepper, and olives. Toss lightly.

Add enough fat-free mayonnaise to desired moistness. Salt and pepper to taste. Mix well. Chill for 30 minutes before serving.

Variation: A good do-ahead dish: Layer the ingredients in a serving dish, starting with tomatoes on the bottom; this keeps any juice from making other items soggy. Put the drained macaroni on top and seal with plastic wrap. The dressing should be added about ½ hour before serving time so flavors may blend. Drain any excess juice off before adding dressing.

LIGHT AND ZESTY PASTA SALAD

SERVES 4

LESS THAN 1 GRAM FAT PER SERVING (ONLY WHAT'S IN PASTA)

Prep :10
Cook :15
Stand 2:00
Total 2:25

½ cup fat-free Zesty Italian salad dressing
½ cup fat-free Miracle Whip salad dressing
1 cup broccoli florets
2 cups cooked corkscrew noodles, drained
½ cup chopped green pepper
½ cup chopped tomato
¼ cup sliced scallions

Combine the dressings in a small bowl and mix well. Steam the broccoli just until crisp-tender. Drain and let cool.

In a large bowl, mix the broccoli florets with the pasta, green pepper, tomato, scallions, and dressing. Mix well. Chill 2 hours.

GARDEN PASTA SALAD

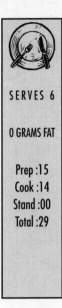

SERVES 6

0 GRAMS FAT

Prep :15
Cook :14
Stand :00
Total :29

Dressing:
½ cup fat-free mayonnaise (such as Miracle Whip)
1 tablespoon vinegar
½ teaspoon Dijon mustard
½ teaspoon dried basil
½ teaspoon dried oregano
Dash ground red pepper
Dash black pepper

1 (16-ounce) package fettuccine, linguine, or spaghetti
½ pound broccoli florets
½ pound asparagus, cut into 1-inch pieces
1 (10-ounce) package frozen green peas, thawed and drained
1 green or red bell pepper, seeded and chopped coarse
½ pound mushrooms, sliced
¼ cup chopped parsley
½ cup grated fat-free Parmesan cheese

Prepare the salad dressing by placing all dressing ingredients in a jar and shaking well.

Prepare the pasta according to package directions, leaving out any oil or margarine called for; drain; place in a large bowl. Toss with about 1 tablespoon of the salad dressing. Set aside.

In a large saucepan, combine the broccoli and asparagus with boiling water to cover. Cook for about 4 minutes or until crisp-tender. Drain well and add to the pasta. Add the peas, bell pepper, mushrooms, parsley, and Parmesan. Toss thoroughly.

Pour remaining salad dressing over all and mix well.

RICE SALAD

SERVES 6

TRACE OF FAT
PER 1-CUP
SERVING

Prep :15
Cook :00
Stand 2:00
Total 2:15

3 cups cooked rice, chilled
¾ cup chopped scallions
½ cup chopped green pepper
½ cup chopped celery
½ cup chopped red bell pepper or pimento (adds color) (optional)

Dressing:
1 cup fat-free mayonnaise
1 tablespoon sugar or sweetener
1 teaspoon prepared mustard
Salt and pepper to taste
1 teaspoon vinegar

Mix the cold rice with the vegetables in a bowl.

In a separate bowl, combine the ingredients for the dressing. Pour the dressing over the rice mixture, and toss to combine thoroughly.

Chill at least 2 hours before serving. Garnish with tomato wedges if desired.

CHICKEN SALAD

4 chicken breast halves, skinned
1 cup chopped celery
1 cup chopped sweet pickles
3 egg whites, boiled and chopped (discard the yolks—*bad!!*)
1 large apple, chopped
¾ cup pecans, chopped (optional)
Fat-free mayonnaise
Salt and pepper to taste

SERVES 6

2 GRAMS FAT
(WITHOUT
PECANS)

Prep :30
Cook :20
Stand :00
Total :50

In a medium saucepan, bring $2\frac{1}{2}$ cups of water to a boil. Add the chicken, return to a boil, and lower the heat. Simmer, covered, until the chicken is fork-tender and the juices run clear, 20 to 30 minutes. When the chicken is cool enough to handle, debone it and chop into small pieces. Reserve the broth in the refrigerator to defat and use later.

Combine chicken in a bowl with the remaining ingredients. Add enough mayonnaise to make as moist as you desire.

MANDARIN CHICKEN SALAD

A very pretty salad, especially for a ladies' luncheon or for your special friends.

SERVES 4

1 GRAM FAT
PER SERVING

Prep :10
Cook :10
Stand :00
Total :20

1 (6-ounce) can mandarin orange segments, chilled
2 tablespoons rice vinegar or wine vinegar
⅓ cup honey
2 tablespoons reduced-sodium soy sauce
1 (8-ounce) can sliced water chestnuts, drained
4 cups shredded napa cabbage or lettuce
1 cup shredded red cabbage
½ cup thinly sliced radishes
4 slices red onion, cut in half and separated into half circles
4 boneless skinless chicken tenders, or any white meat pieces, cooked, cut into thin
   strips

Drain the oranges, reserving ⅓ cup of the liquid in a small mixing bowl. Into this reserved liquid, mix the vinegar, honey, and soy sauce. Blend with a wire whisk. Add the drained water chestnuts and set aside.

Divide the napa cabbage, red cabbage, radishes, and onion evenly onto four salad plates. Top with strips of chicken and orange segments. Remove the water chestnuts from the liquid with a slotted spoon and arrange on salads. Drizzle the remaining dressing over the salads.

CHICKEN WALDORF SALAD

2 cups cooked small shell pasta, cooled
1½ cups sliced celery
2 cups diced cooked or deli-style chicken breast
2 apples, peeled and diced
¼ cup sliced scallions
½ cup chopped and toasted walnuts

Dressing:
½ cup fat-free ranch dressing
3 tablespoons fat-free mayonnaise
1 tablespoon sugar
1 tablespoon cider vinegar
Dash of pepper
Lettuce leaves

Optional garnishes: avocado or mandarin orange slices

SERVES 4

3 GRAMS FAT
PER SERVING

Prep :15
Cook :10
Stand :30
Total :55

In a large bowl, combine the pasta, celery, chicken, apples, scallions, and toasted walnuts.

Prepare the dressing. In a small mixing bowl, combine the ranch dressing with the mayonnaise, sugar, vinegar, and pepper. Blend well and let stand at least 30 minutes, then add to the pasta mixture, tossing to coat thoroughly. To serve, mound on lettuce leaves. A slice of avocado or a few mandarin orange slices on the side are very pretty.

LACY WALDORF SALAD

SERVES 4

0 GRAMS FAT
IF PECANS
OMITTED

Prep :15
Cook :00
Stand :00
Total :15

Salad:
¾ medium head lettuce, chopped fine
¾ cup white grapes, halved
¼ cup chopped celery
1 sliced green onion
½ cup chopped pecans
1 apple, peeled and chopped

Dressing:
1 cup fat-free salad dressing, such as Miracle Whip
2 tablespoons lemon juice
1 tablespoon sugar
2 tablespoons skim milk

Combine the salad ingredients in a large bowl. Blend the dressing ingredients until smooth. Pour over the salad and toss to combine.

Variation: To make your salad prettier when having company, divide the salad between 4 chilled salad plates and lay a very thin slice of avocado on the side of each salad dish.

ORANGE-MELON SALAD

2½ cups honeydew melon cubes or balls
3 oranges, peeled and cut up
⅓ cup (3 ounces) frozen limeade concentrate, thawed

In a serving bowl, combine all the ingredients. Cover; refrigerate until serving time.

SERVES 2

0 GRAMS FAT

Prep :20
Cook :00
Stand :15
Total :35

CREAMY SALAD DRESSING

1 cup fat-free salad dressing, such as Miracle Whip
1 cup fat-free ranch dressing
1 tablespoon lemon juice
1 tablespoon sugar
¼ cup skim milk

MAKES
ABOUT 2¼
CUPS

0 GRAMS FAT

Prep :05
Cook :00
Stand :00
Total :05

Mix all ingredients with a wire whisk until smooth. Serve over your favorite salad greens or fruit.

CREAMY GARLIC DRESSING

½ cup skim milk
2 tablespoons lemon juice
1 tablespoon canola oil
1½ cups fat-free cottage cheese, drained
¼ cup chopped onion
2 cloves garlic, chopped fine
½ teaspoon salt
¼ teaspoon pepper
¼ teaspoon paprika

MAKES
ABOUT 2
CUPS

1 GRAM FAT
PER SERVING

Prep :10
Cook :00
Stand 1:00
Total 1:10

Combine all the ingredients and mix well. Store in a covered container in the refrigerator at least 1 hour before using.

CREAMY COLESLAW DRESSING

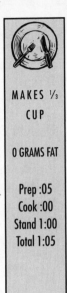

½ cup plain nonfat yogurt
2 tablespoons Dijon mustard
1 tablespoon fat-free mayonnaise
2 teaspoons sugar
Pepper and salt to taste

Mix all ingredients. To serve, pour over shredded cabbage and refrigerate at least 1 hour.

MAKES ⅓
CUP

0 GRAMS FAT

Prep :05
Cook :00
Stand 1:00
Total 1:05

HONEY MUSTARD DRESSING

½ cup lemon juice
¼ cup honey
2 tablespoons prepared mustard
1 teaspoon salt
½ teaspoon paprika
2 cloves garlic, chopped fine
⅔ cup water

Mix all the ingredients and shake well. Store in a covered container at least 1 hour before serving.

MAKES
ABOUT 1½
CUP

0 GRAMS FAT

Prep :10
Cook :00
Stand 1:00
Total 1:10

GARLIC WINE

Good on salad. Excellent to cook with.

SERVES 10

0 GRAMS FAT

Prep :00
Cook :00
Stand :00
Total :00

6 to 8 whole cloves garlic, peeled
1 bottle red wine

Put garlic into wine; let stand for 3 to 4 weeks before using.

Poultry

Chicken

CHICKEN WITH STUFFING—
SHORTCUT METHOD

SERVES 4

**4 GRAMS FAT
PER SERVING**

Prep :20
Cook 1:05
Stand :00
Total 1:25

1 (14-ounce) can fat-free chicken broth
2 tablespoons Butter Buds, liquid form
¾ cup chopped celery
¾ cup chopped onions
5 cups herb-seasoned or chicken-flavored packaged stuffing mix
4 boneless skinless chicken breast halves
2 tablespoons honey
2 tablespoons lemon juice
1 teaspoon parsley flakes

Preheat the oven to 375 degrees.

In a saucepan, combine the broth, Butter Buds, celery, and onions. Heat to boiling; simmer for 5 minutes or until the vegetables are crisp-tender. Remove from heat. Add stuffing mix and toss to combine.

Spray a 3-quart oblong baking dish with vegetable oil cooking spray. Spoon the stuffing mix into the dish and arrange the chicken down the center of the stuffing.

In a small bowl, combine the honey, lemon juice, and parsley flakes. Brush onto the chicken. Bake uncovered for 1 hour or until the chicken is tender. Stir the stuffing before serving.

PAN-ROASTED CHICKEN

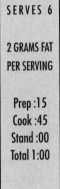

1 chicken, cut up and skinned (or use only breast, for less fat)
7 or 8 small new potatoes, scrubbed
4 or 5 small onions, peeled
4 medium carrots, peeled and cut into 3-inch pieces
½ cup dry white wine
1 (14-ounce) can low-fat reduced-sodium chicken broth
1 tablespoon lemon juice
3 cloves garlic, chopped fine
1 teaspoon oregano
½ teaspoon thyme
¼ teaspoon black pepper
2 tablespoons chopped parsley

SERVES 6

2 GRAMS FAT PER SERVING

Prep :15
Cook :45
Stand :00
Total 1:00

Preheat the oven to 350 degrees.

Arrange the chicken, potatoes, onions, and carrots in a baking dish.

Mix the wine, broth, and lemon juice. Pour over chicken and vegetables.

Sprinkle on garlic, oregano, thyme, and pepper.

Bake uncovered 40 to 45 minutes or until chicken is fork tender. Turn veggies and chicken occasionally and baste with pan juices. (If juices evaporate too quickly, add more chicken broth.)

Transfer to a serving platter, arranging vegetables around chicken, and sprinkle with parsley.

Tip: Dark meat is fattier than white meat. Ounce for ounce, drumsticks have more than twice the fat of chicken breasts.

PAN-ROASTED CHICKEN IN A BAG

No fuss—no muss. Throw away the mess of your stewpot.

SERVES 4

3.5 GRAMS FAT PER SERVING

Prep :15
Cook :50
Stand :00
Total 1:05

1 tablespoon flour
4 boneless skinless chicken breast halves
4 medium carrots, sliced
2 stalks celery, sliced
1 small whole onion, peeled
⅛ teaspoon garlic powder
½ cup brown gravy mix

Preheat the oven to 350 degrees. Place flour in a large (14 x 20-inch) oven bag; shake around to coat the inside of the bag. Place the bag in a 13 x 9-inch baking dish. Cut each chicken breast in half crosswise. Wash the chicken pieces and place in the bag along with the carrots, celery, and onion. Sprinkle garlic powder over all.

In a small bowl, combine the gravy mix with 1½ cups of water. Pour over the chicken and vegetables in the bag. Close the bag with a nylon tie. Cut 6 half-inch slits into the top of the bag to let steam escape.

Bake 45 to 50 minutes or until chicken is tender. Roll and move the bag around a couple of times during cooking to blend and coat all with gravy, being careful not to let it spill through the slits.

Variation: You can use lean pork in place of chicken, if desired.

LEMON HONEY GLAZE FOR BAKED CHICKEN

Dresses up a plain baked chicken to taste like Sunday Company's A Comin'.

¼ cup lemon juice
¼ cup honey
1 teaspoon chopped parsley

Mix the above ingredients and brush over chicken when about $^2/_3$ of the way done when baking.

MAKES ½ CUP

0 GRAMS FAT

Prep :05
Cook :00
Stand :00
Total :05

DRESSING PAN

I have this neat old pan that is my dressing pan. I bet many of you have just such a pan. Mine belonged to my grandmother. My mom had it for many years; I kept borrowing it and finally forgot to take it home. She fussed so that one year I wrapped it up and gave it to her for a Christmas gift. Years later she gave it back to me because I now do all the dressing baking in our family.

Mom is a retired dressing maker. There always seems to be one person in each family that tackles the dressing. This pan is an old beat-up round, deep, ugly pan. I bet you know exactly what I am talking about. Sounds just like that one in your cabinet that you always drag out for dressing, doesn't it? I hope someday my granddaughter will be making dressing in this pan. Dressing day is such a special day with most families, make each one special.

CORN BREAD DRESSING

SERVES 8

VERY LOW FAT

Prep :15
Cook :40
Stand :00
Total :55

1 recipe Corn Bread (page 318), made a day ahead
2 cups chopped onions
2 cups chopped celery
2 to 4 tablespoons sage (some like a stronger sage taste)
2 cups defatted chicken stock (use more if desired)
Salt and pepper to taste
¾ cup egg substitute
Butter Buds

Crumble cold corn bread into a bowl. Add the onions, celery, sage, chicken stock, salt, pepper, and egg substitute. Mix well. Pour into a baking dish that has been coated with vegetable oil cooking spray. Bake in a preheated 350 degree oven for 30 minutes. Pour Butter Buds over the top, as if dotting with butter. Continue baking until desired doneness.

Variation: I cook my onions and celery until crisp tender and use some of the water they were cooked in to help moisten the dressing and give it a nice flavor.

Baked Chicken and Dressing: Boil some boneless, skinless chicken breasts while mixing this. Cut them up into bite-size pieces and place on top of the dressing. Push down just enough to cover the chicken. This keeps it from drying out, and you now have chicken and dressing that looks like you have worked for hours preparing. Don't say a word!

BAG CHICKEN

1 tablespoon flour
4 to 6 boneless skinless chicken breast halves
½ cup chopped onion
½ cup chopped celery
1 cup whole-berry cranberry sauce
½ cup ketchup
1 tablespoon packed brown sugar
2 tablespoons lemon juice
1 tablespoon Worcestershire sauce
1 tablespoon prepared mustard
1 tablespoon red wine vinegar

SERVES 4

2.5 GRAMS FAT PER SERVING

Prep :17
Cook 1:15
Stand :00
Total 1:32

Preheat the oven to 325 degrees. Place the flour in a large (14 x 20-inch) oven bag, shaking it to coat the inside. Put the bag in a 13 x 9 x 2-inch baking pan; set aside.

Dry-fry (in a nonstick skillet without any oil) the chicken breast until browned and tender. Remove with a slotted spoon and blot on paper towels to remove any oil that cooked out of the chicken.

Wipe out the skillet, add a tablespoon or two of water, and cook the onion and celery for 5 minutes, stirring often. Stir in the cranberry sauce and remaining ingredients. Bring to a slow boil. Place the chicken in the bag, spoon the sauce over the chicken, and close the bag as package directions suggest. Punch a few holes in top of the bag to let steam out.

Bake at 325 degrees for 1 hour and 15 minutes. About every 15 minutes, roll the bag around carefully to baste. (Be careful to keep the holes on top.) Serve with rice if desired.

BARBECUED CHICKEN

SERVES 4

4 GRAMS FAT
PER SERVING

Prep :10
Cook :35
Stand :00
Total :45

4 skinless chicken breast halves, rib bone in
1 medium onion, cut into thin slices
1½ cups fat-free barbecue sauce (read label for 0 grams fat)

Preheat the oven to 350 degrees. Spray a 9 x 9-inch square baking dish lightly with vegetable oil cooking spray, or line it with foil. Set aside.

Wash the chicken breasts well and take off all visible fat. I use the bone-in chicken for barbecuing because it is moister than the breast without the bone. Cover the bottom of your baking dish with the onion. Place the chicken pieces bone side down in the baking dish and cover with foil. Bake for about 20 minutes. Uncover, drain off any juices collected in the baking dish, and spoon the barbecue sauce over the chicken generously. Return to the oven and continue to bake uncovered until tender. If you put the sauce on at the beginning it gets too saucy or dries out too much.

You can do this same recipe in a cooking bag for really easy cleanup, and it makes the chicken deliciously tender.

Variation: You can cook these on your grill. First bake them in the oven for 20 minutes, covered, to make them nice and moist and tender. Then drain, coat with sauce, and place them bone side down on a hot grill until cooked through. This method takes a lot less grilling time and you can prepare them ahead of time and finish cooking when the guests arrive. Precooking also keeps them from getting dried out.

OVEN "FRIED" CHICKEN

½ cup egg substitute
1½ cups cornflake crumbs
4 boneless skinless chicken breast halves

SERVES 4

4 GRAMS FAT
PER SERVING

Prep :10
Cook :35
Stand :00
Total :45

Preheat the oven to 375 degrees. Lightly spray a baking sheet with vegetable oil cooking spray.

In two small shallow separate bowls, place the egg substitute and cornflake crumbs. One at a time, dip each piece of chicken into the egg substitute, then roll in the crumbs, patting to make sure they are coated well. This will make them nice and crispy. Place on the cooking sheet. Spray each piece lightly with vegetable oil cooking spray.

Bake for 30 to 35 minutes or until tender and crispy, turning each piece after 15 minutes.

CAJUN OVEN "FRIED" CHICKEN

½ cup egg substitute
1½ cups corn flake crumbs
4 boneless skinless chicken breast halves
½ teaspoon crushed oregano leaves
¼ teaspoon cayenne pepper
½ teaspoon garlic powder
2 tablespoons Creole seasoning

SERVES 4

4 GRAMS FAT
PER SERVING

Prep :10
Cook :35
Stand :00
Total :45

Preheat the oven to 350 degrees. Lightly spray a baking sheet well with vegetable cooking spray; set aside.

Take two small shallow bowls and put the egg substitute in one and the corn flake crumbs in the other. Mix the seasonings with the corn flake crumbs, being sure they are mixed well.

Coat the chicken, one piece at a time, with the egg substitute, then roll in the corn flake crumbs, patting to make sure the pieces are coated well. This will make it nice and crispy.

(continued)

Place on the prepared baking sheet and spray the top of each piece with vegetable cooking spray lightly. Bake for about 30 to 35 minutes, turning each piece when half done. You may want to vary the seasonings—it may be a little too hot for some.

"FRIED" CORNMEAL-COATED CHICKEN

Nice and brown, this chicken gives you the fried satisfaction without the fatisfaction.

SERVES 6

2 GRAMS FAT
PER SERVING

Prep :10
Cook :40
Stand :00
Total :50

1 cup cornmeal
¼ teaspoon oregano
½ teaspoon chili powder
6 boneless, skinless chicken breast halves

Preheat the oven to 350 degrees. Mix the cornmeal, oregano, and chili powder. Coat the chicken with the cornmeal mixture. Arrange the pieces in a baking dish that has been coated with cooking spray. Spray the tops lightly with cooking spray. Bake, without turning, until tender, about 30 to 45 minutes.

Serve with salsa or ketchup.

VEGETABLE-STUFFED CHICKEN BREAST OVER RICE

4 boneless skinless chicken breast halves
2½ cups frozen veggies (broccoli, carrots, water chestnuts, red peppers)
½ cup fat-free chicken broth
¼ teaspoon thyme leaves
¼ teaspoon salt
¼ teaspoon paprika
⅛ teaspoon pepper
2 cups hot cooked rice (1 use Harvest Blend or wild or plain)
2 tablespoons flour
½ cup skim milk

SERVES 4

4 GRAMS FAT
PER SERVING

Prep :20
Cook :40
Stand :00
Total 1:00

Place a chicken breast half between two pieces of waxed paper or plastic wrap. Pound the chicken gently with a meat mallet or rolling pin until it is about ¼ inch thick. Repeat for the remaining chicken breasts.

Thaw the veggies by placing in a sieve and running hot water over them; shake any excess water off. Chop them fine and reserve about 1 cup for the sauce. Spoon some of the remaining veggies into the center of each chicken breast; roll up like a jelly roll.

In a large nonstick skillet, heat the chicken broth, thyme, salt, paprika, and pepper. Add the chicken rolls, seam side down. Bring to a boil, reduce the heat, cover, and simmer 20 to 25 minutes or until chicken is tender. Using a slotted spoon, remove chicken rolls. Arrange over cooked rice on a serving platter; cover to keep warm.

Add the reserved veggies to the mixture in the skillet. Bring to a boil, reduce the heat, and simmer for 5 to 6 minutes or until crisp-tender. In a small bowl, combine flour and milk, blend well, and add to the mixture in the skillet. Cook until thickened, stirring constantly. Spoon over the rice and chicken.

Serve with a nice garden salad.

PICANTE CHICKEN WITH BROWN RICE

SERVES 2

3 GRAMS FAT PER SERVING

Prep :10
Cook :25
Stand :00
Total :35

¾ pound boneless, skinless chicken breasts, cut into strips
1½ teaspoons chili powder
1 teaspoon ground cumin
¼ cup cold water
½ cup sliced green onions
2 cloves garlic, chopped fine
1 (14-ounce) can whole tomatoes, undrained and cut up
1 cup frozen corn kernels
¾ cup uncooked instant brown rice
2 tablespoons chopped green chiles, undrained
½ cup water

Heat a nonstick skillet; add the chicken and sprinkle with chili powder and cumin. Add ¼ cup water, the green onions, and garlic. Sauté until the chicken is no longer pink.

Stir in the tomatoes, corn, rice, chiles, and ½ cup water. Bring to a boil. Reduce the heat, cover, and simmer 5 to 10 minutes, or until the rice is done.

PARMESAN CHICKEN

6 boneless, skinless chicken breast halves
2 tablespoons fat-free margarine, melted
½ cup grated fat-free Parmesan cheese (see Note)
¼ cup dry bread crumbs
1 teaspoon oregano
1 teaspoon parsley
¼ teaspoon paprika
Salt and pepper to taste

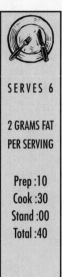

SERVES 6

2 GRAMS FAT
PER SERVING

Prep :10
Cook :30
Stand :00
Total :40

   Heat the oven to 400 degrees. Spray a baking dish with vegetable oil cooking spray.

   Dip the chicken in the melted margarine (use liquid Butter Buds if you prefer). Combine the remaining ingredients and coat the chicken with the crumb mixture. Place in the baking dish and bake uncovered for 25 to 30 minutes, or until tender and golden brown.

Note: Weight Watchers makes a fat-free Parmesan.

CHICKEN DIJON

½ cup fat-free salad dressing, such as Miracle Whip
¼ cup Dijon mustard
4 to 6 boneless, skinless chicken breast halves
1¼ cups dry bread crumbs, fat-free
¼ cup Butter Buds, liquid form

SERVES 4

ULTRA LOW-
FAT

Prep :10
Cook 1:00
Stand :00
Total 1:10

   Preheat the oven to 350 degrees.

   Combine salad dressing and mustard, blending well. Brush chicken with the mixture and coat with crumbs. Place in a baking dish that has been coated with vegetable oil cooking spray. Drizzle with Butter Buds.

   Bake uncovered for 45 minutes to 1 hour, or until chicken is done to desired tenderness.

CHICKEN CORDON BLEU

SERVES 8

4 GRAMS FAT
PER SERVING

Prep :25
Cook :35
Stand :00
Total 1:00

8 boneless, skinless chicken breast halves
1/4 cup chopped parsley
4 ounces fat-free mozzarella cheese, sliced
4 slices low-fat ham
3/4 cup egg substitute
1 cup seasoned bread crumbs
White Wine Sauce (recipe follows)
1 tablespoon minced fresh parsley

Preheat the oven to 400 degrees.

Pound the chicken breast pieces until they are thin. Sprinkle with parsley. Top each piece with a thin layer of cheese, then a half slice of ham. Roll up tightly.

Roll each breast in egg substitute and coat with bread crumbs. Spray a baking dish with cooking spray. Arrange chicken rolls in the dish with the seam sides down (secure with a toothpick if desired).

Bake for 30 minutes, or until browned and cooked through. Pour a small amount of white wine sauce over each chicken breast when served and sprinkle with parsley.

White Wine Sauce

MAKES
ABOUT 3 1/2
CUPS

LOW-FAT

Prep :05
Cook :10
Stand :00
Total :15

2 cups fat-free chicken broth
1/2 cup white wine
6 tablespoons all-purpose flour
3/4 cup skim milk
Onion powder and pepper to taste (optional)

Combine the broth and wine in a nonstick saucepan. Heat to boiling; reduce heat. Mix flour and milk in a small cup until smooth; stir into broth. Cook and stir until mixture is thick. Thin with a little water if necessary. Add onion powder and pepper if desired.

CHICKEN BREASTS WITH SWEET ORANGE SAUCE

8 boneless skinless chicken breast halves
1½ cups herb-seasoned stuffing mix
¼ cup Butter Buds, liquid form
½ cup orange juice
4 cups hot cooked wild rice
Sweet Orange Sauce (see below)

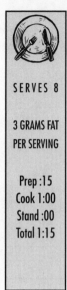

SERVES 8

3 GRAMS FAT
PER SERVING

Prep :15
Cook 1:00
Stand :00
Total 1:15

Preheat the oven to 350 degrees. Lightly coat a 13 x 9-inch baking dish with vegetable oil cooking spray. Arrange the chicken breasts in the dish and sprinkle some of the stuffing mix over each. Drizzle with Butter Buds and then with the orange juice. Cover the dish tightly with foil and bake for 1 hour. Serve with wild rice and sweet orange sauce.

Sweet Orange Sauce

1 (6-ounce) can frozen orange juice concentrate, thawed and undiluted
½ cup orange marmalade
2 tablespoons steak sauce

Combine all ingredients in a microwave-safe container. Microwave on high 6 minutes or until hot and bubbly, stirring once. Spoon over chicken on a bed of wild rice.

CHEESY OAT-BAKED CHICKEN

SERVES 6

2 GRAMS FAT
PER SERVING

Prep :15
Cook :40
Stand :00
Total :55

2 cups quick-cooking oats
¼ cup fat-free Parmesan cheese
1 teaspoon paprika
½ teaspoon pepper
6 boneless, skinless chicken breast halves
2 egg whites or egg substitute

Preheat the oven to 350 degrees. Spray a 13 x 9 x 2-inch baking pan with cooking spray. Combine the oats, Parmesan, paprika, and pepper. Dip the chicken in the egg whites; coat with the oat mixture. Arrange the chicken pieces in the prepared pan; spray lightly with cooking spray. Bake uncovered until tender, approximately 30 to 45 minutes.

CHICKEN CREOLE

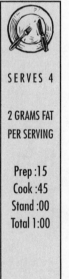

SERVES 4

2 GRAMS FAT
PER SERVING

Prep :15
Cook :45
Stand :00
Total 1:00

1 medium onion, chopped
1 medium bell pepper, seeded and chopped
1 stalk celery, chopped
2 cloves garlic, chopped fine
2 whole chicken breasts, halved and skinned
1 teaspoon paprika
½ teaspoon cayenne pepper
1 (12-ounce) can low-sodium stewed tomatoes
1 teaspoon dried rosemary
½ teaspoon dried marjoram
1 bay leaf
1 tablespoon flour
¼ cup defatted chicken broth or water

Sauté the onion, pepper, celery, and garlic in ¼ cup water in a medium-size skillet. (If using frozen onions and peppers you don't need to use any water; enough will cook out of them to do the job.)

Sauté until the onion is just tender, about 3 minutes. Transfer to a small dish.

Sprinkle the chicken with paprika and cayenne pepper. Put the chicken in the skillet and cook about 5 minutes, turning occasionally.

Add half the cooked vegetables to the skillet along with tomatoes, rosemary, marjoram, and bay leaf. Reduce the heat, cover, and simmer for 20 to 25 minutes, or until fork tender.

Dissolve the flour in the chicken broth. Stir into the pan juices and cook, stirring constantly, until thickened. Add the reserved cooked vegetables and heat for 3 to 4 minutes. Discard bay leaf. Serve with rice and steamed okra.

MUSHROOM DILL CHICKEN

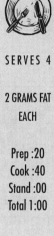

SERVES 4

2 GRAMS FAT
EACH

Prep :20
Cook :40
Stand :00
Total 1:00

4 boneless, skinless chicken breast halves
2 tablespoons Butter Buds, liquid form
1 cup hot water
2 cups Stove Top stuffing, chicken flavor
1 green or red bell pepper (optional), seeded and chopped fine
¼ cup egg substitute
Pepper to taste
1 (10¾-ounce) can Healthy Request cream of mushroom soup
½ teaspoon dried dill weed

Preheat the oven to 350 degrees. Lay the chicken breast halves on a flat surface and pound with a rolling pin or meat mallet to ¼-inch thickness.

Combine the Butter Buds, hot water, stuffing mix, chopped bell pepper if using, and egg substitute. Mix until moistened. Spoon evenly over the chicken. Roll up tightly, starting with a long end. Secure with toothpicks. Place seam side down in a square baking dish that has been sprayed with vegetable oil cooking spray. Spray the chicken lightly and sprinkle with pepper.

Bake uncovered, without turning, until tender, about 30 to 40 minutes. Heat the soup with ½ cup water and the dill in a saucepan. Serve spooned over the chicken.

■ ■

QUICK CHICKEN CACCIATORE

SERVES 6

3 GRAMS FAT EACH

Prep :10
Cook :50
Stand :00
Total 1:00

6 to 8 breaded chicken tenders
12 ounces spaghetti
Prepared low-fat spaghetti sauce

Brown chicken tenders in a nonstick skillet; pat excess fat off with a paper towel. Cut into bite-size pieces. Set aside.
Prepare spaghetti according to package directions and drain.
Heat spaghetti sauce (I use Healthy Choice; it is very low in fat).
Add chicken. Serve over spaghetti with salad and garlic toast.

> *Garlic Toast:* To make garlic toast without a lot of fat, spray your bread with vegetable oil cooking spray and sprinkle with garlic salt or garlic powder. Brown in a nonstick skillet.

SPICY MEXICAN CHICKEN

SERVES 8

4 GRAMS FAT PER SERVING

Prep :10
Cook :40
Stand :00
Total :50

½ cup fine dry bread crumbs
¼ cup fat-free Parmesan cheese
1 teaspoon chili powder
¼ teaspoon ground cumin
¼ teaspoon pepper
8 boneless skinless chicken breast halves
2 cups shredded fat-free Monterey Jack cheese
½ cup egg substitute

Preheat the oven to 375 degrees. Lightly coat an 11 x 7-inch baking dish with vegetable oil cooking spray.

In a shallow dish, combine the bread crumbs, Parmesan cheese, chili powder, cumin, and pepper. Set aside.

Place each chicken breast between two sheets of wax paper; flatten to a thickness of ¼ inch with a meat mallet or rolling pin. Place ¼ cup of shredded cheese in the middle of each piece of chicken, roll up from short side, and secure with a wooden pick. Dip the chicken rolls in the egg substitute and dredge in the bread crumb mixture. Place rolls seam side down in the prepared baking dish. Spray the pieces of chicken very lightly with vegetable oil cooking spray and bake for 35 to 40 minutes. Depending on the size of chicken pieces, cooking time may vary.

Variation: If you don't have time to flatten the chicken, just skip that step. Dip the chicken in the egg substitute, then dredge in bread crumbs, spray, and bake. About the last 5 minutes of baking time, put the shredded cheese on the top of each piece and melt. A little dollop of chopped green chiles on top of the cheese is also very good.

RUSSIAN CHICKEN

6 to 8 boneless, skinless chicken breast halves
1 (8-ounce) bottle low-fat Russian salad dressing
1 envelope dry onion soup mix, such as Lipton's
1 (8-ounce) jar apricot preserves

SERVES 6

4 GRAMS FAT

Prep :15
Cook :15
Stand :00
Total :30

Preheat the oven to 350 degrees. Spray a baking pan with vegetable oil cooking spray. Arrange the chicken pieces in the pan and spray them lightly. Bake uncovered, without turning, for 30 minutes. Drain off the pan juices.

Mix together the Russian dressing, soup mix, and apricot preserves. Pour over the drained cooked chicken and bake another 20 to 30 minutes, or until hot and bubbly.

HAWAIIAN STUFFED CHICKEN

SERVES 4

2 GRAMS FAT
EACH

Prep :20
Cook :40
Stand :00
Total 1:00

4 boneless, skinless chicken breast halves
1/3 cup hot water
2 tablespoons Butter Buds
2 cups Stove Top stuffing, chicken flavor
1 medium green bell pepper, seeded and chopped
1 (8-ounce) can crushed pineapple, undrained
2 tablespoons brown sugar
2 tablespoons vinegar
1/4 teaspoon ground ginger

Preheat the oven to 400 degrees. Lay the chicken breasts on a flat surface and pound with a rolling pin or meat mallet to 1/4-inch thickness.

Mix the hot water and Butter Buds in a bowl. Stir in the stuffing mix, green pepper, and half the pineapple and juice.

Spoon the stuffing mix evenly over the chicken. Roll up tightly, starting with a long end. Secure with toothpicks. Place seam side down in a square baking dish that has been coated with vegetable oil cooking spray. Place any leftover stuffing in the middle.

Mix the remaining pineapple and juice with the brown sugar, vinegar, and ginger. Spoon over the chicken.

Bake uncovered, without turning, for 30 to 40 minutes, or until tender.

POLYNESIAN CHICKEN

2½ pounds meaty chicken pieces, skinned
1 (14-ounce) can crushed pineapple, undrained
1 small jar peach or apricot preserves

SERVES 4

2 GRAMS FAT
EACH

Prep :10
Cook :60
Stand :00
Total 1:10

Preheat the oven to 400 degrees. Spray a rectangular baking pan with vegetable oil cooking spray. Arrange the chicken pieces in the pan and spray them lightly. Bake uncovered for 30 minutes. Turn the chicken pieces and bake for an additional 15 or 20 minutes, or until tender. Drain off the pan juices.

Mix the pineapple with the peach preserves. Pour over the drained chicken and bake for another 15 to 20 minutes, or until hot and bubbly.

KRISPY CHICKEN

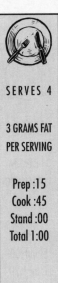

4 cups Rice Krispies
1 teaspoon paprika
½ teaspoon salt (optional)
¼ teaspoon pepper
4 boneless skinless chicken breast halves
¾ cup fat-free mayonnaise

SERVES 4

3 GRAMS FAT
PER SERVING

Prep :15
Cook :45
Stand :00
Total 1:00

Preheat the oven to 400 degrees. Spray a baking sheet lightly with vegetable oil cooking spray.

In a large zipper-lock plastic bag, place the Rice Krispies; close the bag and crush with a rolling pin. Add the paprika, salt, if desired, and pepper. Set aside.

Wash chicken pieces and pat dry. Cover each piece with mayonnaise and place, one at a time, in the bag of Rice Krispies. Shake to cover well. Place the chicken on the prepared baking sheet and bake for 40 to 45 minutes, until crisp and brown.

MIRACLE CHICKEN

4 boneless skinless chicken breast halves
¾ cup fat-free Miracle Whip salad dressing
1 cup fat-free Italian salad dressing
¼ cup dry white wine

SERVES 4

3 GRAMS FAT PER SERVING

Prep :10
Cook :15
Stand 6:00
Total 6:25

Place the chicken breast halves in one layer in a baking dish or deep platter.

Stir together the Miracle Whip, Italian dressing, and wine. Pour this marinade over the chicken pieces. Cover and refrigerate for several hours or overnight.

Preheat a gas grill or an oven broiler, or start a charcoal fire. Spray the grill or broiler rack lightly with vegetable oil cooking spray before lighting the fire.

Drain the chicken, reserving the marinade, and arrange on the grill. Cook about 5 to 7 minutes on each side, brushing frequently with the reserved marinade. Discard the remaining marinade.

CHICKEN CASSEROLE

10 slices low-fat (1 gram per slice) white bread, cut into 1-inch cubes
1½ cups fat-free cracker crumbs
3 cups fat-free chicken broth
¾ cup egg substitute, lightly beaten
¾ cup diced celery
3 tablespoons chopped onion
3 cups cubed cooked chicken breast
1 (8-ounce) can sliced mushrooms, drained
1 cup whole-kernel corn (optional)
Salt to taste (about 1 teaspoon)

SERVES 8

3 GRAMS FAT PER SERVING

Prep :20
Cook 1:00
Stand :00
Total 1:20

Preheat the oven to 350 degrees. Lightly coat a 2-quart casserole with butter-flavored vegetable oil cooking spray.

In a large mixing bowl, combine the bread cubes and 1 cup of the cracker crumbs. Stir in the chicken broth, egg substitute, celery, onion, chicken, and mushrooms. Add corn if desired and salt to taste. Spoon into the prepared casserole.

In a nonstick skillet, place the remaining ½ cup of cracker crumbs. Spray with butter-flavored cooking spray, stirring to coat evenly. Cook, stirring, until lightly browned. Sprinkle over the casserole. Bake uncovered for 1 hour.

Note: You may make this a day ahead. Leave off the top cracker crumbs until time for baking

CREAMY CHICKEN AND NOODLES

2 cups water
4 boneless, skinless chicken breast halves
6 ounces cholesterol-free noodles
2 cups skim milk, or as needed
2 tablespoons cornstarch
2 cups cooked fresh vegetables (cut-up asparagus, corn kernels, green peas, etc.)

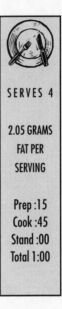

SERVES 4

2.05 GRAMS
FAT PER
SERVING

Prep :15
Cook :45
Stand :00
Total 1:00

Bring the water to a boil in a large saucepan over high heat. Add the chicken breasts, return to a boil, and lower the heat. Cover and simmer to desired degree of doneness, about 30 minutes. Remove from pan with a slotted spoon. Defat the stock; set chicken aside.

Return the stock to the pan and bring to a boil. Add the noodles and boil until tender but still firm, about 15 minutes. Drain in a colander (reserve stock for another purpose).

Return noodles to the pan, cover with 1 cup skim milk, and turn heat on to medium. While noodles are heating, mix 2 tablespoons of cornstarch with 1 cup cold milk. When noodles are hot, add the cornstarch mixture while stirring. Add the chicken and vegetables. Remove from the heat when the dish reaches the desired thickness.

Variation: Omit the cooked vegetables. Serve cut-up raw vegetables on the side.

CHICKEN AND DUMPLINGS

SERVES 6

VERY LOW-FAT

Prep :15
Cook :35
Stand :00
Total :50

3 cups water
6 to 8 boneless, skinless chicken breast halves
½ cup egg substitute
1 cup skim milk
2 cups self-rising flour

In a large saucepan, bring the water to a boil over high heat. Add the chicken pieces, return to a boil, and lower the heat. Cover and simmer until chicken is fork tender, 20 to 30 minutes.

Defat the stock. Return the chicken and stock to the saucepan and bring to a boil while you mix the dumplings.

In a medium bowl, mix the egg substitute and skim milk into the flour to form a soft dough. Drop by spoonfuls into the hot broth. Let boil 15 minutes without stirring. Do not cover.

Variations: Turn the dough out onto a floured board and roll to the desired thickness. Cut into squares and drop into the boiling broth; boil for 15 minutes. The broth may be thickened with 1 tablespoon cornstarch mixed in ¼ cup of cold water or cold skim milk. Season to taste.

If you like a tougher type of dumpling, let the dough rest for ½ to 1 hour after you have rolled it out on a floured board. Cut into strips or squares and cook as directed above.

CHICKEN, VEGETABLES, AND DUMPLINGS

6 boneless skinless chicken breast halves
½ cup chopped onion
1 cup chopped celery
1 cup chopped carrots
2 cups skim milk

Dumplings:
1½ cups self-rising flour
¾ cup skim milk
2 tablespoons cornstarch
Salt and pepper to taste

SERVES 6

3 GRAMS FAT
PER 1-CUP
SERVING

Prep :35
Cook :45
Stand :00
Total 1:20

Wash the chicken and trim off any visible fat. In a large saucepan, cover the chicken with water, bring to a boil, and lower the heat to medium. Add the onion, celery, and carrots; cook 25 minutes or until tender.

Strain through a colander, reserving broth and solids separately.

Defat the broth with a defatting pitcher or dipper, or if none is available, cool the broth and place in the refrigerator overnight or for a few hours and remove any excess fat, which will come to the top.

About a half hour before you want to serve, return the chicken and vegetables to the defatted broth. Add 2 cups of skim milk and bring all to a boil. While the chicken and vegetables are heating, prepare the dumplings.

Dumplings: In a mixing bowl, combine the self-rising flour with ¾ cup of milk. Stir the milk in gradually, ¼ cup at a time. Mix with a fork until a soft dough forms.

Drop the dumplings by the tablespoonful into the boiling liquid. Let boil without stirring for 15 minutes. Do not cover.

In a small bowl, combine the cornstarch and 2 tablespoons *cold* water. Turn heat off, carefully stir this into the chicken and dumpling broth—not too vigorously or you'll mush up the dumplings and vegetables. Add salt and pepper to taste.

(continued)

Serve directly from the pot or transfer to a platter and pass the sauce separately.

> *Variation:* Chicken Potpie: You may roll the dough out thin on a floured surface, adding enough flour to make the dough workable. Cut into 1½-inch squares with a sharp knife. If you like tender potpie dumplings, cook immediately. If you like tougher dumplings like Grandma used to make, let them sit for about 1 hour after you roll them out and cut them. You may not need to thicken the broth, as the excess flour will probably make it thick enough. If not, then use the cornstarch.

CHICKEN NOODLE CASSEROLE

SERVES 6

2 GRAMS FAT

Prep :10
Cook 1:00
Stand :00
Total 1:10

6 to 8 breaded chicken tenders
2 cups cholesterol-free noodles
1 (8-ounce) can cream of mushroom soup, Healthy Request
1 (14-ounce) can fat-free chicken broth

Preheat the oven to 350 degrees. Brown the chicken on both sides in a dry nonstick skillet. Blot up any excess fat that has cooked out of the chicken.

Cook the noodles in a large pot of boiling salted water until tender, about 15 to 20 minutes. Drain. Coat a casserole dish with vegetable oil cooking spray. Add the noodles. Cut the chicken in bite-size pieces and place over the noodles.

Mix the soup and broth together with a whisk until smooth. Pour over the chicken and noodles. Bake about 45 minutes, until thick and creamy.

> *Chicken Rice Casserole:* Rice may be substituted for noodles, if desired. Cook 1 cup regular or converted rice according to package directions and proceed with the recipe.

CHICKEN AND RIGATONI

6 to 8 breaded chicken tenders
½ cup chopped onion
¼ cup chopped green pepper
½ pound rigatoni (about 2½ cups)
2 (10¾-ounce) cans pasta-style tomatoes
1 (4-ounce) can V-8 juice
½ tomato can water
½ teaspoon basil
½ teaspoon oregano
Salt and pepper to taste

SERVES 6

4 GRAMS FAT

Prep :10
Cook :30
Stand :00
Total :40

Sauté the chicken tenders, onion, and green pepper in a large nonstick skillet that has been sprayed with vegetable oil cooking spray. Cook until lightly browned.

Meanwhile, cook the rigatoni according to package directions until just tender. Drain and keep warm.

When the chicken is done, blot off any fat that cooked out. Add the tomatoes, V-8 juice, water, and pasta. Stir in the seasonings and simmer until well blended.

CHICKEN AND PASTA SKILLET DINNER

SERVES 4

1.5 GRAMS FAT PER 2-CUP SERVING

Prep :10
Cook :35
Stand :00
Total :45

1½ cups pasta (I use ziti or any large tubular pasta)
6 frozen breaded chicken tenders
½ cup chopped onions
¾ cup chopped celery
½ cup chopped green peppers
1 (14-ounce) can stewed tomatoes
½ tomato can water (about ¾ cup)
½ teaspoon crushed dried basil
½ teaspoon lemon pepper
½ teaspoon crushed dried oregano
¼ teaspoon pizza (mild Italian) seasoning
2 cups chopped raw cabbage
1 cup frozen green peas

In a medium saucepan, cook the pasta according to package directions, leaving out salt and oil if called for. Drain. Set aside.

While the pasta is cooking, start your dish. In a large or deep nonstick skillet or dutch oven, brown the chicken tenders lightly.

Add the chopped onions, celery, and peppers; sauté until just starting to soften. Cut the chicken into bite-size pieces with a spatula. Add the stewed tomatoes, water, basil, lemon pepper, oregano leaves, and pizza seasoning. Simmer for about 5 minutes; add the cabbage and green peas. Continue simmering, stirring occasionally, until vegetables are desired tenderness.

Carefully stir in the pasta and simmer a few minutes longer. Add a little more water if the mixture seems too thick or dry.

CHICKEN WITH BROCCOLI AND RICE CASSEROLE

4 boneless skinless chicken breast halves
Garlic powder and pepper
1 (10 ¾-ounce) can Healthy Request cream of broccoli soup
½ soup can water (swish water around to get all the soup)
4 cups cooked rice or pasta

Preheat the oven to 375 degrees.

Lightly spray a 2-quart cooking dish with vegetable oil cooking spray; arrange the chicken in a single layer in the dish. Sprinkle with garlic powder and pepper to taste.

Bake for about 30 minutes. Drain off any juices (they will contain some fat that has cooked out of the chicken).

Combine the soup and water and mix with a wire whisk. Pour over the chicken and bake an additional 30 minutes or until the chicken is done.

Serve with rice cooked according to package directions.

SERVES 4

4.25 GRAMS FAT PER SERVING

Prep :10
Cook 1:00
Stand :00
Total 1:10

CHICKEN BROCCOLI BAKE

SERVES 6

3 GRAMS FAT
PER 1½-CUP
SERVING

Prep :20
Cook :35
Stand :00
Total :55

2 cups chopped broccoli florets
2 cups diced cooked chicken (white meat)
1 (10¾-ounce) can Healthy Request low-fat cream of mushroom soup
1 cup fat-free mayonnaise
1 teaspoon lemon juice
1½ cups shredded fat-free Cheddar cheese

Preheat the oven to 350 degrees. Lightly spray a 9 x 13-inch baking dish with vegetable oil cooking spray.

Steam the broccoli just until crisp-tender. Drain. Layer the broccoli in the prepared baking dish. Layer the chicken on top of the broccoli.

In a mixing bowl, combine the soup, mayonnaise, and lemon juice. Spread evenly over the chicken. Top with cheese. Bake uncovered for 30 minutes, or until bubbly.

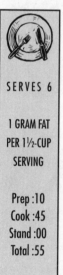

LADIES' LUNCHEON CASSEROLE

I buy frozen diced chicken at a wholesale store to have on hand at all times for just this kind of a recipe, which you can throw together in a hurry and look like you have been working for hours. I'll never tell if you don't.

SERVES 6

1 GRAM FAT
PER 1½-CUP
SERVING

Prep :10
Cook :45
Stand :00
Total :55

2 cups diced cooked chicken (white meat)
2 cups cooked rice
1 (10¾-ounce) can Healthy Request cream of mushroom soup
1 (10¾-ounce) can Healthy Request cream of broccoli soup
1 (8-ounce) can sliced water chestnuts, drained
1 (11-ounce) can white shoepeg corn, drained
Salt and pepper to taste

Preheat the oven to 350 degrees. Lightly spray a 2-quart baking dish with vegetable oil cooking spray.

In a large bowl, combine the cooked chicken with the rice and cream of mushroom soup. Fill the soup can ½ full of water, swish it around to loosen any soup left behind, and add to above. Repeat with the cream of broccoli soup. Add the water chestnuts, corn, and salt and pepper to taste. Stir to blend all ingredients.

Spoon into the prepared baking dish and bake uncovered for about 45 minutes, until bubbly and heated through.

BAKED CHICKEN REUBEN

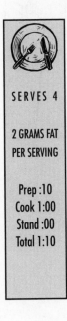

4 boneless, skinless chicken breast halves
¼ teaspoon salt
⅛ teaspoon pepper
2 cups sauerkraut, drained
1¼ cups low-calorie Russian salad dressing
4 slices fat-free Swiss cheese
1 tablespoon chopped parsley
Chopped chives

SERVES 4

2 GRAMS FAT PER SERVING

Prep :10
Cook 1:00
Stand :00
Total 1:10

Preheat the oven to 325 degrees. Coat a small glass or ceramic baking dish with vegetable oil cooking spray.

Arrange the chicken pieces in the dish and sprinkle with salt and pepper. Cover the chicken with sauerkraut. Pour the dressing evenly over all and top with the cheese and parsley.

Cover with foil and bake 1 hour, or until fork tender. Sprinkle with chopped chives to serve.

CREOLE CHICKEN AND RICE

SERVES 4

VERY LOW-FAT

Prep :15
Cook :15
Stand :05
Total :35

¼ teaspoon salt
¾ cup instant rice, uncooked
4 boneless, skinless chicken breast halves
1 (8-ounce) can tomato sauce
¼ cup chopped onion
2 tablespoons chopped green pepper
1 clove garlic, chopped fine
½ teaspoon dried basil
⅛ teaspoon pepper

Combine ¾ cup water and the salt in a small saucepan. Bring to a boil. Remove from the heat, stir in the rice, cover, and let stand 5 minutes. Keep warm while you make the chicken.

Coat a large nonstick skillet with vegetable oil cooking spray. Place over medium heat until hot. Add the chicken and cook until brown and tender, about 10 to 12 minutes, turning once. Add the tomato sauce, onion, green pepper, garlic, basil, pepper, and ¼ cup water. Bring to a boil, cover, reduce the heat, and simmer 6 minutes, stirring occasionally. Serve with the rice.

CANADIAN BACO CHICKO

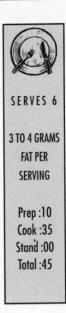

6 to 8 breaded chicken tenders (or boneless, skinless chicken tenders)
½ cup chopped onion
½ cup chopped green pepper
¾ cup shredded Canadian bacon
1 teaspoon minced garlic
2 (8-ounce) cans low-salt stewed tomatoes
1½ cups frozen green peas
1½ cups cholesterol-free noodles or macaroni
Salt and pepper to taste

SERVES 6

3 TO 4 GRAMS
FAT PER
SERVING

Prep :10
Cook :35
Stand :00
Total :45

Brown the chicken on both sides in a nonstick skillet. Add the onion, green pepper, Canadian bacon, and garlic. Sauté for 5 to 6 minutes, stirring to let onions, peppers, and bacon cook evenly.

Add the tomatoes and peas. Simmer for 10 to 12 minutes, stirring occasionally.

Meantime, cook noodles or macaroni (I use spiral macaroni) in a large pot of boiling water until nearly tender. Drain. Add to the chicken and sauce and continue to simmer about 10 more minutes. Correct seasoning.

BUSY DAY CROCK-POT CHICKEN SPECIAL

This is for the working person who savors the flavor as well as their time.

SERVES 4

3 GRAMS FAT PER SERVING

Prep :12
Cook 6:00
Stand :00
Total 6:12

4 boneless skinless chicken breast halves
1 (10-ounce) package frozen mixed vegetables (mixture of diced carrots, green beans, etc.)
1 medium onion, cut into thick slices or chunks
¾ to 1 cup sliced fresh mushrooms
1 (14-ounce) can stewed tomatoes
1 (8-ounce) can tomato sauce
1 teaspoon dried Italian seasoning, crushed
2 cloves garlic, minced

Cut the chicken into 1-inch pieces. Place the mixed vegetables, onion, and mushrooms in a Crock-Pot (about 4 quarts or larger). Place the chicken pieces on top of the vegetables.

In a medium-size mixing bowl, combine the tomatoes with their juice, the tomato sauce, Italian seasoning, and garlic. Pour over the chicken and vegetables.

Cover and cook for 6 hours on low heat setting or 3 hours on high.

Serve this over hot rice or fettuccine, cooked and drained, along with garlic bread or toast. (Spray bread slices with vegetable oil cooking spray and sprinkle with garlic salt. Toast on both sides in a nonstick skillet or grill until golden.)

WHITE CHICKEN CHILI

1 teaspoon lemon pepper
1 teaspoon cumin seed
4 boneless, skinless chicken breast halves
1 clove garlic, chopped fine
1 cup chopped onion
2 (8-ounce) cans white shoepeg corn, drained
2 (4-ounce) cans chopped green chiles, undrained
1 teaspoon ground cumin
2 to 3 tablespoons lime juice
2 (14-ounce) cans white or Great Northern beans, undrained
⅔ cup crushed tortilla chips
⅔ cup shredded fat-free Monterey Jack cheese

SERVES 8

2 GRAMS FAT
PER 1½-CUP
SERVING

Prep :20
Cook 1:30
Stand :00
Total 1:50

In a large saucepan, combine 2½ cups of water with the lemon pepper and cumin seed. Bring to a boil. Add the chicken breast halves and return to a boil. Reduce the heat to low and simmer 20 to 30 minutes, or until the chicken is fork tender and the juices run clear.

Remove the chicken from the pan and cut into tiny pieces. Defat the broth, return to the saucepan, and place the chicken back in the stock.

Spray a medium skillet with vegetable oil cooking spray, add the garlic, and cook and stir over low heat 1 minute (careful not to burn garlic—it is terrible). Add to the chicken, then sauté the onions in the same skillet, cooking until tender. Add the cooked onions, corn, chiles, cumin, and lime juice to the chicken mixture. Bring to a boil.

Add beans and simmer until thoroughly heated, about 45 minutes. To serve, place about 1 tablespoon each of tortilla chips and cheese in 8 individual soup bowls, ladle hot chili over, and serve with salsa.

ZUCCHINI, CHICKEN, AND RICE

SERVES 4

**2 GRAMS FAT
PER SERVING**

Prep :15
Cook :25
Stand :00
Total :40

6 breaded chicken tenders
½ cup chopped onion
¼ cup chopped green pepper
¾ cup chopped celery
1 cup chopped zucchini
1 (16-ounce) can stewed tomatoes
½ teaspoon minced garlic, or to taste
¼ teaspoon crushed oregano leaves
¼ teaspoon crushed basil leaves
¼ teaspoon adobo seasoning
¼ teaspoon Creole seasoning
3 cups hot cooked rice

Brown chicken on one side in a nonstick skillet. Add the onion, green pepper, and celery. Sauté for a short while, adding about ¼ cup of water. Move the chicken around a little to move the flavor around.

Turn the chicken over and add the zucchini, tomatoes, and spices. Simmer for about 20 minutes, stirring a little now and then. As you stir, cut the chicken with a spatula into bite-size pieces. The breading on the chicken will thicken the sauce as you simmer and move it around.

When all is tender and thickened somewhat, serve on a bed of rice.

SEASONED RICE AND CHICKEN CASSEROLE

1 (8-ounce) can condensed Special Request cream of mushroom soup, low-fat and low-sodium
1 cup skim milk
1 (8-ounce) can sliced water chestnuts, drained
1 (6-ounce) package long-grain and wild rice mix
1 (4-ounce) can mushroom stems and pieces, drained
1 (2-ounce) jar sliced pimientos, drained
3 cups cooked chicken or turkey, cubed

SERVES 4

3 GRAMS FAT

Prep :10
Cook :60
Stand :00
Total 1:10

Preheat the oven to 350 degrees. In a mixing bowl, combine the soup, milk, and 1 cup of water. Stir with a whisk until smooth. Add all the remaining ingredients. Mix well.

Pour into an ungreased 3-quart casserole. Cover and bake for 30 minutes. Uncover, stir, and bake for an additional 30 to 45 minutes, or until rice is tender, stirring once again halfway through baking.

CHICKEN TORTILLA CASSEROLE

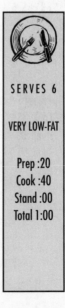

6 boneless, skinless chicken breast halves, cut into thin strips
½ cup sliced green onions
1 clove garlic, minced
3 tablespoons cornstarch
4 cups cold chicken broth, defatted
1½ cups shredded fat-free Monterey jack cheese
½ cup fat-free salad dressing, such as Miracle Whip
½ cup fat-free sour cream
1 (4-ounce) can chopped green chiles, undrained
½ cup ripe olives
¼ cup chopped parsley
12 (7-inch) flour tortillas

SERVES 6

VERY LOW-FAT

Prep :20
Cook :40
Stand :00
Total 1:00

(continued)

Preheat the oven to 350 degrees.

Heat a nonstick skillet and spray with vegetable oil cooking spray. Add the chicken, onions, and garlic. Cook, stirring frequently, until the chicken is golden and cooked through, about 10 minutes. Remove the skillet from the heat and set aside.

In a saucepan stir together the cornstarch and cold chicken broth. Bring to a boil, stirring constantly. Boil 1 minute. Mix in 1 cup of the cheese, the salad dressing, sour cream, chiles, ¼ cup of the olives, and parsley. Stir the sauce until smooth.

Remove 1 cup of sauce and stir into the chicken mixture. Spoon 2 tablespoons of the chicken mixture into each tortilla; roll to enclose. Place the tortillas seam side down in a 9 x 13-inch baking dish. Pour the remaining sauce over and top with the remaining cheese and olives. Bake for 25 minutes, or until thoroughly heated.

ALMOND CHICKEN CASSEROLE

SERVES 6

8 GRAMS FAT
ENTIRE DISH

Prep :15
Cook :35
Stand :00
Total :50

1 cup fresh bread cubes
1 tablespoon Butter Buds liquid
3 cups chopped cooked white-meat chicken
1½ cups chopped celery
1 cup fat-free salad dressing, such as Miracle Whip
1 cup shredded fat-free Swiss cheese
1 cup green bell pepper strips
¼ cup slivered almonds, toasted
¼ cup chopped onion

Preheat the oven to 350 degrees. Combine the bread cubes and Butter Buds; toss lightly. Set aside.

In a mixing bowl, combine the remaining ingredients; mix lightly. Spoon into a medium baking dish. Top with bread cubes. Bake uncovered for 30 to 35 minutes, or until lightly browned.

CHICKEN POTATO CASSEROLE

This is a good Sunday morning quick casserole to leave cooking while in church. Just adjust the temperature of the oven down to about 300 degrees, depending on how long you will be gone. Do you have a short-winded preacher or does yours get his second wind around 12:00? If so, adjust down to about 250 degrees. You know your oven and your preacher!

6 to 8 breaded chicken tenders
3 to 4 potatoes, peeled and sliced thin
1 (10-ounce) package frozen green peas
2 (10¾-ounce) cans Healthy Request condensed cream of mushroom soup

Preheat the oven to 350 degrees. Brown the chicken on both sides in a nonstick skillet. Spray a medium-size casserole with vegetable oil cooking spray. Put the potatoes in the bottom of the casserole; add the peas for the second layer and the chicken for the third layer. (Blot any excess fat that cooked out of the chicken with paper towels before adding.)

Mix the cream of mushroom soup and 1 can of water with a wire whisk until smooth. Pour over casserole.

Bake about 45 minutes to 1 hour, or until golden and potatoes are tender.

MEXICAN CHICKEN CASSEROLE

SERVES 6

2.09 GRAMS
FAT PER
SERVING

Prep :15
Cook :45
Stand :00
Total 1:00

1 large onion, chopped
3 medium tomatoes, peeled and chopped
2 cups chopped cooked white meat chicken
½ cup fat-free chicken broth
2 teaspoons chili powder
1 teaspoon salt
1 teaspoon ground cumin
1 teaspoon dried oregano
6 corn tortillas, cut into fourths
1 cup shredded fat-free Cheddar cheese

Lightly spray an 11 x 7 x 1½-inch baking dish with vegetable oil cooking spray. Preheat the oven to 350 degrees.

Sauté the onion in ¼ cup water in a medium skillet until tender, stirring often. Add the tomato, chicken, broth, chili powder, salt, cumin, and oregano. Bring to a boil, reduce the heat, and simmer 5 to 6 minutes. Layer half the chicken mixture, half the tortillas, and half the cheese in the baking dish and repeat with the remaining chicken and tortillas. Reserve the remaining cheese. Cover the casserole and bake for 25 to 30 minutes.

Uncover and sprinkle evenly with the remaining ½ cup cheese. Bake an additional 5 minutes, or until the cheese is bubbly.

STIR-FRY CHICKEN AND VEGGIES

3 boneless skinless chicken breast halves
¼ cup low-sodium soy sauce
1 teaspoon sesame seeds
1 medium onion, chopped
1 medium green pepper, chopped
4 cups frozen stir-fry vegetables
1 (4-ounce) can mushroom pieces, drained
1 (4-ounce) can sliced water chestnuts, drained

SERVES 4

2 GRAMS FAT
ENTIRE DISH

Prep :15
Cook :10
Stand :00
Total :25

Cut the chicken breast into 1-inch squares. In a nonstick skillet or wok, brown the chicken pieces until light brown. Add the soy sauce and sesame seeds; continue to cook until tender. With a slotted spoon remove the chicken to a platter; set aside.

To the juices in the same pan, add the onions and green pepper; cook until crisp-tender. Add the frozen vegetables, mushroom pieces, and water chestnuts. Cook, stirring constantly, until all is hot. Return the chicken to the vegetable mixture and stir in. Serve with hot rice if desired.

CHICKEN VEGETABLE SPECIAL

I use a large electric nonstick skillet for this and serve it with a pone of cornbread along-side a small green salad.

SERVES 4

**3.0 GRAMS FAT
ENTIRE DISH**

**Prep :25
Cook :30
Stand :00
Total :55**

6 frozen chicken tenders
¾ cup uncooked flat noodles
1½ cups okra
1½ cups chopped cabbage
1 tablespoon vinegar
⅔ cup chopped onion
⅔ cup chopped green pepper
1 cup chopped celery
1 (14-ounce) can stewed tomatoes, pasta style
¾ cup picante sauce (commercial)
½ teaspoon minced garlic
½ teaspoon crushed oregano leaves
½ teaspoon crushed dried basil
¼ teaspoon Creole seasoning
¼ teaspoon adobo seasoning
½ teaspoon lemon pepper

In a nonstick skillet, dry-fry the chicken tenders until brown. In a medium saucepan, cook the noodles according to package directions, leaving out any oil or margarine called for. (Salt may also be omitted.)

If using fresh okra, trim the ends, slice ½ inch thick, and cover with water in a saucepan. Add about 1 tablespoon vinegar and boil 4 to 5 minutes, until crisp-tender. Drain in a colander and rinse with warm water.

Cut the chicken into bite-size pieces, return to the skillet, and add the onions, green pepper, and celery. Sauté until slightly tender (add ¼ cup water if needed).

Add the tomatoes and ½ can of water, the picante sauce, and seasonings. Simmer for about 5 minutes. Add the noodles, okra, and cabbage; continue to simmer about 5 more minutes—the cabbage should be crisp-tender. Be careful when stirring not to break up the noodles too much.

BAYOU MAGIC CHICKEN

4 to 6 frozen chicken tenders
¾ cup chopped onion
3⅓ cups chopped celery
1 small green pepper, chopped
1 (10¾-ounce) can Healthy Request cream of mushroom soup
1 (10¾-ounce) can Healthy Request cream of celery soup
1 (16-ounce) can Healthy Request (or fat-free) chicken broth
1 (14-ounce) package Bayou Magic Cajun rice mix

SERVES 8

3 GRAMS FAT
PER SERVING

Prep :10
Cook 1:40
Stand :00
Total 1:50

Put the chicken tenders, onion, celery, and pepper in a nonstick skillet over medium heat. When they start to brown, add 1 cup water. Simmer 20 minutes, or until tender and thick. Cut the chicken tenders into bite-size pieces.

Add the mushroom and celery soups, 2 soup cans of water, and the chicken broth. While this is heating a little, put the rice into a colander or strainer and shake some of the pepper out (it is seasoned too hot for us Okies; if you are in Cajun country, then just leave all spices in). Add the rice to the above mixture. Place in a casserole about 11 x 13 inches, cover with foil, and bake at 350 degrees for 1 hour and 10 minutes or until the rice is tender.

QUICK SPICY CHICKEN GUMBO

Be creative in the summer when the fresh veg-etables are plentiful. Add all your favorites.

SERVES 4

3.0 GRAMS FAT
ENTIRE DISH

Prep :10
Cook :20
Stand :00
Total :30

1 cup sliced fresh or frozen okra (optional)
1 teaspoon vinegar
6 boneless skinless chicken tenders
½ pound fat-free smoked sausage such as Butterball, cut into ½-inch slices
½ cup chopped onion
½ cup chopped green peppers
½ teaspoon chopped garlic
1 (16-ounce) package frozen vegetables, such as broccoli, corn, peppers, etc.
1 (14-ounce) can stewed tomatoes
Salt and pepper

If using okra, cover it with water in a saucepan, add 1 teaspoon of vinegar, and boil 4 or 5 minutes, or until just tender. Rinse in a colander. (This process will eliminate any slimy texture in your gumbo.) Set aside.

In a large deep nonstick skillet, cook the chicken tenders and sausage pieces until tender and lightly browned. Remove from the skillet and cut the chicken into ½-inch chunks.

In the same skillet, sauté the onion, peppers, and garlic in ¼ cup of water for 5 minutes. Return the chicken and sausage to the skillet and add the frozen vegetables, the okra, the tomatoes, and 1 cup of water. Cover and cook over medium heat about 3 to 5 minutes. Season with salt and pepper; serve hot.

QUICK CHICKEN GUMBO

1½ to 2 cups frozen fully cooked hickory-flavored chicken, thawed and cut into
    bite-size pieces (or cubed uncooked white meat chicken)
¼ cup chopped green peppers
1 (12-ounce) package frozen gumbo mix
1 (8-ounce) can stewed tomatoes
½ teaspoon garlic flakes
1 cup cooked macaroni

In a nonstick skillet, cook the chicken in ¼ cup water along with
the peppers until tender.

In a separate saucepan cover the gumbo mix with ¼ cup of water
and simmer for 4 to 5 minutes. Drain in a colander and add to the
chicken in the skillet along with the tomatoes and garlic flakes.
Simmer for 15 to 20 minutes. Add cooked macaroni; stir in gently
to avoid breaking.

Variation: A touch of Cajun seasoning may be added to your
taste. Omit the macaroni and serve on rice.

CREOLE CHICKEN AND PASTA

6 fresh or frozen chicken tenders
¾ cup chopped onion
¾ cup chopped green pepper
1 (12-ounce) package frozen gumbo mix
1 tablespoon vinegar
2 cups uncooked ziti
1½ cups tomato juice
½ cup fat-free spaghetti sauce
½ teaspoon crushed dried basil
½ teaspoon crushed dried oregano
Dash lemon pepper
Dash adobo seasoning

(continued)

Dry-fry the chicken tenders in a nonstick skillet. Add the onion and green pepper when the chicken is about ¾ of the way done and lightly browned. Take the chicken out of the skillet (so as not to scratch the skillet), cut it into bite-size pieces, and return to the skillet.

While the chicken is cooking, in a separate saucepan cook the vegetable gumbo mix according to package directions. Add a tablespoon of vinegar to keep the okra from being slick. Drain in a colander when tender. Set aside.

Cook the pasta until tender in a separate pan; drain and set aside.

To the chicken and vegetables in the skillet, add the tomato juice and spaghetti sauce and stir in ¾ cup of water. Bring to a boil and add the seasonings, the reserved gumbo mix, and the pasta. Stir carefully, lower the heat, and simmer for about 20 minutes, until the flavors are blended.

CHICKEN CHILI

The corn gives this and other chilies, soups, and chowders a wonderful crunch.

SERVES 4

6 GRAMS FAT
PER 1¼-CUP
SERVING

Prep :20
Cook :30
Stand :00
Total :50

2 cups ground chicken or turkey (use freshly ground for less fat)
1 cup chopped onion
¾ cup chopped green pepper
1 cup chopped carrot
2 Roma or other small tomatoes, chopped
4 rings jalapeño pepper, chopped fine
1 (15-ounce) can Great Northern beans, drained
1 (11-ounce) can white shoepeg corn, drained
2 (14-ounce) cans fat-free chicken broth
2 teaspoons chili powder, or more to taste
½ teaspoon ground cumin

In a large nonstick skillet or saucepan, brown the chicken, onion, and green pepper over medium heat, stirring often. Transfer to a colander and run hot water over to rinse away any excess fat. Shake to remove water and return to the skillet after wiping out any fat. Add the carrots and remaining ingredients, bring to a boil, reduce the heat, cover, and simmer for 15 minutes.

HURRY-SCURRY CHICKEN CHILI

4 frozen chicken tenders
½ cup chopped onions
1½ cups Harvest Blend rice
1 (14-ounce) can fat-free vegetable chili
2 (12-ounce) cans chili beans
1 tablespoon chili powder
Dash of adobo seasoning

SERVES 2

4 GRAMS FAT
PER 2½-CUP
SERVING

Prep :20
Cook :15
Stand :00
Total :35

In a nonstick skillet, dry-fry the chicken tenders and onions 5 to 8 minutes, or until tender. You may add about 2 tablespoons of water to speed up and tenderize. Cut into bite-size pieces (I use the rubber or plastic spatula).

In a small saucepan, cook the rice according to package directions, leaving out the margarine or butter.

In a large heavy saucepan, pour the chili right from the can, as well as the two cans of beans. Add the rice and chicken. Stir in the seasonings and simmer for 15 to 20 minutes.

BAKED CHICKEN CHILI CASSEROLE

SERVES 4

4 GRAMS FAT PER SERVING

Prep :15
Cook 1:10
Stand :00
Total 1:25

½ cup uncooked Harvest Blend rice
1 (14-ounce) can fat-free chicken broth
2 cups chopped cooked chicken breast
1½ cups medium salsa
1 (10¾-ounce) can Healthy Request cream of chicken soup
1 cup whole-kernel corn, frozen or canned, drained
½ cup finely chopped onion
1 tablespoon lite Worcestershire sauce
2 tablespoons chili powder, or to taste
1 teaspoon dried oregano
¼ teaspoon pepper

Preheat the oven to 350 degrees. Lightly coat a 2-quart baking dish with vegetable oil cooking spray.

In a saucepan, combine the rice and chicken broth; bring to a boil. Cover, reduce the heat, and simmer 40 minutes or until rice is tender.

Combine the chicken and remaining ingredients in a large bowl; stir in the rice. Spoon the mixture into the prepared baking dish and bake for 30 minutes or until bubbly.

CHICKEN ENCHILADAS

5 boneless skinless chicken breast halves
2 (3-ounce) packages fat-free cream cheese, at room temperature
⅓ cup evaporated skim milk
¾ cup chopped onion
½ teaspoon salt (optional)
2 cups tomatillo sauce
12 (6-inch) corn tortillas
1 cup shredded fat-free Cheddar cheese
1 cup shredded fat-free Monterey Jack cheese

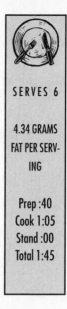

SERVES 6

4.34 GRAMS
FAT PER SERV-
ING

Prep :40
Cook 1:05
Stand :00
Total 1:45

In a large saucepan, cover the chicken with water, bring to a boil, reduce the heat, and simmer about 40 minutes, or until tender. Remove the chicken and, when cool enough to handle, chop fine.

Preheat the oven to 350 degrees. Spray a 9 x 13-inch baking dish lightly with vegetable oil cooking spray.

Combine the softened cream cheese and the milk in a mixing bowl and whisk together until smooth. Stir in the chicken, onion, and salt, if desired. Set aside.

Spread ¾ cup tomatillo sauce in the prepared baking dish.

Soften the tortillas by dipping each, one at a time, in a shallow dish of warm water briefly, or wrap the stack in foil and warm in oven ahead of time.

Spoon about 1½ tablespoons tomatillo sauce over each tortilla, spreading to the edge; spoon ¼ cup of the chicken mixture evenly down center of each. Roll up the tortillas and place seam side down in the baking dish.

Cover with foil and bake the enchiladas for about 25 minutes. Uncover, sprinkle with cheeses, and return to the oven long enough to melt the cheese. Serve garnished with fat-free sour cream.

SWEET-AND-SOUR CHICKEN AND RICE

SERVES 4

1.25 GRAMS
FAT PER SERV-
ING

Prep :10
Cook :20
Stand :00
Total :30

1 (8-ounce) bottle fat-free French dressing
1 (8-ounce) jar apricot preserves
½ cup honey
1 envelope Lipton onion soup mix
6 boneless skinless chicken tenders
1 cup rice, prepared according to package directions, leaving out the butter or
    margarine and salt

In a medium-size mixing bowl, combine the French dressing, preserves, honey, and soup mix. Set the sauce aside.

In a nonstick skillet, dry-fry the chicken tenders until done. Add the sauce, simmer for about 5 minutes, and stir in the rice, if desired; or the chicken and sauce may be served on top of the rice.

CHICKEN CHILES CASSEROLE

*Cooked turkey or ham may be substituted for
the chicken in this easy day-ahead dish.
Prepare, cover, and refrigerate until ready
to bake.*

SERVES 6

1 GRAM FAT
PER 1-CUP
SERVING

Prep :10
Cook 1:15
Stand :00
Total 1:25

1 cup fat-free sour cream
1 cup Healthy Request cream of chicken soup
1 cup chopped onion
1 (4-ounce) can chopped green chiles
½ cup chopped green pepper
1 teaspoon salt
½ teaspoon pepper
1 (2-pound) package frozen hash brown potatoes, with peppers and onions
2½ cups chopped cooked white meat chicken
2½ cups shredded fat-free Cheddar cheese

Preheat the oven to 350 degrees. Lightly coat a 13 x 9-inch baking dish with vegetable oil cooking spray.

In a large bowl, mix the sour cream, soup, onion, chiles, green pepper, salt, and pepper. Stir in the potatoes, chicken, and 2 cups of the cheese. Pour into the prepared baking dish. Bake uncovered for 1 hour and 15 minutes or until golden brown. Sprinkle with the remaining cheese before serving.

GRILLED CHICKEN CHEESE SANDWICH

Quick, easy, and good. Serve with chips and salsa if desired.

SERVES 4

2 GRAMS FAT PER SERVING

Prep :10
Cook :08
Stand :00
Total :18

8 slices low-fat bread (1 gram per slice)
4 teaspoons fat-free sandwich spread (such as Miracle Whip)
4 slices fat-free deli-style chicken (such as Healthy Choice)
2 thin slices onion separated into rings
4 tablespoons salsa
4 slices fat-free Cheddar or American cheese

Heat a nonstick skillet or a grill over medium heat. Spread each slice of bread with sandwich spread. On four of the slices layer a slice of chicken, some onion rings, 1 tablespoon of salsa, and a slice of cheese. Top with the remaining slices of bread.

Spray the skillet lightly with vegetable oil cooking spray, place the sandwiches in the skillet, and spray the top of each lightly with cooking spray. When lightly browned, turn over with a spatula. Brown lightly on the other side. Transfer to a platter and cut in half diagonally.

CHICKEN CHEESEBURGERS

These taste great! Your craving for a burger has been taken care of and so has your fat gram count.

SERVES 4

5 GRAMS FAT PER SERVING

Prep :10
Cook :15
Stand :00
Total :25

4 boneless skinless chicken breast halves
4 slices fat-free Cheddar cheese
4 light hamburger buns
Lettuce, onion, pickles, tomatoes, mustard

Remove any fat from chicken breast. Grill on a preheated outdoor grill or cook in a nonstick skillet, turning once, for about 5 minutes per side, until just cooked through.

Carefully, so as not to burn your fingers, split the chicken pieces almost through, butterfly fashion. Open and lay them flat on the grill or in the skillet. Place a slice of cheese on top and cook only until the cheese is melted. You don't want to dry out the chicken.

Meanwhile, while the cheese is melting, open the buns and place on the grill or around the chicken in the skillet. When all is hot and melted, place each opened bun on a serving plate and top with a piece of chicken. Add all the trimmings as you would a regular hamburger.

Turkey

TURKEY AND DRESSING

Cooking in an oven bag makes the turkey come out so moist and beautifully browned. It doesn't sit and swim in fat while cooking. The dressing is baked separately in a dressing pan or baking dish.

1 (8- to 12-pound) turkey
2 tablespoons flour

Dressing:
2 to 3 quarts crumbled dry fat-free corn bread
2 cups chopped onions
2 cups chopped celery
2 to 4 cups defatted turkey broth
2 to 4 tablespoons ground sage
Salt and pepper to taste
¾ cup egg substitute
Fat-free margarine or Butter Buds, liquid form

Giblet Gravy:
Reserved cooked giblets, chopped fine
1 cup uncooked dressing
3 tablespoons flour, or as needed
Defatted turkey broth

(continued)

Turkey

Day ahead: Take turkey out of its original packing package, clean the neck and giblets, place in twice as much water as you need to cover the giblets, and boil until tender. When done, remove from the heat and cool. Cut giblets into small bite-size pieces for gravy. Place broth in the refrigerator overnight to defat. Store giblets in a zipper-lock plastic bag and refrigerate.

Trim all visible fat possible from the neck and tail area of turkey. Wash well in cold water. Drain.

Prepare a large (4 x 20-inch) oven bag by placing 2 tablespoons of flour in the bag and shaking to coat the inside. This will keep the turkey from sticking to the bag. Place a wire cake rack in the bottom of your roasting pan. (Don't forget to spray your roaster or roasting pan with vegetable oil cooking spray; it makes cleanup a snap.) (If you don't have a wire rack, you may use a pie plate or pan, turned upside down.) Place the turkey in the bag and tie as instructed on the package. Set the turkey, in its bag, on the rack or pan in the roaster. Place in refrigerator until time to cook. Before placing in the oven, punch holes in the bottom of the bag; this will let any excess fat drip out and into the pan. Also punch a few holes in the top of the bag, to let excess steam out. Cook according to directions on turkey timetable (included with turkey).

Dressing

Day ahead: Cook your corn bread. Clean and chop the onions and celery.

Day of preparation: Place onions and celery in a saucepan and cover with water. Cook until crisp-tender. Drain, reserving cooking water. Set aside.

Skim off any fat congealed on top of the broth and heat the broth to boiling. Preheat the oven to 350 degrees. Lightly spray your largest casserole with vegetable oil cooking spray.

In a big mixing bowl, combine the corn bread, sage, salt, and pepper. Add the celery and onions, using some of the water they were cooked in, and 2 cups of defatted broth. Stir until well blended. Don't add all your broth at once; add slowly, until desired consistency. Some like dressing drier than others.

Add the egg substitute and stir well. Pour into the prepared baking dish (reserve 1 cup for gravy) and dot with fat-free margarine or stream Butter Buds over the top. Bake, uncovered, about 30 to 45 minutes, until about half done; don't stir. Again add margarine or Butter Buds over top. Continue baking for another 30 to 45 minutes or until the desired doneness.

Giblet Gravy

Combine the giblets and defatted broth, about 4 cups, with 1 cup of uncooked dressing; bring to a boil and reduce heat. In a small bowl, mix about 3 tablespoons flour and 1 cup of hot broth with a small wire whisk or fork; when smooth, start adding to the gravy. Stir in a small amount at a time, until desired thickness. Remove from heat to stop thickening.

Tip: (Buy turkey when prices are low or they are on sale; keep in freezer several weeks before holidays.) Three to four days ahead, take turkey out of freezer, place in an ice chest full of cold water, breast down, and change water approximately every 5 hours, keeping water cold. When thawed, drain and place in refrigerator. The size of your turkey will determine how far ahead you need to start this thawing process.

Turkey or Chicken Gravy

2 to 2½ cups defatted chicken broth, or skim milk and water, mixed
¼ cup poultry drippings, defatted as much as possible
¼ cup flour
½ cup cold water
Salt and pepper to taste

SERVES 5

4 GRAMS FAT
PER ½-CUP
SERVING

Prep :05
Cook :10
Stand :00
Total :15

Heat the broth and add the hot liquid to the poultry drippings in the skillet or roasting pan. In a jar with a tight-fitting lid, combine the flour and cold water; shake vigorously until smooth. Add the flour mixture to the hot liquid while stirring with a whisk. Cook until mixture boils and thickens, stirring constantly. Season with salt and pepper.

Cranberry Sauce

1 (12-ounce) package fresh or frozen cranberries, thawed if frozen
½ cup plus 2 tablespoons sugar

SERVES 4

0 GRAMS FAT

Prep :05
Cook :06
Stand :15
Total :26

Rinse fresh cranberries and pick over to remove bits of stem.

In a medium-size saucepan, combine sugar, cranberries, and 1 cup of water. Bring to a boil; continue cooking uncovered, stirring occasionally, for 5 to 6 minutes or until the berries pop and the mixture thickens slightly.

Transfer to a small serving bowl; cool slightly. Cover and refrigerate several hours or until cold.

ZITI TURKEY CASSEROLE

This is a great do-ahead dish for entertaining or for family-night supper at church. You can use lean beef instead of turkey, although it will add more fat grams.

2 cups chopped onions
1½ pounds lean ground turkey
1 (8-ounce) can tomato sauce
¼ cup chopped fresh parsley
½ teaspoon dried oregano
½ teaspoon salt
½ teaspoon pepper
1 pound ziti (or other tubular pasta), prepared according to package directions
  (about 10 cups)

Sauce:
1 (8-ounce) can tomato sauce
Pinch of oregano
Pinch of dried basil
1 cup fat-free Parmesan cheese

SERVES 8

2 GRAMS FAT
PER SERVING

Prep :35
Cook 1:20
Stand :15
Total 2:10

Preheat the oven to 350 degrees. Lightly spray a deep 3-quart casserole with vegetable oil cooking spray.

In a large nonstick skillet, dry-fry the onions, adding about 2 tablespoons water if needed, for 5 to 6 minutes, or until translucent. Add the turkey, stirring to break up lumps, and cook 8 to 10 minutes or until lightly browned. Transfer to a colander; rinse with hot water to remove any excess fat. Wipe the skillet clean of any fat with paper towels.

Return the meat to the skillet; add ¼ cup water, the can of tomato sauce, and the parsley, oregano, salt, and pepper. Simmer over medium heat 2 to 3 minutes or until the liquid is almost gone. Remove from heat.

Spread half of the cooked, drained ziti evenly in the prepared casserole. Spread the meat mixture over the pasta. Top with the remaining ziti. *(continued)*

In a small mixing bowl, mix the remaining can of tomato sauce with a pinch each of oregano and basil and half the Parmesan cheese. Pour over the casserole; top with the remaining Parmesan. Bake uncovered for 1 hour, or until lightly browned. Let stand 15 minutes before serving.

> *Note:* You can make this ahead. After assembling, refrigerate uncovered until cool, then cover with plastic wrap and refrigerate up to 3 days. If made ahead, allow to stand at room temperature for 20 minutes before putting in the oven. Bake 1 hour and 15 minutes. Let stand 15 minutes before serving.

TURKEY LO MEIN

SERVES 4

0.5 GRAMS FAT PER 1⅓-CUP SERVING

Prep :10
Cook :10
Stand :00
Total :20

2 cups cooked turkey breast strips
1 (14-ounce) can fat-free chicken broth
2 tablespoons light soy sauce
½ teaspoon sugar
½ to ¾ teaspoon ground ginger
¼ teaspoon garlic powder
1 (16-ounce) package frozen broccoli, carrots, water chestnuts, and peppers
1 (4-ounce) package uncooked angel hair pasta or vermicelli
2 teaspoons cornstarch
2 tablespoons water

In a large skillet, combine the turkey, broth, soy sauce, sugar, ginger, garlic powder, and vegetables. Bring to a boil. Stir in the pasta. Reduce the heat to low, cover, and simmer 5 to 8 minutes, or until the pasta is tender.

In a small bowl combine the cornstarch and water; blend until smooth. Stir into the hot mixture in the skillet. Cook 1 minute, or until thickened, stirring constantly. Serve with additional soy sauce if desired.

TURKEY AND HAM À LA KING

A good recipe for that leftover holiday turkey and ham.

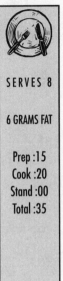

SERVES 8

6 GRAMS FAT

Prep :15
Cook :20
Stand :00
Total :35

¼ cup chopped onion
2 tablespoons chopped green bell pepper
6 tablespoons flour
¼ teaspoon white pepper
2 cups defatted chicken broth
1 cup skim milk
1½ cups diced cooked turkey or chicken
1½ cups diced lower-salt, 95% fat-free boneless ham
1 (2-ounce jar) sliced pimientos, drained
2 tablespoons sherry

Sauté the onion and green pepper in ¼ cup water until tender. Stir in the flour and white pepper. Cook until smooth and bubbly. Gradually add the broth and milk. Cook until the mixture boils and thickens, stirring constantly. Boil 1 minute.

Stir in the turkey, ham, and pimientos; cook until thoroughly heated. Stir in the sherry just before serving.

Variation: Serve in patty shells if desired; this is also very good over rice.

SOUTH OF THE BORDER TURKEY CASSEROLE

SERVES 4

6 GRAMS FAT
PER SERVING

Prep :15
Cook :35
Stand :00
Total :50

8 or 9 (6-inch) corn tortillas
½ pound lean (93% fat-free) fresh ground turkey
¾ cup chopped onion
1 cup mild or medium taco sauce
1 (4-ounce) can chopped green chiles
¾ cup frozen whole-kernel corn, thawed
¾ cup shredded fat-free Cheddar cheese
Fat-free sour cream, if desired for garnish
2 green onions, chopped, if desired for garnish

Preheat the oven to 350 degrees. Lightly coat a 1½-quart casserole with vegetable oil cooking spray.

Place the tortillas on a cookie sheet, not overlapping, and bake until crisp, about 4 minutes on one side; turn and bake 2 more minutes on the other. Cool on a wire rack. (Leave the oven on.)

In a nonstick skillet, dry-fry the turkey and onion, stirring to break up lumps, until the turkey is brown. Transfer to a colander and rinse off any fat with hot water. Shake to remove water. Wipe the skillet with paper towels to remove any fat that cooked out of the turkey. Return the turkey and onion to the skillet; add the taco sauce, chiles, and corn. Bring to a boil, reduce the heat, and simmer for about 5 minutes.

Break up 3 of the tortillas and arrange over the bottom of the prepared casserole.

Spoon half the turkey mixture over the tortillas; sprinkle with half the cheese. Repeat layers. Bake 15 minutes, or until the cheese is melted and the casserole is heated through. Break up the remaining tortillas and sprinkle over the casserole. Garnish with dollops of fat-free sour cream and sprinkle ½ cup chopped scallions over all.

QUICK TURKEY POTPIE

2 (10¾-ounce) cans Healthy Request cream of mushroom soup
1 (16-ounce) package frozen mixed vegetables
3 cups cooked turkey or chicken, diced into small cubes
1 teaspoon poultry seasoning
½ teaspoon garlic salt
2 cups Bisquick reduced-fat baking mix
1½ cups skim milk
½ teaspoon parsley flakes

SERVES 8

**3 GRAMS FAT
PER SERVING**

Prep :25
Cook :35
Stand :00
Total 1:00

Preheat the oven to 400 degrees. Lightly spray a 13 x 9-inch baking pan with vegetable oil cooking spray.

In a large mixing bowl, combine the soup, vegetables, turkey, poultry seasoning, and garlic salt. Spoon into the prepared pan.

In a separate mixing bowl, stir together the baking mix and milk until blended. Pour over the turkey mixture. Sprinkle with parsley.

Bake uncovered 35 minutes or until the crust is light golden brown.

Leftover frozen or deli turkey or chicken can be used.

TURKEY, RICE, SAUSAGE, AND CRANBERRIES ALL IN ONE

Great for leftover holiday turkey, or make from scratch.

1 (6-ounce) package long grain and wild rice mix
½ pound lean bulk pork sausage (3 grams fat per patty)
1 cup sliced fresh mushrooms
½ cup chopped celery
1 tablespoon cornstarch
1 cup skim milk
3 cups chopped cooked turkey
1 cup dried cranberries or 1 (12-ounce) bag chopped fresh berries

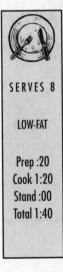

SERVES 8

LOW-FAT

Prep :20
Cook 1:20
Stand :00
Total 1:40

(continued)

Preheat the oven to 375 degrees. Lightly spray an 11 x 7-inch baking dish with vegetable oil cooking spray.

Prepare the rice according to package directions, omitting any butter, margarine, or salt. Set aside.

Dry-fry the sausage, mushrooms, and celery in a large nonstick skillet until the sausage is browned, stirring to crumble meat. Place in a colander and rinse with hot water; shake off excess water. Remove all but 1 teaspoon of pan drippings. In the skillet, place the cornstarch and gradually add the milk, stirring constantly with a wire whisk until the mixture is smooth and starts to thicken. Turn heat off.

Combine the rice, sausage mixture, sauce, turkey, and cranberries. Spoon the mixture into the prepared baking dish. Bake uncovered about 40 to 45 minutes.

To store: Cover and refrigerate up to 2 days. Or cover and freeze up to 2 weeks, thaw in refrigerator, and bake as directed above.

TURKEY TAMALE PIE

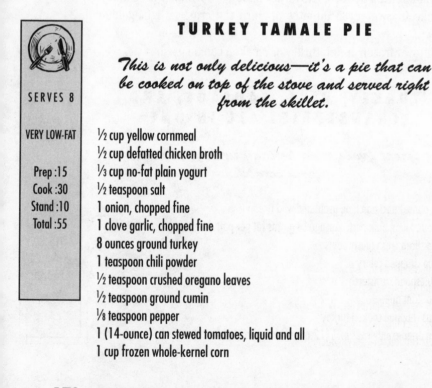

This is not only delicious—it's a pie that can be cooked on top of the stove and served right from the skillet.

SERVES 8

VERY LOW-FAT

Prep : 15
Cook : 30
Stand : 10
Total : 55

½ cup yellow cornmeal
½ cup defatted chicken broth
⅓ cup no-fat plain yogurt
½ teaspoon salt
1 onion, chopped fine
1 clove garlic, chopped fine
8 ounces ground turkey
1 teaspoon chili powder
½ teaspoon crushed oregano leaves
½ teaspoon ground cumin
⅛ teaspoon pepper
1 (14-ounce) can stewed tomatoes, liquid and all
1 cup frozen whole-kernel corn

½ cup black olives, sliced
1 cup shredded fat-free Cheddar cheese

Combine the cornmeal, chicken broth, yogurt, and ¼ teaspoon salt in a bowl. Set aside.

Sauté onion in ¼ cup of water in a large skillet until tender. Add the garlic and cook 1 minute longer. Crumble the turkey into the skillet, sprinkle with chili powder, oregano, cumin, remaining ¼ teaspoon salt, and pepper. Cook, stirring, until no pink remains. Blot with a paper towel to remove any excess fat.

Add the tomatoes and corn. Bring to a boil. Lower the heat to a simmer. Pour two-thirds of the cornmeal mixture into the simmering turkey mixture. Stir and simmer 3 minutes. (Do not let boil.)

Smooth the top with a spatula and scatter over ¼ cup of the olives. Drizzle the remaining cornmeal mixture over the top. Sprinkle with the cheese. Cover and simmer over very low heat, without stirring, for 15 to 20 minutes, or until set. Sprinkle with the remaining olives.

Remove from the heat. Let stand covered for 10 minutes. Serve hot, spooning onto plates.

TURKEY TORTILLA CASSEROLE

2 pounds ground turkey
1 cup chopped onion
1 clove garlic, minced
1 (15-ounce) can tomato sauce
1 (2-ounce) package taco seasoning
1 (4-ounce) can green chiles
1 teaspoon chili powder, or more to taste
Salt and pepper to taste (optional)
12 (6-inch) corn tortillas
1 (10¾-ounce) can Healthy Request low-fat cream of chicken soup
¾ cup skim milk
2 cups shredded fat-free cheddar cheese

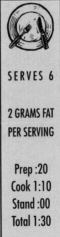

SERVES 6

2 GRAMS FAT
PER SERVING

Prep :20
Cook 1:10
Stand :00
Total 1:30

(continued)

Preheat the oven to 350 degrees.

Brown the turkey, onion, and garlic in a nonstick skillet over medium heat, stirring frequently. Transfer to a colander, rinse under hot water to remove any fat, and shake excess water off. With a paper towel, remove any fat in the skillet. Return the turkey to the skillet; add the tomato sauce, taco seasoning, green chiles, chili powder, and salt and pepper if desired. Mix well and heat thoroughly.

Line a 9 x 13-inch baking dish with half the tortillas. Spoon the turkey mixture over the tortillas. Layer the remaining tortillas over the turkey mixture and pour the soup over the tortillas. Pour the milk over the soup. Sprinkle cheese over all and bake uncovered for 45 minutes. Serve with salsa and fat-free sour cream if desired.

TURKEY TORTILLA CASUAL

SERVES 4

LOW-FAT

Prep :15
Cook :45
Stand :10
Total 1:10

1 pound lean ground turkey
½ cup chopped onion
1 (8-ounce) jar Mexican salsa, green or red
½ cup fat-free sour cream
1 (10¾-ounce) can Healthy Request cream of chicken soup
1 (2-ounce) jar sliced pimientos, drained
6 corn tortillas, cut into 1-inch strips
2 cups shredded fat-free Cheddar cheese
Sliced olives (optional)

Preheat the oven to 350 degrees.

Cook and stir the ground turkey and onion in a nonstick skillet until brown. Transfer to a colander and rinse with hot water to wash away any excess fat. Shake dry.

Spread ½ cup of the salsa in the bottom of an ungreased square baking dish.

Mix the remaining salsa, the sour cream, soup, and pimientos. Layer half the tortilla strips, turkey mixture, soup mixture, and cheese in the baking dish. Repeat.

Bake uncovered until the casserole is hot and bubbly, about 30 minutes. Let stand 10 minutes. Garnish with olives if desired.

SAUSAGE SCALLOPED POTATOES

1 pound turkey sausages
1 (10¾-ounce) can Healthy Request cream of mushroom soup
¾ cup skim milk
½ cup chopped onion
½ teaspoon salt
¼ teaspoon pepper
3 cups thinly sliced potatoes
Butter Buds
½ pound shredded fat-free Cheddar cheese

SERVES 8

VERY LOW-FAT

Prep :20
Cook 2:00
Stand :00
Total 2:20

Preheat the oven to 350 degrees. Cook the sausages in a nonstick skillet, breaking apart and stirring frequently until lightly browned. Transfer to a colander and run hot water over to wash away any excess fat. Drain well.

In a mixing bowl, combine the soup, milk, onion, salt, and pepper. In a large casserole sprayed with vegetable oil cooking spray, layer half the potatoes, half the soup mixture, and half the sausage. Repeat the layers, ending with sausage.

Stream Butter Buds over the top lightly. Bake for 1½ hours or until potatoes are tender. Sprinkle with cheese, and return to the oven for another 15 minutes.

SERVES 6

VERY LOW-FAT

Prep :20
Cook :45
Stand :00
Total 1:05

SAUSAGE AND NOODLE CASSEROLE

1 pound turkey sausages
½ cup chopped onion
¼ cup chopped green pepper
1 (10¾-ounce) can Healthy Request cream of chicken soup
1 (8-ounce package) noodles (no yolk, no cholesterol, fat-free), cooked and
    drained
Salt and pepper to taste

Preheat the oven to 350 degrees.

Crumble the sausage in a large nonstick skillet; add the onion and green pepper. Cook, stirring, over medium heat until the meat is browned and vegetables are tender. Drain and rinse under hot water in a colander; shake off excess water.

Combine soup with 1⅓ cups of water in a large bowl. Stir until smooth. Add the meat mixture, noodles, salt, and pepper. Mix well. Spoon into a 9 x 11-inch baking dish. Bake uncovered for 30 minutes, or until bubbly.

SERVES 6

VERY LOW-FAT

Prep :15
Cook 1:30
Stand :00
Total 1:45

SAUSAGE AND RICE CASSEROLE

1 pound turkey sausages
1 green bell pepper, seeded and chopped
1 onion, chopped
4 stalks celery, chopped
1 (10¾-ounce) can Healthy Request cream of chicken soup
1 cup brown rice
3 tablespoons slivered almonds

Preheat the oven to 350 degrees. Heat a large nonstick skillet and cook the sausage, breaking apart and stirring frequently, until it begins to brown. Add the pepper, onion, and celery and continue cooking until the vegetables are tender. Transfer to a colander and rinse under hot water; shake dry.

Combine the soup in a saucepan with enough water to measure 4 cups. Add the turkey and vegetables, bring to a boil, and simmer 5 minutes. Add the raw rice and almonds. Pour into a 9 x 13 x 2-inch baking dish, cover, and bake for 1 hour.

SPAGHETTI PIE

6 ounces spaghetti
3 tablespoons Butter Buds
½ tablespoon egg substitute
½ cup grated fat-free Parmesan cheese
1 pound turkey sausages
½ cup chopped onion
¼ cup chopped green pepper
1 (8-ounce) can tomatoes, cut up, with their juice
1 (6-ounce) can tomato paste
1 teaspoon sugar
1 teaspoon oregano
¼ teaspoon garlic salt
1 cup fat-free cottage cheese, drained
½ cup shredded fat-free mozzarella cheese

SERVES
4 TO 6

8 GRAMS FAT

Prep :15
Cook 1:00
Stand :00
Total 1:15

Preheat the oven to 350 degrees.

In a saucepan, cook the spaghetti according to package directions; drain and return to the pan. Stir in the Butter Buds, egg substitute, and Parmesan cheese. Press the spaghetti into a pie plate that has been sprayed with vegetable oil cooking spray, forming a crust.

In a nonstick skillet, cook the turkey sausage with the onion and green pepper, stirring to break apart the sausage, until brown. Drain, place in a colander, and rinse with hot water to remove any excess fat. Place in a saucepan; stir in the tomatoes, tomato paste, sugar, oregano, and garlic salt. Heat thoroughly. Spread cottage cheese over the bottom of the spaghetti crust. Top with the meat mixture.

Bake uncovered for 20 minutes. Sprinkle with mozzarella and bake 5 minutes more, or until the cheese is melted.

SANTA FE TURKEY TOSTADAS

SERVES 3

5 GRAMS FAT

Prep :15
Cook :25
Stand :00
Total :40

6 flour tortillas (8-inch)
1 pound ground turkey breast
½ cup chopped onion
1 (16-ounce) package frozen corn with red and green peppers
1 (14-ounce) can tomato sauce
3 to 4 teaspoons chili powder
1½ teaspoons cumin
½ teaspoon garlic powder
3 cups shredded lettuce
1 large tomato, diced
½ cup shredded fat-free Cheddar cheese
Salsa if desired
Fat-free sour cream if desired

Heat the oven to 375 degrees. Place the tortillas on an ungreased cookie sheet. Bake for 7 to 10 minutes, or until crisp and lightly browned.

Meanwhile, spray a large nonstick skillet with vegetable oil cooking spray. Brown the turkey with the onion; drain well. Pat out any excess fat or rinse in a colander under hot water.

Return the turkey to the pan. Add the corn, tomato sauce, chili powder, cumin, and garlic powder. Bring to a boil, reduce the heat, and simmer 6 to 8 minutes, stirring occasionally.

To assemble: Place baked tortillas on individual serving plates, top with ⅙ of lettuce, spoon ⅙ of meat mixture over lettuce. Top each with tomato and cheese. Serve with salsa and a dollop of fat-free sour cream.

Meat
and Fish

SWISS STEAK

SERVES 4

4 GRAMS FAT PER SERVING

Prep :15
Cook 1:30
Stand :00
Total 1:45

1 pound lean boneless sirloin steak, trimmed of all fat
1 cup tomato juice or stewed tomatoes
1 large onion, sliced thin and separated into rings
1 large green bell pepper, sliced into thin rounds
Salt and pepper to taste

Spray a nonstick skillet with vegetable oil cooking spray. Brown the steak well on both sides. Pour off or blot away any fat. Return the meat to the skillet and add the remaining ingredients. Cover and simmer about 1¼ hours, or to desired doneness.

Note: The meat may be transferred to a covered baking dish and cooked in a 350 degree oven until tender if so desired.

MEXICALI PORK CHOP CASSEROLE

SERVES 4

8 GRAMS FAT PER SERVING

Prep :15
Cook :27
Stand :00
Total :42

Studies say that pork chops (butterfly and center-cut) are equal to chicken in fat content if trimmed of all fat. You be the judge. I'm very careful and seldom serve pork, but it is nice for a change, and won't hurt you if you serve it in moderation.

1 large onion, halved and sliced thin
½ medium green bell pepper, chopped
½ medium red bell pepper, chopped
1 (12-ounce) can low-sodium stewed tomatoes, drained and chopped
1 cup frozen whole-kernel corn, thawed and drained
¼ teaspoon dried marjoram
4 lean pork chops, trimmed of all fat

Preheat the oven to 350 degrees. Spray a nonstick skillet with vegetable oil cooking spray.

Sauté the onion and peppers in the skillet for about 5 minutes. Add the tomatoes, corn, and marjoram, raise the heat, and cook uncovered 5 minutes longer. Pour into 1½-quart casserole coated with cooking spray.

In the same skillet brown the chops for 2 minutes on each side. Lay the chops on top of the vegetable mixture.

Cover the casserole and bake 12 to 15 minutes, or until the chops are done.

GLAZED PORK CHOPS

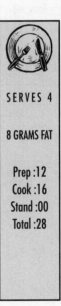

4 lean pork chops, about 1-inch thick
Salt and pepper to taste
¼ cup lemon juice
¼ cup honey

SERVES 4

8 GRAMS FAT

Prep :12
Cook :16
Stand :00
Total :28

Trim the chops of all fat.

Heat a nonstick skillet and coat lightly with vegetable oil cooking spray. Brown the chops for 2 minutes on each side. Sprinkle with salt and pepper.

Stir the lemon juice and honey together in a measuring cup. Pour over the chops and simmer, partially covered, for 6 minutes. Turn the chops and continue cooking until the meat is still juicy and tender and the sauce is reduced to a glaze, about 6 minutes longer.

HAM, NOODLE, AND
GREEN PEA CASSEROLE

SERVES 4

3 GRAMS FAT

Prep :10
Cook :30
Stand :00
Total :40

6 ounces cholesterol-free noodles
1½ tablespoons flour
1 teaspoon dry mustard
¼ teaspoon ground sage
⅛ teaspoon grated nutmeg
⅛ teaspoon pepper
1½ cups skim milk
6 ounces 98% fat-free ham, cubed
2 cups frozen green peas
2 tablespoons Butter Buds liquid
2 tablespoons bread crumbs, fat-free bread (1 slice)

Preheat the oven to 350 degrees.

Cook the noodles according to package directions, but leave out the salt. Drain well and set aside.

In a saucepan or skillet, combine the flour, mustard, sage, nutmeg, and pepper. Slowly whisk in the milk and set aside.

In a mixing bowl, combine the noodles, ham, and frozen peas. Pour the milk mixture over and mix well. Transfer to a shallow baking dish. Pour the Butter Buds over.

Cover with foil. Bake 10 to 15 minutes. Uncover, sprinkle with the bread crumbs, and bake 10 to 15 minutes longer.

HAM AND POTATOES AU GRATIN

1 pound frozen hash brown potatoes (check label for fat content)
1½ cups cubed 98% fat-free ham
1 cup shredded fat-free Cheddar cheese
½ cup fat-free salad dressing, such as Miracle Whip
½ cup skim milk
½ cup dry bread crumbs
1 tablespoon Butter Buds, liquid form
Salt and pepper to taste

SERVES 4

VERY LOW-FAT

Prep :10
Cook :45
Stand :00
Total :55

Preheat the oven to 350 degrees.

Combine the potatoes, ham, and cheese; mix lightly. Combine the salad dressing and milk; mix well. Add the dressing mixture to the potato mixture and mix lightly. Spoon into a 1-quart casserole.

Combine the bread crumbs and Butter Buds. Sprinkle over the potato mixture. Bake uncovered for 40 to 50 minutes, or until thoroughly heated.

CAMPFIRE DELIGHT

This is not only for cooking over an open fire, but very good for an easy breakfast at home.

¾ cup diced low-fat ham (98% fat-free)
1 (16-ounce) package frozen potatoes, onions, and peppers, thawed
2 cups egg substitute
Salt and pepper (optional)
6 drops hot pepper sauce
¼ cup shredded fat-free Monterey Jack cheese
¼ cup shredded fat-free Cheddar cheese

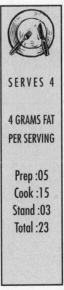

SERVES 4

4 GRAMS FAT
PER SERVING

Prep :05
Cook :15
Stand :03
Total :23

Heat a nonstick skillet (if using a cast-iron skillet over an open fire, spray lightly with vegetable oil cooking spray). Add the ham and the potatoes with onions and peppers, cooking and stirring

(continued)

about 5 minutes. If they start to stick in the cast-iron pan, add a little water.

In a mixing bowl, combine the egg substitute, salt and pepper if desired, and hot pepper sauce. Pour into the skillet. Cover and cook for 8 to 10 minutes on medium-low heat or until set, lifting edges occasionally to let the uncooked part under as you would an omelet. Remove from heat, cover with cheeses, and let stand covered for 2 to 3 minutes, or until the cheeses are melted.

BREAKFAST HAM CASSEROLE

SERVES 4

4 GRAMS FAT
PER 1-CUP
SERVING

Prep :10
Cook :30
Stand 8:30
Total 9:10

3 cups cubed French bread
¾ cup diced 98% fat-free ham
2 tablespoons diced sweet red bell pepper
1 cup shredded fat-free Cheddar cheese
1⅓ cups skim milk
¾ cup egg substitute
¼ teaspoon dry mustard
¼ teaspoon onion powder
¼ teaspoon white pepper
Paprika

Arrange bread cubes evenly in an 8-inch square baking dish. Layer the ham, red bell pepper, and cheese over the bread. Set aside.

Combine the milk, egg substitute, mustard, onion powder, and white pepper. Pour over the cheese. Cover and refrigerate at least 8 hours. Remove from the refrigerator and let stand 30 minutes. Meantime, heat the oven to 350 degrees.

Bake the casserole uncovered for 30 minutes, or until puffy and golden. Sprinkle with paprika. Serve immediately.

Variation: One pound of turkey sausage, cooked, drained, and crumbled, may be substituted for the ham. (Pat out any and all excess fat with a paper towel, or place the browned meat in a colander and rinse with hot water.) Twelve grams of fat per serving.

POTATOES AND HAM AND PEAS IN A HURRY

This is my shortcut to a casserole-type dish made on top of the stove in a flash. Don't tell me you have no time to cook. Make your salad while this meal-in-one is cooking.

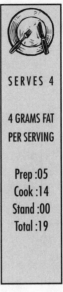

SERVES 4

4 GRAMS FAT
PER SERVING

Prep :05
Cook :14
Stand :00
Total :19

1 (24-ounce) package frozen hash-brown potatoes with peppers and onions
1½ cups cubed cooked 99% fat-free ham
1 (10¾-ounce) can Healthy Request cream of mushroom soup
1 cup frozen green peas
1 cup whole-kernel corn
½ teaspoon garlic salt
½ teaspoon Italian seasoning
Salt and pepper to taste

In a large nonstick skillet, combine the potatoes and ¾ cup of water. Bring to a boil, stirring often, reduce the heat, cover, and cook about 7 or 8 minutes or until the potatoes are tender. Stir in the ham, mushroom soup and half a soup can of water. Add the peas, corn, and seasonings. Cover and cook 5 to 6 minutes or until thoroughly heated, stirring occasionally.

BREAKFAST SAUSAGE CASSEROLE

SERVES 8

VERY LOW-FAT

Prep :20
Cook :30
Stand 8:00
Total 8:50

1 (4-ounce) can chopped green chiles
1½ cups shredded fat-free Cheddar cheese
1 pound low-fat sausage, cooked, crumbled, rinsed with hot water, and drained
2 cups egg substitute
1 cup skim milk

Line the bottom of an 8-inch square baking dish with half the green chiles. Add half the cheese, then the remaining chiles, then all the sausage. Top with the remaining cheese. Refrigerate overnight.

The next morning, preheat the oven to 400 degrees. Beat together the egg substitute and milk. Pour over the casserole and bake uncovered for 30 minutes.

BREAKFAST SAUSAGE BAKE

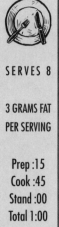

SERVES 8

3 GRAMS FAT
PER SERVING

Prep :15
Cook :45
Stand :00
Total 1:00

1 pound fresh mushrooms, chopped fine
1 cup fine dry bread crumbs
1 pound low-fat sausage (3 grams fat per patty) or turkey breakfast sausages
1 green or red bell pepper, cored and chopped
1 tablespoon dried parsley flakes
¼ teaspoon cayenne pepper
2 (8-ounce) cartons egg substitute

Preheat the oven to 350 degrees.

Heat ¼ cup of water in a nonstick skillet and add the mushrooms. Cook and stir until the mixture boils and the moisture evaporates. Remove from the heat. Stir in the bread crumbs.

Spray a 9 x 13 x 2-inch baking dish with vegetable oil cooking spray. Press the mushroom mixture onto the bottom of the prepared baking dish to form crust.

In the same nonstick skillet cook the sausage, breaking apart or crumbling into small pieces and stirring frequently until lightly browned. Remove from the heat. Put into a colander and rinse with hot water; shake well.

In a mixing bowl, combine the sausage, chopped pepper, parsley, and cayenne. Spread the sausage mixture over crust. Pour the egg substitute evenly over the sausage. Bake uncovered 25 to 30 minutes, or until the mixture is set.

SAUSAGE BAKE

1 pound low-fat sausage (3 grams per patty)
¾ cup chopped onion
½ cup chopped bell pepper
1 cup uncooked white rice
½ teaspoon lemon pepper
¼ teaspoon oregano
½ teaspoon adobo seasoning
¼ teaspoon dried basil
Salt and pepper to taste
1 (8-ounce) can sliced water chestnuts, drained
2 (10¾-ounce) cans Healthy Request cream of mushroom soup
1 (14-ounce) can fat-free chicken broth
1 (4-ounce) can mushroom pieces and stems, drained
1 (10-ounce) package frozen broccoli (run hot water over to thaw)

SERVES 6

VERY LOW-FAT

Prep :30
Cook 1:00
Stand :00
Total 1:30

Preheat the oven to 350 degrees. Lightly coat a 13 x 9-inch baking dish with vegetable oil cooking spray.

Crumble and cook the sausage in a nonstick skillet. When the meat is about half done, add the onion and pepper. Cook 8 to 10 minutes, until tender. Blot any excess fat from the meat with paper towels.

Add the rice and all remaining ingredients. Pour into the prepared dish. Bake for 45 minutes to 1 hour, until the rice is tender and liquid is absorbed.

SNAKE MEAT

SERVES 4

16 GRAMS FAT
ENTIRE DISH

Prep :15
Cook 2:00
Stand :00
Total 2:15

1 (12-ounce) bottle chili sauce
1 (16-ounce) can cranberry sauce
1 (16-ounce) package low-fat Healthy Choice smoked sausage

In a large saucepan mix all ingredients together. Place over low heat and simmer for at least 2 hours.

I use a Crock-Pot and let it cook all day. Put it on before you leave in the morning. Great over rice.

Those girls in the hills really come up with some different dishes. Wait until you tell your friends what you are having for dinner when you invite them over. Makes me nervous when Jean invites us up into the hills for dinner.

Fish

IN FISH, FAT IS NOT A DIRTY WORD

A lean high-quality protein source, fish contains three fatty acids
that are thought to help lower blood cholesterol.

LOW-FAT FISH (LESS THAN 5%)

Catfish	Halibut
Black sea bass	Monkfish
Cod	Orange roughy
Flounder	Pollock
Grouper	Red snapper
Haddock	Rockfish
Sole	Sea trout
Striped bass	Swordfish
Whiting	Tilapia
Perch	

Source: USDA Handbook 8

MODERATELY FAT FISH (5–10%)

Bluefish	Trout
Butterfish	Tuna
Carp	Whitefish

HIGHER FAT FISH (OVER 10%)

Herring	Salmon
Mackerel	Sardine
Pompano	

CAJUN OVEN-FRIED FISH

This looks and tastes fried, but with no fat!
The types of fish may be catfish, grouper,
orange roughy, perch, bass, or just about any
type of fillets.

SERVES 6

ULTRA LOW-
FAT

Prep :10
Cook :10
Stand :00
Total :20

½ cup cornmeal
½ cup dry bread crumbs
Dash of salt
1 teaspoon Cajun seasoning
1 pound fish fillets
⅔ cup skim milk or skim or low-fat buttermilk (1 gram per cup)

Preheat the oven to 450 degrees. Lightly spray a baking sheet with vegetable oil cooking spray.

Combine the cornmeal, bread crumbs, salt, and Cajun seasoning. Dip the fish in the skim milk or buttermilk and dredge in the cornmeal mixture. Place on the prepared baking sheet and spray the top of the fish lightly with cooking spray.

Bake for 10 minutes or until the fish flakes easily when tested with a fork. I usually turn mine over with a spatula after about half done. This makes it nice and brown on each side.

BAKED "FRIED" CATFISH

Catfish fillets
Egg substitute
Cornflake crumbs

2 GRAMS FAT

Prep :10
Cook :25
Stand :00
Total :35

Preheat the oven to 400 degrees.

Spray a heavy metal baking sheet or pan with vegetable oil cooking spray.

Dip the fillets in the egg substitute. Roll in cornflake crumbs. Place on the baking sheet and spray the fillets lightly with cooking spray.

Bake about 25 minutes, or until crisp and flaky. Turn over when half done to brown and crisp both sides nicely.

BOB'S "FRIED" FISH SPECIAL

This may be done in a mixing bowl the same way, but this is the way Bob does it. He throws the bag away and there's no bowl to wash.

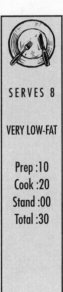

SERVES 8

VERY LOW-FAT

Prep :10
Cook :20
Stand :00
Total :30

2 cups cornmeal
¼ cup lemon pepper
1 teaspoon Creole seasoning
8 fish fillets

Preheat the oven to 400 degrees. Lightly spray a baking sheet with vegetable oil cooking spray.

In a small paper bag, mix the cornmeal, lemon pepper, and Creole seasoning. Rinse and drain the fish fillets. Put one or two fillets at a time in the paper bag and shake to coat evenly. Place on the baking sheet, spray the top of each piece lightly, and cook for about 20 minutes. Turn the fish when about half done.

Eggs, Cheese, Dried Beans, and Rice

Eggs

HOMEMADE EGG SUBSTITUTE

This is good for an emergency, but I have found the commercial egg substitutes that are now on the market and are fat-free to be much faster and easier.

MAKES
¾ CUP

2.4 GRAMS FAT

Prep :10
Cook :00
Stand :00
Total :10

6 egg whites
¼ cup instant nonfat dry milk powder
2 tablespoons water
1½ teaspoons vegetable oil
¼ teaspoon ground turmeric

Combine all the ingredients in the container of electric blender. Process 30 seconds. Refrigerate up to 1 week or freeze in an airtight container for up to 1 month.

EASY GARDEN QUICHE

2 cups chopped fresh broccoli
½ cup chopped onion
½ cup chopped green bell pepper
1 cup shredded fat-free Cheddar cheese
1½ cups skim milk
¾ cup low-fat biscuit mix, such as Bisquick
1 teaspoon salt
¼ teaspoon pepper
¾ cup egg substitute

SERVES 2

6 GRAMS FAT

Prep :10
Cook :40
Stand :05
Total :55

Heat the oven to 400 degrees. Lightly spray a pie plate with vegetable oil cooking spray. In a saucepan, heat 1 cup water with ½ teaspoon salt to boiling. Add the broccoli and cook until tender; drain thoroughly.

Toss together the broccoli, onion, green pepper, and cheese and turn into the prepared pie plate. Beat the remaining ingredients until smooth (about 15 seconds in a blender). Pour over the veggies in the pie plate. Bake 35 to 40 minutes, or until golden brown and a knife inserted halfway between the center and the edge comes out clean. Let stand 5 minutes before cutting.

Variation: 1 package (10-ounce) frozen chopped broccoli or cauliflower, thawed and drained, can be substituted for fresh broccoli. Do not cook.

FIESTA QUICHE

SERVES 2

2.5 GRAMS FAT
PER SERVING

Prep :10
Cook :35
Stand :05
Total :50

4 flour tortillas
½ cup shredded fat-free Cheddar cheese
1 (4-ounce) can green chiles, drained and chopped
¼ cup sliced green onions
½ cup picante sauce
1 cup egg substitute
⅓ cup skim milk
1 teaspoon chili powder
1 teaspoon pepper
Tomato wedges
Fat-free yogurt or sour cream
Cilantro

Preheat the oven to 350 degrees. Spray a 12-inch quiche dish with vegetable oil cooking spray. Arrange the tortillas in dish. Sprinkle the cheese, chiles, and green onions over the tortillas. Dollop with picante sauce.

Combine the egg substitute, milk, chili powder, and pepper. Pour into the quiche dish.

Bake uncovered for 30 to 35 minutes. Remove from the oven. Arrange tomato wedges around the edge; top with a dot of fat-free yogurt or sour cream and a sprig of cilantro. Let stand 5 minutes before cutting into wedges to serve.

RICE AND TURKEY QUICHE

Good for leftover turkey from the holidays.

3 cups cooked rice, cooled
1½ cups chopped cooked turkey
1 medium tomato, seeded and chopped
¼ cup sliced green onions
¼ cup chopped green bell pepper
1 teaspoon dried basil
½ teaspoon seasoned salt
⅛ teaspoon cayenne pepper
½ cup skim milk
¾ cup egg substitute
1 cup shredded fat-free Cheddar cheese

SERVES 4

**6 GRAMS FAT
ENTIRE DISH**

Prep :10
Cook :20
Stand :05
Total :35

Preheat the oven to 375 degrees. In a mixing bowl, combine the rice, turkey, tomato, onion, green pepper, basil, seasoned salt, cayenne, milk, and egg substitute. Pour into a square baking dish that has been coated with vegetable oil cooking spray. Top with the cheese.

Bake for 20 minutes, or until a knife inserted halfway between the edge and the center comes out clean. Let stand 5 minutes before serving.

CRUSTLESS ZUCCHINI QUICHE

SERVES 6

0 GRAMS FAT

Prep :15
Cook 1:05
Stand :00
Total 1:20

2 cups coarsely shredded zucchini
½ cup chopped onion
1 cup egg substitute
1½ cups skim milk
1 tablespoon flour
¼ teaspoon salt
⅛ teaspoon pepper
⅛ teaspoon ground nutmeg
1½ cups shredded fat-free Monterey Jack cheese
1 (4-ounce) can sliced mushrooms, drained

Preheat the oven to 325 degrees.

In a covered saucepan, cook the zucchini and onion in a small amount of water for 5 minutes. Drain well; press out excess liquid.

In a bowl, combine the egg substitute, milk, flour, and seasonings. Stir in the cheese, mushrooms, and zucchini mixture. Pour into an ungreased 10 x 6 x 2-inch baking dish.

On an oven rack, place the baking dish in a larger baking pan. Pour hot water into the larger pan to a depth of 1 inch. Bake at 325 degrees for 1 hour, or until a knife inserted in the center comes out clean.

ITALIAN OMELET

1 cup egg substitute
¼ teaspoon salt
¼ teaspoon Italian seasoning
⅛ teaspoon pepper
½ cup chopped onion
2 tablespoons chopped green pepper
1 clove garlic, chopped fine
¾ pound potatoes (about 4 small), peeled and cut into small dice
1 tablespoon fat-free Parmesan cheese
Salsa (optional)

SERVES 2

LESS THAN 1
GRAM FAT PER
SERVING

Prep :10
Cook :20
Stand :00
Total :30

Combine the egg substitute, salt, Italian seasoning, and pepper and set aside.

Heat 2 tablespoons of water in a skillet; add the onion, pepper, and garlic. Sauté until crisp tender. Add the potatoes and cook 5 to 8 minutes, stirring often, until they begin to brown. Spray lightly with vegetable oil cooking spray a couple of times to help brown.

Reduce the heat. Pour the egg substitute mixture over the vegetables in the skillet and sprinkle with Parmesan cheese. Cover and cook 7 to 8 minutes, or until set. Invert onto a plate and serve with salsa, if desired.

POCKET BREAKFAST

SERVES 4

0 GRAMS FAT

Prep :10
Cook :10
Stand :00
Total :20

1 (8-ounce) carton egg substitute
¾ cup frozen or canned corn with red and green peppers
1 tablespoon chopped cilantro
Salt and pepper
¼ cup shredded fat-free Cheddar cheese
2 whole wheat fat-free pocket (pita) breads, halved

Combine the egg substitute, vegetables, cilantro, and salt and pepper to taste. Mix well.
Spray a nonstick skillet with vegetable oil cooking spray. Add the egg mixture and cook until firm but moist, stirring occasionally. Sprinkle with the cheese. Spoon into pocket bread halves.

BREAKFAST ROLL-UPS

SERVES 4

**3 GRAMS FAT
PER SERVING**

Prep :10
Cook :20
Stand :00
Total :30

4 thin slices lean Canadian bacon, chopped
1½ cups fat-free frozen hash brown potatoes
Salt and pepper to taste (optional)
1½ cups egg substitute
4 (6-inch) flour tortillas
Picante sauce (optional)
Fat-free sour cream (optional)

Brown the bacon in a large nonstick skillet until desired doneness. Turn out of the pan and blot any excess fat on a paper towel. Set aside.
Using the same skillet, wipe out any fat with a paper towel, and cook the potatoes until done, stirring often. Add salt and pepper to taste if desired. Return the bacon to the skillet and mix slightly with potatoes. Pour the egg substitute over the potatoes and bacon. After it begins to set, with a rubber spatula move it around a little to form large curds. Do not stir, or it will become too dry. Re-

peat this cooking procedure until done, or egg substitute is set and no longer runs. Remove from heat. Keep warm.

Warm the tortillas according to package directions and lay them on a work surface. Spoon some of the egg mixture evenly down the center of each tortilla, top with picante sauce, if desired, roll up, and serve immediately. A dollop of fat-free sour cream is also a nice touch.

Variation: Chopped onions and bell peppers may be added to the potatoes to give a Western flair to the roll-ups. Use about 1/4 cup each.

BAKED GRITS

1 1/2 cups fat-free chicken broth
1 1/2 cups skim milk
2/3 cup hominy grits
1/4 teaspoon salt
1/4 cup egg substitute
1 large egg white
Dash pepper
1 teaspoon Butter Buds, liquid form

SERVES 4

0 GRAMS FAT

Prep :15
Cook 1:05
Stand :05
Total 1:25

Preheat the oven to 350 degrees. Lightly spray a 1 1/2-quart baking dish with vegetable oil cooking spray. Set aside.

In a medium-size heavy saucepan, bring the chicken broth and 1 cup of the milk to a boil. Stir in the grits and salt, reduce the heat to low, and cook, stirring, for 5 minutes or until thickened. Let cool for about 5 minutes.

In a small bowl, whisk together the remaining 1/2 cup of milk, the egg substitute, and egg white. Stir the egg mixture into the grits along with pepper and Butter Buds. Spoon the grits into the baking dish and bake uncovered for 1 hour or until golden brown.

(continued)

Note: May make a day ahead, cool completely, cover with plastic wrap, and refrigerate. Bake as directed.

Variations: Add ¼ cup each sautéed onions and peppers. Or sprinkle ½ cup fat-free shredded cheese over the top; bake an additional 3 to 4 minutes or until cheese is melted. Cheese and/or chopped green chiles may be added to the mixture with either variation before baking. This is a recipe you can have fun and be creative with.

Cheese

MOCK SOUR CREAM

1 cup nonfat cottage cheese
2 tablespoons fat-free mayonnaise
Juice and grated zest of ½ lemon
¼ cup skim buttermilk

Blend all ingredients together until smooth.

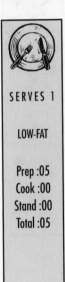

SERVES 1

LOW-FAT

Prep :05
Cook :00
Stand :00
Total :05

BREAKFAST ON THE RUN

1 slice fat-free bread
2 to 3 tablespoons fat-free cream cheese
1 banana
Cinnamon

Toast the bread, spread cream cheese over, slice the banana over
the top, and sprinkle with cinnamon.

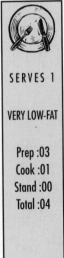

SERVES 1

VERY LOW-FAT

Prep :03
Cook :01
Stand :00
Total :04

BAKED CHEESE GRITS

SERVES 8

LESS THAN 1
GRAM FAT

Prep :15
Cook :45
Stand :00
Total 1:00

4 cups skim milk
1½ cups quick-cooking hominy grits
1 cup shredded nonfat Cheddar cheese (4 ounces)
⅓ cup Butter Buds liquid
¾ cup egg substitute, slightly beaten
½ teaspoon salt
½ teaspoon crushed red pepper

Heat the oven to 350 degrees. Spray a shallow 2½-quart baking dish, or eight 1½-cup individual baking dishes, with vegetable oil cooking spray.

Bring the milk and 2 cups of water to a boil in a large heavy saucepan. Watch carefully or it will boil over. Slowly stir in the grits. Stir until boiling, reduce the heat to low, and cook 4 to 6 minutes, stirring often, until thick.

Remove from the heat, stir in the cheese, then add the remaining ingredients. Stir until well blended and smooth.

Pour into the prepared dish or dishes. Bake until puffed and lightly browned, 25 to 30 minutes for individual dishes, 35 to 45 minutes for large baking dish.

GRILLED CHEESE SPECIAL

1 tomato
1 onion
4 slices low-fat bread (less than 1 gram each)
Fat-free mayonnaise-type dressing
2 slices fat-free cheese

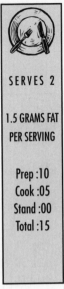

SERVES 2

1.5 GRAMS FAT
PER SERVING

Prep :10
Cook :05
Stand :00
Total :15

Slice the tomato and onion into thin slices. Spread each slice of bread on one side with mayonnaise. Put one slice of cheese on two of the slices, add slices of onion and tomato. Place the top of the sandwiches on; spray the bread lightly with vegetable oil cooking spray.

Spray a heated grill or nonstick skillet lightly with cooking spray. With a spatula place a sandwich in the skillet and brown slightly; turn sandwich over and brown on other side. Cut in half diagonally. Repeat with the remaining sandwich.

CHEESE ENCHILADAS

1 cup salsa
1½ cups fat-free cottage cheese
1 cup shredded fat-free Cheddar cheese
½ cup sliced scallions
¼ teaspoon crushed oregano
8 (6-inch) flour tortillas, warmed

SERVES 8

1 GRAM FAT
PER SERVING

Prep :20
Cook :25
Stand :00
Total :45

Preheat the oven to 375 degrees. Spread ¼ cup salsa in the bottom of a 12 x 9-inch baking dish that has been lightly sprayed with vegetable oil cooking spray.

Combine the cottage cheese with ¼ cup Cheddar cheese, the scallions, and the oregano. Lay the tortillas on a work surface and spoon ¼ cup of the cottage cheese mixture down the center of each tortilla. Roll up and place seam side down over the salsa. Top with the remaining ¾ cup of Cheddar cheese and ¾ cup of salsa.

(continued)

Cover with foil; bake for 20 to 25 minutes or until thoroughly heated.

Garnish with a few pieces of chopped green chiles.

CORNY CORNMEAL CASSEROLE

SERVES 8

0 GRAMS FAT

Prep :10
Cook :50
Stand :00
Total 1:00

2 (16-ounce) cans cream-style corn
2 cups shredded fat-free Cheddar cheese
1 (4-ounce) can chopped green chiles
½ cup chopped onion
1 cup skim milk
½ cup egg substitute
1 cup yellow cornmeal
1½ teaspoons garlic salt
½ teaspoon baking soda

Preheat the oven to 350 degrees. Lightly spray an 11 x 7-inch baking dish with vegetable oil cooking spray.

In a large mixing bowl, combine all ingredients, mixing until well blended. Pour into prepared baking dish.

Bake uncovered for about 50 minutes, or until a knife inserted in the center comes out clean.

BAKED SAUSAGE AND CHEESE GRITS

1½ pounds low-fat sausage (3 grams per patty), crumbled
½ cup quick-cooking grits, uncooked
3 cups shredded fat-free sharp Cheddar cheese
1 cup egg substitute
1 cup skim milk
½ teaspoon thyme leaves
⅛ teaspoon garlic powder
Garnishes: parsley sprigs, orange slices

SERVES 8

6.75 GRAMS
FAT PER
SERVING

Prep :25
Cook :62
Stand :00
Total 1:27

Preheat the oven to 350 degrees.

In a nonstick skillet, brown the sausage over medium-low heat, stirring to break up lumps. Transfer to a colander and rinse with hot water to remove all traces of fat. Drain well.

Bring 2 cups of water to a boil in a medium-size saucepan; stir in the grits. Return to a boil, reducing the heat to low, and continue cooking for about 4 minutes, stirring occasionally. Add the cheese, stirring until melted.

In a mixing bowl, combine the egg substitute, milk, thyme, and garlic powder; stir well. Gently and slowly stir the grits mixture into the egg mixture, stirring constantly. Stir in the sausage. Pour into an 11 x 7-inch baking dish lightly sprayed with vegetable oil cooking spray.

Bake uncovered at 350 degrees for 50 to 55 minutes or until set. Garnish with parsley sprigs and orange slices.

Variation: This makes a very good breakfast casserole. Cover the unbaked casserole with plastic wrap and refrigerate overnight. Next morning, let it stand at room temperature for ½ hour before baking as directed.

SERVES 4

0 GRAMS FAT

Prep :15
Cook 4:00
Stand :00
Total 4:10

RED BEANS AND RICE

1 package Cajun red beans, spices reserved (I shake about half the pepper off before using; it's too hot for Okies!)
Defatted ham stock or water
1 cup chopped celery
1 cup chopped onions
¾ cup chopped green pepper
Pepper and salt to taste
Hot cooked rice

Boil the beans in ham stock to cover until tender, about 3 to 3½ hours. Meanwhile, sauté the celery, onions, and green pepper in ¼ cup of water for 3 to 5 minutes.

When the beans are almost done, add the vegetables and simmer. Add 2 tablespoons of the Cajun seasoning (careful, just add a little at a time, it gets hot quick). Pepper and salt to taste. Simmer until very thick. Serve over rice.

SHORTCUT BEANS AND RICE

½ cup thinly sliced scallions
1 (8-ounce) can tomato sauce
1 (14-ounce) can spicy chili beans, undrained
½ teaspoon dried basil
2 cloves garlic, minced
½ teaspoon Cajun seasoning (more may be added according to your desired temperature)
2½ cups cooked rice

<table>
<tr><td>SERVES 4</td></tr>
</table>

SERVES 4

LESS THAN 1 GRAM FAT PER SERVING

Prep :20
Cook :10
Stand :00
Total :30

In a nonstick skillet, sauté the scallions in about ¼ cup water for about 2 minutes. Add the tomato sauce, beans, basil, and garlic. Stir in the Cajun seasoning, using the "add and taste" method until desired spiciness is reached. Simmer about 4 minutes and add the cooked rice, stirring until thoroughly heated.

Variation: This may be made ahead according to the above instructions, placed in a baking dish, covered with plastic wrap, and refrigerated. Remove plastic wrap and heat in the oven at 350 degrees for 20 to 25 minutes, until thoroughly heated, or microwave on high for 4 to 6 minutes, stirring twice during the heating period.

MEXICAN BEAN PIE

SERVES 6

2.3 GRAMS FAT
PER SERV-
ING—⅙ OF
PIE

Prep :15
Cook :30
Stand :15
Total 1:00

Crust:
1½ cups yellow cornmeal
¼ teaspoon salt (optional)
2 teaspoons canola oil
½ to ¾ cup hot water, or more as needed

Filling:
1 (16-ounce) can fat-free refried beans
½ cup commercial salsa, green or red
1½ cups cooked rice
2 scallions, chopped fine
1 tablespoon chopped cilantro leaves
1 (4-ounce) can chopped green chiles
¼ cup shredded fat-free Monterey Jack cheese

Preheat the oven to 350 degrees.

Combine the cornmeal and salt, if desired, in a mixing bowl. Add the oil, blend with a fork, and stir in enough hot water so that a dough forms, pulling away from sides of bowl and balling up in the center.

Spray a 9-inch pie plate lightly with vegetable oil cooking spray. Press the dough evenly on the bottom and sides, pinching a finished edge around top. If time allows, chill before filling. (The pie crust may be made ahead of time and filled at the last minute.)

Spread ⅓ of the beans over the bottom of the crust. Spread 1 to 2 tablespoons of salsa over the bean layer.

Toss the rice with the scallions and cilantro. Spread evenly over bean layer and pat gently to pack just a tiny bit. Make a layer of the chiles on top of the rice. Layer the remaining beans and salsa over the chiles.

Bake uncovered 25 to 30 minutes, sprinkling the cheese over the pie for the last 5 minutes of baking time. Let stand 15 minutes before slicing.

Garnish with fat-free sour cream and a slice of avocado and a slice of tomato for your salad on the side. Here you have your bread, vegetables, dairy, and salad all in one dish.

QUICK CHILI

3 cups chopped onion
1 carrot, chopped
1 teaspoon minced jalapeño
3 to 4 teaspoons chili powder
1 teaspoon minced garlic, prepared or fresh
1½ teaspoons ground cumin
3 (14-ounce) cans stewed tomatoes, undrained
2 (16-ounce) cans kidney or chili beans, drained
⅓ cup fine- or medium-grain bulgur

SERVES 4

0 GRAMS FAT

Prep :20
Cook :28
Stand :00
Total :48

In a heavy nonstick dutch oven or saucepan, heat ¼ cup of water; add the onions, carrot, jalapeño, chili powder, garlic, and cumin. Sauté for 5 to 8 minutes, or until the onions and carrots are soft.

Add the tomatoes with their juice, the beans, and the bulgur. Cook for 5 more minutes and reduce the heat to low. Simmer the chili uncovered for 15 minutes or until thickened.

VEGETABLE BEAN CHILI

If you like your chili just a little hotter you might like to experiment with this and add 1½ or 2 packages of chili seasoning. My brother says chili isn't hot unless it makes the top of your bald head itch.

SERVES 6

0 GRAMS FAT

Prep :25
Cook :50
Stand :00
Total 1:15

1 cup coarsely chopped onion
1 medium green bell pepper, chopped coarse
1 cup chopped celery
2 cloves garlic, minced
1 (14-ounce) can stewed tomatoes, undrained

(continued)

1 (15-ounce) can white beans or Great Northern beans
2 (16-ounce) cans chili-seasoned beans
2 (11-ounce) cans white shoepeg corn
1 (4-ounce) can chopped green chiles
1 (15-ounce) can tomato sauce
1 (1.25-ounce) package chili seasoning mix (such as McCormick)

In a deep nonstick saucepan or skillet, sauté the onion, pepper, celery, and garlic in ¼ cup water for 5 minutes or until softened. Stir frequently to keep garlic from burning.

Add the tomatoes, juice and all, the beans, corn, green chiles, and tomato sauce. Stir to mix ingredients well. Stir in the chili seasoning, mixing well. Lower the heat and simmer for 30 to 45 minutes.

CHILI VEGETABLE STEW

SERVES 6

LESS THAN 0.5
GRAM FAT PER
SERVING

Prep :20
Cook :20
Stand :05
Total :45

2½ cups chopped zucchini
3⅓ cups chopped green pepper
¾ cup chopped onions
1 (1¾-ounce) package chili seasoning mix
1 (15-ounce) can kidney beans, undrained
1 (15-ounce) can tomato sauce
1 (7-ounce) can whole-kernel corn, drained
2 cups uncooked instant rice

In a large nonstick skillet, sauté the zucchini, peppers, and onions in ¼ cup of water for 5 to 8 minutes, until crisp-tender. Add the seasoning mix and stir in 2 cups of water, the beans, and tomato sauce. Bring to a boil. Lower the heat to a simmer and cook for 10 more minutes, stirring occasionally.

Stir in the corn. (I like shoepeg corn the best, but regular corn is fine), return to a boil, stir in rice, and cover. Remove from heat. Let stand for about 5 minutes. Serve with shredded cheese, chopped onions, sour cream, and salsa.

COOKING FOR MY KIDS

Let me tell you about cooking for my five kids.

I have one boy and one girl. Bob has three boys. I already had my two children when we got married. We were only married six weeks when the first of his boys came to live with us, and within six months we had them all. *All five.* Wow! I was only thirty-two. Can you just imagine a thirty-two-year-old with five kids, ages eleven, twelve, thirteen, fourteen, and fifteen? Neither can I.

We had a normal three-bedroom house with seven people living in it. I had the furniture taken out of the dining room to put beds in. We then cleaned out the garage, paneled, carpeted, and fixed it all up with black lights, and all the beads and junk that were so popular at that time. We bought four twin-size beds and now had our own dormitory. I was all set up to run this institution.

We had a very good group of kids. We really got a lot of attention when we went places with these five, looking like the Brady Bunch. Remember that TV show? Well, this was the Rohde Bunch.

The boys played football, wrestled, and did all the things that seemed to create appetites that teenage boys do not need any help creating.

My friends would ask me, "How do you cook for that bunch?" My reply: "In a big pot." I would think nothing of cooking four pounds of bacon and two dozen eggs and making thirty-six big homemade biscuits for a Saturday breakfast, plus a big bowl of gravy.

I would come home from work and fry two large chickens, cook eight to ten pounds of potatoes, four cans of green beans, four cans of corn, and a large pan of corn bread and never even bat an eye. During that time I would be shouting orders left and right, doing forty tons of laundry, and picking up the place as I awaited the arrival of my Bob. Now I am out of breath at the thought. Youth!

As luck would have it, these four new men I had to feed would eat anything if it didn't crawl off the plate before they could stab it. They liked my cooking so much, that it got to the point where I had to limit each one. I would fill the platters with what I had figured as portion sizes and set them on the table, all the while shouting out limitations. Each kid could have three pieces of this, two of that, one of this, and so forth down the line. If anyone would reach for his not-commissioned piece of food, I would jokingly pretend to stab their hand with my fork. We couldn't buy enough milk to satisfy their undying thirst—we had to limit them to one gallon a day. We had a milk delivery man at that time. He loved us.

We had a lot of fun and a lot of discipline. We got through it, penniless, alive, and well. Five graduated from school. Bob and I graduated into an empty nest.

Those were the young days of grease and cholesterol. Well, now we pay the price. No more of that. I wish that I had been as fat-smart as I am now so that I could have cooked a much healthier meal for those human garbage disposals. Their pipes would have been much better off. By the way, Bob is a mechanical engineer (plumbing, heating, air conditioning). I'll tell you how I met him in another story. Feeding this group is a story all of its own. You should have seen us go to the grocery story once a week. Oh, my!

QUICK-THE-KIDS-ARE-COMING CASEROLE

(Throw Something in the Pot)

SERVES 8

2 GRAMS FAT
PER SERVING

Prep :25
Cook 1:30
Stand :00
Total 1:55

8 ounces low-fat smoked sausage (such as Healthy Choice), sliced and each slice quartered
2 medium-size onions, halved lengthwise, sliced thin
6 boneless skinless chicken tenders, cut into 1½-inch pieces
1 tablespoon minced garlic
Pinch of oregano
Pinch of dried basil
½ teaspoon pepper
1 (16-ounce) can tomatoes, undrained
¾ cup dry white wine or canned fat-free chicken broth
3 (16-ounce) cans white beans, rinsed and drained (sometimes I mix two or three kinds of beans, whatever I have on hand)
2 cups coarse fresh bread crumbs (can use dried crumbs)

Preheat the oven to 325 degrees. Lightly spray a 4-quart casserole with vegetable oil cooking spray.

Dry-fry the sausage and onions in a nonstick skillet, stirring occasionally, for 5 to 7 minutes, until onions are translucent. Add the chicken, garlic, oregano, basil, and pepper. Cook 5 minutes or so, until the chicken is tender. Add the tomatoes and the wine. Bring to a boil and boil about 3 minutes. Stir in the beans. Spoon the mixture into the prepared casserole. Cover with foil and bake for 1 hour.

Prepare the crumb mixture: Place crumbs in a mixing bowl and spray lightly with cooking spray; stir and spray again; stir and spray again until very lightly coated.

Uncover the casserole, sprinkle the crumb mixture over evenly, and continue to bake for 30 additional minutes or until the crumbs are lightly browned.

Note: If making ahead, cook 1 hour, remove cover, and cool 30 to 40 minutes. Refrigerate uncovered until cool. Cover and refrigerate up to 3 days. When ready to serve, remove cover, top with crumb mixture, and bake 30 to 40 minutes or until the crumbs are browned and the casserole is heated through.

HAM AND BEANS (WITHOUT THE FAT)

SERVES 8

0 GRAMS FAT

Prep :15
Cook 3:30
Stand :00
Total 3:45

Ham hock, or chunk of ham
2 pounds white navy or brown pinto beans

The day before bean cooking day, place the ham hock in a large stockpot, cover with water, and simmer until tender, about 1½ hours. Remove the ham from the stock, let cool. Refrigerate the stock overnight; all the fat will collect to the top and congeal; you can just lift it off and throw it away. (I have often thought of getting into the refrigerator overnight myself and seeing if I would congeal enough to lift off a couple or three pounds from several unsightly areas.)

Look over the beans carefully for bits of dirt and pebbles, and wash thoroughly. Place in a deep stockpot or dutch oven, cover with the defatted stock, and bring to a boil. Lower the heat to a slow boil, cooking ½ to 2 hours or until the beans are tender and the liquid has thickened.

You may add lean chunks of ham if desired, but this will add fat grams, and you already have the flavor from the broth. If you are adding the ham, do so when beans are about half done.

Some people like to wash their beans and soak them overnight before cooking. I have heard arguments both ways. You write and tell me. I personally do not soak my beans ahead of time.

OKLAHOMA LAZY DAZE
TEX-MEX CASSEROLE

SERVES 6

1.5 GRAMS FAT
ENTIRE DISH

Prep :20
Cook :50
Stand :00
Total 1:10

1 (14-ounce) can stewed tomatoes, undrained
1 (16-ounce) can fat-free refried beans
1 (16-ounce) can fat-free vegetable chili
1 (4-ounce) can chopped green chiles
2 cups yellow cornmeal
1 (16-ounce) can chili beans
½ cup chopped onion
1 cup shredded fat-free Cheddar cheese
1 cup crushed baked low-fat tortilla chips (1 gram fat per 13 chips)
1 cup commercial salsa
¾ cup chopped scallions, tops and all, plus more as needed
1 cup fat-free sour cream (optional)
Optional garnish: chopped lettuce, chopped tomatoes, carrot sticks, celery sticks

Preheat the oven to 350 degrees. Lightly spray a deep casserole or baking dish with vegetable oil cooking spray.

Pour the tomatoes, juice and all, into the baking dish. Spoon refried beans on top of the tomatoes, spreading to make a fairly even layer. Pour the vegetable chili over the refried bean layer. Spread the green chiles over all.

In a separate bowl, mix the cornmeal and 1½ cups boiling water, making a mushy consistency. (You may need to add a little more water.) Spread this mixture over the green chiles. Pour the chili beans over the cornmeal mixture. Spread chopped onion over the chili beans; sprinkle shredded cheese over onions.

Bake uncovered for 40 to 50 minutes. Sprinkle crushed chips over all. Pour salsa over the chips, sprinkle on the chopped scallions, and dollop sour cream over all, if desired.

To serve, make a nice circle of chopped lettuce around the outside of each dinner plate; place a serving of the casserole in the center of the plate, and garnish the lettuce ring with tomatoes. Place a couple of carrot sticks and celery sticks alongside the lettuce. Makes a very pretty plate and meal in one.

MOCK TAMALE PIE

SERVES 6

1 GRAM FAT PER TAMALE

Prep :20
Cook :20
Stand :00
Total :40

1 package 6-inch corn tortillas (12 tortillas)
1 (14-ounce) can fat-free refried beans
2½ cups shredded fat-free Cheddar cheese
1 medium onion, chopped
2 cups fat-free vegetable chili—use leftovers from recipe on page 209 (see Note)

Preheat the oven to 350 degrees.

Warm the tortillas by dipping one at a time in hot water. Pat dry. Place 2 to 3 tablespoons of refried beans down the center of each. Top the beans with 2 tablespoons of shredded cheese and 1 teaspoon of onion.

Fold the tortillas around the filling and place seam side down in a 9 x 13 x 2-inch baking dish that has been sprayed with vegetable oil cooking spray. Pour the chili over the top and sprinkle with the remaining cheese.

Bake for about 20 minutes, or until the cheese inside the tortillas is melted. Serve with salad and baked flour tortilla chips.

Note: There is a fat-free canned chili available at the market that will work very nicely if no leftover chili is on hand.

BEAN BURRITOS

8 (6-inch) flour tortillas
1 cup chopped onion
1 (16-ounce) can fat-free refried beans
1 (4-ounce) can diced green chiles, drained
4 dashes hot pepper sauce
¾ cup salsa
1½ cups shredded fat-free Cheddar cheese
For garnish: fat-free sour cream, diced fresh tomato, diced green chiles

SERVES 8

1 GRAM FAT
PER SERVING

Prep :20
Cook :25
Stand :00
Total :45

Stack tortillas one on top of the other, wrap in foil, and heat in the oven at 350 degrees for about 10 minutes.

In a nonstick skillet, sauté the onion in 2 tablespoons of water for 5 minutes or until tender. Do not drain. Add the refried beans, green chiles, and hot pepper sauce. Cook and stir until heated through.

Spoon about ⅓ cup of the bean mixture onto each tortilla just down the center. Spoon about 1½ tablespoons of salsa over the bean mixture. Sprinkle about 3 tablespoons of cheese over the salsa. Roll up the tortilla and place on a foil-lined cooking sheet. Bake loosely covered in a 350-degree oven for about 10 minutes, or until thoroughly heated.

Serve with a dollop of fat-free sour cream, some diced fresh tomato, and diced green chiles if desired.

SPICY BEAN BURRITO EXPRESS

SERVES 2

1 GRAM FAT
PER SERVING

Prep :20
Cook :28
Stand :00
Total :48

1 (16-ounce) can fat-free refried beans
4 (8-inch) flour tortillas
1½ cups shredded fat-free Cheddar cheese
4 tablespoons chopped onion
1 (10-ounce) can red enchilada sauce
¼ cup fat-free sour cream
½ cup salsa

Preheat the oven to 350 degrees. Lightly spray an 8-inch square pan with vegetable oil cooking spray.

Spoon ¼ of the refried beans into the center of each tortilla. Sprinkle each with ¼ cup cheese and a tablespoon of the onion. Roll each tortilla, fold the ends under, and place seam side down in the prepared pan. Pour enchilada sauce over the burritos; cover the pan with foil.

Bake at 350 degrees for 25 minutes. Uncover, sprinkle with remaining cheese, and return to the oven for an additional 2 or 3 minutes, until the cheese is melted. Serve with sour cream and salsa.

BEAN BURRITO CASSEROLE

Great make-ahead dish. Oh! This is so good
and so good for you.

SERVES 4

LOW-FAT

Prep :25
Cook 1:10
Stand :00
Total 1:35

8 (8-inch) flour tortillas
½ pound lean ground turkey
1½ cups tomato juice
1 (1¼-ounce) package taco seasoning mix
1 (16-ounce) can fat-free refried beans
2 cups shredded fat-free Cheddar cheese
For garnish: shredded lettuce, chopped tomato, sliced scallions, fat-free sour cream, commercial salsa

Preheat the oven to 350 degrees. Lightly spray a 13 x 9-inch baking dish with vegetable oil cooking spray.

Stack the tortillas, wrap in foil, and place in the oven for 10 minutes, or until warmed and workable. (You can also dip them in hot water one at a time and pat dry if you're in a hurry, as I always am.)

Brown the turkey in a nonstick skillet, stirring to crumble. Meanwhile, in a saucepan, combine the tomato juice and seasoning mix, bring to a boil, reduce heat, and simmer about 5 minutes while turkey is cooking. Transfer the cooked turkey to a colander, rinse with hot water, and shake excess water off. Return to skillet (wipe the skillet with paper towels to rid of any fat). Stir in the beans and half the tomato juice mixture.

To assemble: Place ¼ cup of the turkey mixture down the center of each tortilla. Roll up the tortillas and place seam side down in the prepared baking dish and top with 2 tablespoons of cheese.

To store: If making ahead, cover with plastic wrap at this point, and refrigerate up to 8 hours. Refrigerate the remaining tomato juice mixture in a tightly covered container.

To bake and serve: Pour the remaining juice over the casserole, cover with foil, and bake at 350 degrees for 35 to 40 minutes. Uncover, sprinkle with the remaining cheese, and bake an additional 5 minutes or until the cheese melts.

Serving suggestions: Make a circle of shredded lettuce around your plate about 2 inches wide. Layer with a ring of chopped tomatoes; top with scallions. Sprinkle cheese over for more color if desired. Place 2 burritos in the center of each. Dollop fat-free sour cream on burritos if desired.

BAKED BEAN STORY

I created my recipe for baked beans in the days when my aunts were coming in the summer. Dad had seven sisters, and they would all come to see him at the same time in the summer and stay at my house (which could be called Roadway Inn or Do Drop In). They are all old and either gone or in nursing homes, including Dad, except three. No more summer get-togethers. We always had a big cookout and party. One aunt from Louisiana would bring shrimp, oysters, and crawfish. My brother did the steaks, and I did the down-home country cooking—not always fat-free until the last two years. The Washington aunt would bring apples and onions. California aunt would bring English walnuts, figs, oranges, lemons, etc. New Mexico brought a thirst. You should see some of the pictures of the preparation going on for one of these parties. Aunts all over the cabinets cooking all kinds of things. Mom was the hush puppy queen; my sister-in-law inherited that title. My brother was the fry captain for the fish, which came out of my dad's catfish pond. Sometimes there would be thirty or more of us.

We would even have themes. My cousin from Louisiana brought Cajun music and we would be dancing on the patio or driveway, wherever we were cooking. We had big cookers that we would cook in outside. These are stories that need to be remembered and I am sure that we will all do just that. I just wanted to share with you that this type of thing really happened and still happens. Do some of the same type of getting together with your family. It is worth the effort.

Beans are packed with protein, low in fat and cholesterol. Beans are one of the best sources of complex carbohydrates and dietary fiber. Beans contain more fiber per serving than most vegetables, fruits, grains, or cereals. A diet high in fiber has been linked to lowering cholesterol, maintaining blood sugar levels for body energy, and curbing the hunger bug.

BAKED BEANS

This is an excellent picnic or church-function recipe but you can halve it and use it just for your family. It has more of a barbecue taste than sweet.

1 (1-gallon) can pinto beans (just drain off if any fat has collected)
1 cup chopped celery
1 cup chopped onion
1 cup chopped green bell pepper
½ cup honey
1 cup salsa
¾ cup cubed 98% fat-free ham
¼ cup prepared mustard

Mix all ingredients well and bake uncovered in a large casserole about 1½ to 2 hours at 350 degrees. Stir once midway.

SERVES 10

1 GRAM FAT

Prep :15
Cook 1:30
Stand :00
Total 1:45

VEGETABLE CHILI

1 cup chopped onion
1 cup chopped celery
1 cup chopped green pepper
1 clove garlic, chopped
1½ cups chopped zucchini
1 (14-ounce) can low-sodium stewed tomatoes
1 (14-ounce) can tomato sauce
1 package chili seasoning, such as McCormick
2 cans kidney beans (or your favorite beans even leftover) (I like to use chili beans, canned)

Cover the bottom of a large saucepan with 3 or 4 tablespoons of water. Add the chopped onion, celery, green pepper, and garlic. Sauté until wilted, 3 to 4 minutes. Add the zucchini and cook until tender, 5 to 10 minutes.

SERVES 6

0 GRAMS FAT

Prep :30
Cook 1:15
Stand :00
Total 1:45

(continued)

Add the tomatoes, juice and all, the tomato sauce, chili seasoning, and beans. Simmer for about 1 hour, just as you would any chili.

> When Vidalia onions are in season I buy up several pounds and store in an old refrigerator we have in the garage for drinks and veggies. They will keep all winter long. Just be sure they are nice and dry before storing them. At Christmas time I always have nice Vidalia onions.

HOBO CASSEROLE

SERVES 6

LESS THAN 1 GRAM FAT IN ENTIRE DISH

Prep :30
Cook :40
Stand :00
Total 1:10

Beans:
1 cup chopped onion
½ cup chopped green pepper
2 cloves garlic, chopped fine
1 (14-ounce) can kidney beans, drained
1 (14-ounce) can pinto beans, drained
1 (16-ounce) can tomatoes, chopped, juice and all
1 (8-ounce) can tomato sauce
1 teaspoon chili powder
½ teaspoon prepared mustard
⅛ teaspoon hot pepper sauce

Corn Bread:
1 cup yellow cornmeal
1 cup all-purpose flour
2½ teaspoons baking powder
½ teaspoon salt
1 tablespoon sugar
1 cup skim milk
½ cup egg substitute
1 tablespoon canola oil (optional)
1 (8-ounce) can cream-style corn

Preheat the oven to 375 degrees.

Spray a large skillet with vegetable oil cooking spray, and sauté the onion, green pepper, and garlic 3 to 5 minutes, or until tender. (Add ¼ cup water if desired.) Stir in the beans, tomatoes, tomato sauce, chili powder, mustard, and hot sauce. Cover and cook 5 minutes. Pour into a 9 x 13 x 2-inch baking dish. Set aside.

Mix the corn bread: Combine the cornmeal and flour with the baking powder, salt, and sugar. In a separate bowl, mix the milk, egg substitute, oil, and corn. Stir into the dry ingredients until combined.

Spoon the corn bread mixture evenly over the bean mixture to within 1 inch of the edge all around.

Bake for 30 to 35 minutes, or until the corn bread is golden. Serve hot.

THREE BEAN BAKE

1 (16-ounce) can Great Northern beans, drained
1 (16-ounce) can spicy chili beans, undrained
1 (16-ounce) can light or dark kidney beans, drained
½ cup ketchup
⅓ cup firmly packed brown sugar
½ teaspoon ginger

SERVES 4

1 GRAM FAT

Prep :10
Cook :30
Stand :00
Total :40

Combine all the ingredients and mix well. Place in an uncovered casserole and bake at 350 degrees for 30 to 40 minutes, until thoroughly heated. Stir a couple of times during the baking period.

Rice

RICE CASSEROLE

2 (10¾-ounce) cans Healthy Request cream of broccoli soup
1 (8-ounce) can sliced water chestnuts, drained
1½ cups whole-kernel corn
Salt and pepper to taste
2 cups cooked rice

SERVES 8

1.25 GRAMS
FAT PER
SERVING

Prep :25
Cook :45
Stand :00
Total 1:10

Preheat the oven to 350 degrees. Lightly spray an 8 x 10-inch baking dish with vegetable oil cooking spray.

In a large mixing bowl, combine the cream of broccoli soup, half a soup can of water, the water chestnuts, corn, salt, and pepper. Stir in the rice. Mix well.

Spoon into the prepared dish and bake uncovered for about 30 minutes.

RICE SALAD

1 cup cold cooked rice
1 (8-ounce) can kidney beans, drained and rinsed
1 tomato, peeled, seeded, and chopped
½ cup frozen whole-kernel corn (see Note)
1 tablespoon chopped green onion
2 tablespoons red wine vinegar
2 teaspoons canola oil
1 teaspoon dried basil
Salt and pepper to taste
Fresh spinach leaves (optional)

SERVES 2

2 GRAMS FAT
PER SERVING

Prep :10
Cook :00
Stand :00
Total :10

In a serving bowl, combine the rice, beans, tomato, corn, and chopped onion.

Whisk together the vinegar, oil, basil, salt, and pepper. Pour the dressing over the salad and toss lightly to mix. Serve on spinach leaves if desired.

> *Note:* To quick-thaw the corn, run hot water over it while in a strainer.

VEGETARIAN FRIED RICE

½ cup sliced scallions
¼ cup chopped green pepper
½ cup sliced fresh mushrooms
¼ cup shredded carrot
¼ teaspoon ground ginger
1 clove garlic, minced
3 cups cooked rice
2 tablespoons light soy sauce
¼ cup egg substitute
Dash pepper
¾ cup frozen green peas, thawed

SERVES 4

1 GRAM FAT
PER 1-CUP
SERVING

Prep :15
Cook :10
Stand: :00
Total :25

Lightly spray a large nonstick skillet with vegetable oil cooking spray. Place over medium heat until just hot. Toss in the scallion slices, green pepper, mushrooms, carrot, ginger, and garlic. Cook and stir about 1 minute. Stir in rice and soy sauce. Lower the heat; cook while stirring occasionally with a fork for about 5 minutes.

Push the rice mixture to one side of the skillet. Add the egg substitute and pepper to the vacant spot; cook for about 4 minutes, stirring constantly. With a spatula, chop the egg mixture into small pieces. Add the peas to the rice and egg mixture, stirring gently to combine. Cook until thoroughly heated. Serve with additional soy sauce if desired.

MEXICAN RICE

**SERVES
2 TO 3**

1 GRAM FAT

**Prep :10
Cook :20
Stand :00
Total :30**

½ cup chopped onion
½ cup chopped green bell pepper
2 cloves garlic, chopped fine
2 tablespoons Butter Buds liquid
1 cup rice
1 tomato, peeled, seeded, and chopped
2 cups defatted chicken broth
1 teaspoon cumin seeds

Sauté the onion, peppers, and garlic in 2 to 4 tablespoons of water until crisp but tender. Add the Butter Buds and rice; cook until the onions are soft but not brown. Stir in the tomatoes and cook 30 seconds more; add the broth and cumin. Bring to a boil; stir once or twice. Reduce the heat, cover, and simmer 15 minutes, or until the rice is tender.

QUICK SPANISH RICE

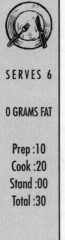

SERVES 6

0 GRAMS FAT

**Prep :10
Cook :20
Stand :00
Total :30**

1 cup finely chopped onion
1 cup chopped celery
1 cup chopped green bell pepper
1 (8-ounce) can tomato sauce
1 (8-ounce) can tomatoes with their juice
1¼ cups low-fat reduced-sodium chicken broth
1 teaspoon prepared mustard
1 bay leaf
½ teaspoon oregano
2 cups instant rice

In a saucepan, combine the onion, celery, green pepper, tomato sauce, tomatoes, broth, mustard, bay leaf, and oregano. Simmer for 10 to 12 minutes. Stir in the rice and simmer, covered, over very low heat for 5 to 6 minutes, stirring occasionally.

PINEAPPLE RICE

This is very good with grilled chicken.

1 can pineapple tidbits in juice, undrained
1½ cups instant rice
¼ teaspoon salt (optional)
¼ teaspoon grated nutmeg
¼ cup chopped fresh parsley

SERVES 4

0 GRAMS FAT

Prep :10
Cook :05
Stand :00
Total :15

In a saucepan, combine the pineapple, rice, salt, nutmeg, and ½ cup water. Bring to a boil, reduce the heat, cover, and simmer about 5 minutes, or until rice is tender. Stir in the parsley.

RICE-STUFFED PEPPERS

Serve these hot, with a nice green salad on the same plate.

2 cups fat-free chicken broth
1 cup raw rice
½ pound mushrooms, chopped
2 cloves garlic, minced
4 scallions, chopped (about 1 cup)
1 stalk celery with leaves, chopped
1 tablespoon fresh mixed herbs or 1 teaspoon dried (chives, oregano, dill, cilantro, tarragon, marjoram, or parsley)
8 ounces shredded fat-free Cheddar cheese
4 bell peppers, green, yellow, or red

SERVES 4

0 GRAMS FAT

Prep :20
Cook :15
Stand :05
Total :40

In a large saucepan over high heat, bring the chicken broth to a boil. Add the rice and cook according to the directions on the package, leaving out the butter or margarine and salt. Drain and set aside.

(continued)

In a microwave-safe dish lightly sprayed with vegetable oil cooking spray, mix the mushrooms and garlic. Cover and cook on high power for 8 minutes. Let stand covered for 2 minutes. Stir in scallions, celery, and herbs. Add the rice and shredded cheese. Toss to combine.

Slice the tops off the peppers very close to the top; remove membranes and seeds. Stuff the pepper cavities with the rice mixture. Place the peppers in a microwave-safe round or oval baking dish. Pour ½ cup water around the peppers, cover, and cook on high power for 8 minutes. Let stand covered 3 minutes. Serve hot.

JAMBALAYA

This is a nice-size casserole for a crowd—or it can be cut in half.

SERVES 8

4.19 GRAMS FAT PER 1-CUP SERVING

Prep :35
Cook 1:10
Stand :00
Total 1:45

4 chicken breast halves, skin removed
1 (16-ounce) package Healthy Choice smoked sausage
1 (10¾-ounce) can French onion soup
1 (14-ounce) can vegetable broth
1 (10¾-ounce) can Healthy Request cream of celery soup
1 (14-ounce) can stewed tomatoes
1 (16-ounce) package Bayou Magic Cajun jambalaya rice mix (or any Cajun jambalaya rice mix)

Cover the chicken with water and boil 20 to 30 minutes, until tender. Debone and cut into 1-inch cubes. Defat the broth and reserve.

Preheat the oven to 350 degrees. Lightly spray a deep casserole or a 4-quart roasting pan with vegetable oil cooking spray.

Cut the sausage into 1-inch pieces and brown in a nonstick skillet. Pat off any excess fat with paper towels.

Mix together the onion soup, vegetable broth, celery soup, reserved chicken broth, and tomatoes. Before you add the rice from the package, put it in a strainer and, using *hot* water, rinse off some of the pepper seasoning; it is just too hot for us Okies. (If you live in Cajun country, add just as is.) I reserve the water in a bowl with the seasoning to make sure it has enough; if not hot enough, add some of the Cajun-seasoned water. Don't run too much water over the rice—just about 2 cups.

Add the chopped meats to the above mixture, place in the prepared casserole, and bake for 30 to 35 minutes, until all the rice is tender.

SMOKED SAUSAGE, BEANS, AND RICE

Most sausage, bean, and rice dishes take half a day to cook; this one takes half an hour.

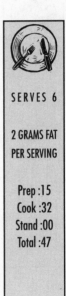

SERVES 6

2 GRAMS FAT PER SERVING

Prep :15
Cook :32
Stand :00
Total :47

1 pound low-fat smoked sausage such as Healthy Choice (1.5 grams fat per 2 ounces), sliced and each slice quartered

¾ cup chopped onion (may use frozen)

½ cup chopped green pepper (may use frozen)

¾ cup chopped celery

1 tablespoon chopped garlic, prepared or fresh

1 (16-ounce) can fat-free refried beans with salsa, such as Rosarita

2 (15-ounce) cans ranch-style pinto beans, undrained

½ cup medium or hot prepared salsa

4 drops hot sauce, or to taste

1 tablespoon Cajun spice

1 teaspoon chili powder

2 cups instant rice, prepared according to package directions, leaving out the butter or margarine and salt

In a large deep nonstick skillet, brown the sausage; add the onions, green peppers, celery, and garlic. Add about ¼ cup water and sauté over medium heat for 5 to 7 minutes or until the vegetables are tender. If using frozen vegetables you may not need to add as much water.

Pour in 1 cup of water, the refried beans, and the 2 cans of pinto beans; stir until well mixed. (Refried beans will thicken your dish;

(continued)

water is to make a nice consistency. You may need to add a little more, according to your own preference.)

Add the salsa, hot sauce, Cajun spice, and chili powder. Stir to mix. Simmer the dish for about 10 minutes, add the rice, and mix well. Continue to simmer for 5 to 10 minutes, until hot.

CORN AND RICE CASSEROLE

SERVES 4

1 GRAM FAT

Prep :20
Cook :45
Stand :00
Total 1:05

1 green bell pepper, seeded and chopped
1 large onion, chopped
1½ cups rice
2 (14-ounce) cans cream-style corn
1 small jar pimientos, drained and chopped
¼ cup egg substitute
2 tablespoons sugar
½ cup Butter Buds

Preheat the oven to 350 degrees.

Sauté the pepper and onion for 3 minutes in ¼ cup water. Cook the rice according to package directions (leave out the butter).

Combine the pepper and onion, rice, and corn with the pimientos, egg substitute, sugar, and Butter Buds. Pour into a baking dish that has been sprayed with vegetable oil cooking spray. Spray the top lightly and bake uncovered for 25 to 30 minutes.

Pasta and Pizza

Pasta

PASTA TIPS

Pasta is easy to cook, but you should pay attention because it is also easy to have a "pot of paste" if you aren't following the basics. Use a large pot and plenty of water. The pasta needs room to move and circulate.

Bring the water to a rapid boil before you add the pasta. A lid on the pot at this stage will hold the heat and help the water to boil faster.

Add the pasta slowly. If it is short pasta, such as macaroni, stir the boiling water with a long-handled spoon as you add the pasta. When cooking long pasta, such as spaghetti, hold a handful at one end and gradually bend the pasta around the inside of the pot as it softens. Stir now and then so the pasta doesn't stick together or settle in a lump on the bottom. A lump of pasta is nothing to write home about, for sure. Keep the pasta moving and the pot *un*covered. Adjust the heat so the pasta keeps boiling and moving, but not so high that it boils over.

Follow the recommended cooking time on the package, but check two or three minutes before to make sure you don't overcook. Remove a piece of pasta, rinse with cold water to keep from burning your mouth, and bite into it. Perfect pasta should be slightly firm in the center. If it's not quite done, check again in a minute or two. If the pasta is to be used in a casserole and cooked again, cook it slightly firmer than pasta to be eaten right away.

Pour the pasta into a colander set in the sink. Shake the colander gently to drain off excess water. If the pasta is to be eaten right away, just drain and serve. If it is to be used in a salad or such, rinse with cold water to stop the cooking. Pasta can be cooked ahead of time, drained, and stored in a plastic bag or bowl in the refrigerator until it's needed.

FETTUCCINE

8 ounces uncooked wide no-egg noodles
1 cup fat-free cottage cheese, at room temperature (see Note)
½ cup fat-free Parmesan cheese
Salt and pepper to taste (optional)
¼ cup minced fresh parsley

Boil the noodles according to package directions. Drain and return to the same pot. Quickly toss together with the remaining ingredients. Serve immediately.

Note: I mash my cottage cheese a little to avoid larger lumps.

SERVES 4

0.5 GRAM FAT
PER SERVING

Prep :10
Cook :10
Stand :00
Total :20

STUFFED MANICOTTI

1 (8-ounce) box manicotti shells
1 (16-ounce) carton ricotta cheese, soft
Dab of nutmeg
1 (10-ounce) package frozen spinach, cooked, squeezed dry, and chopped
Spaghetti sauce (Healthy Choice is good and low in fat)

Preheat the oven to 350 degrees. Spray a rectangular baking dish with vegetable oil cooking spray.

Cook and drain the pasta shells according to package directions. Set aside.

Mix the ricotta, nutmeg, and spinach. Stuff shells with the mixture. Arrange in the baking dish. Pour spaghetti sauce over and bake uncovered for 25 minutes, or until hot and bubbly.

SERVES 4

2 GRAMS FAT

Prep :20
Cook :40
Stand :00
Total 1:00

SPICY ANGEL HAIR PASTA

SERVES 4

LESS THAN 1
GRAM FAT PER
SERVING

Prep :15
Cook :45
Stand :00
Total 1:00

1 medium onion, sliced thin
1 clove garlic, minced
1 (28-ounce) can tomatoes, coarsely chopped or crushed
2 tablespoons minced fresh cilantro
Few drops of hot pepper sauce, or to taste
¼ teaspoon salt (optional)
¼ teaspoon sugar (optional)
12 ounces uncooked angel hair pasta
Grated fat-free Parmesan cheese (optional)

In a large heavy saucepan, over medium heat, sauté the onion and garlic in about ¼ cup of water. Sauté until tender, stirring constantly. Be careful not to burn the garlic.

Add the tomatoes, cilantro, hot pepper sauce, salt, and sugar, if desired. Bring to a slow boil, reduce the heat to low, and simmer uncovered for about 30 minutes, or until slightly thickened.

While the sauce is cooking, prepare the pasta according to package directions, leaving out any oil or margarine called for. Drain. Transfer to a heated platter and keep warm.

To serve, spoon the sauce over the pasta and sprinkle with Parmesan cheese.

PASTA ROLL-UPS

A good make-ahead dish. Make it one day and cook the next, or freeze and bake when desired.

SERVES 4

**1 GRAM FAT
PER ROLL-UP**

Prep :25
Cook 1:20
Stand :00
Total 1:45

1 large onion, chopped fine
1 teaspoon crumbled dried basil
½ teaspoon crumbled dried marjoram
2 cloves garlic, minced
½ teaspoon black pepper
1 boneless skinless chicken breast half, chopped fine (about 8 ounces)
1 (26-ounce) jar fat-free pizza sauce
8 uncooked lasagne noodles, ruffle-edge type (for prettier appearance)
½ (10-ounce) package frozen chopped spinach, thawed and drained (squeeze out all water possible)
½ cup grated fat-free Parmesan cheese
1 cup fat-free cottage cheese

In a nonstick skillet, sauté the onion, basil, marjoram, half the garlic, and half the pepper until the onion is soft, about 3 to 5 minutes. Remove 2 tablespoons and set aside.

Add the chopped chicken to the skillet and cook, stirring, for 4 minutes. Reduce the heat to low and add the pizza sauce. Cook uncovered for 15 to 20 minutes, stirring occasionally. Set aside.

Meanwhile, cook the lasagne noodles according to package directions, omitting salt and oil if called for. Rinse and drain.

Preheat the oven to 375 degrees. Lightly spray a 9 x 9-inch baking dish with vegetable oil cooking spray.

For the filling, in a medium-size bowl combine the spinach with ¼ cup of the Parmesan cheese and all the cottage cheese. Add the remaining garlic and pepper, and the reserved onion mixture. Mix well.

Spoon half the tomato sauce into the prepared baking dish. Spread 3 tablespoons or so of the cheese filling on each noodle, roll up as you would a jelly roll, and place seam side down in the

(continued)

baking dish. Repeat until all the noodles are used. Top with the remaining sauce.

Cover with foil and bake for 25 to 30 minutes. Uncover, sprinkle the remaining Parmesan cheese on top, and bake uncovered 5 to 6 minutes longer.

TEX-MEX LASAGNE

1 (14-ounce) can fat-free chili, with or without beans
1 (16-ounce) jar Mexican salsa, drained
1 (4-ounce) can mushroom stems and pieces, drained
¾ cup grated fat-free Parmesan cheese
1½ teaspoons Italian seasoning
1½ cups fat-free cottage cheese
1½ teaspoons parsley flakes
9 cooked lasagne noodles
2½ cups shredded fat-free mozzarella cheese

Preheat the oven to 350 degrees. Lightly spray a 9 x 9-inch baking dish with vegetable oil cooking spray.

Combine the chili, drained salsa, mushroom pieces, Parmesan cheese, and Italian seasoning. In a small bowl, combine the cottage cheese and parsley flakes.

Line the bottom of the prepared baking dish with ⅓ of the noodles. Dot with ⅓ of the cottage cheese. Spread evenly with ⅓ of the chili mixture and sprinkle with ⅓ of the mozzarella. Repeat to make three layers.

Bake uncovered for 30 to 40 minutes, or until the lasagne is thoroughly heated. Let stand 10 minutes before serving.

VEGETARIAN LASAGNE

1 medium onion, chopped
1 medium green pepper, seeded and chopped
1 (16-ounce) can tomatoes, undrained
1 (16-ounce) can kidney beans, drained and rinsed
3 tablespoons tomato paste
Dash of salt and pepper
1 teaspoon sugar
2 medium zucchini, chopped
1½ packages (about 18) no-boil lasagne noodles
16 ounces fat-free mozzarella cheese, shredded (2 cups)

SERVES 6

LESS THAN 1
GRAM FAT
ENTIRE DISH

Prep :30
Cook 1:25
Stand :10
Total 2:05

Sauté the onion and pepper in ¼ cup water in a large nonstick skillet until tender.

Add the tomatoes, liquid, and all the beans, tomato paste, salt, pepper, sugar, and 2½ cups water. Heat to a boil. Reduce heat and simmer 15 minutes. Stir occasionally.

Sauté the zucchini in ¼ cup water in a separate pan until crisp-tender, about 5 minutes. Drain well.

Preheat the oven to 350 degrees. Spoon a third of the sauce evenly over the bottom of a 9 x 13 x 2-inch baking dish. Arrange half the noodles in a single layer overlapping to fit. Top with the zucchini, 3 cups of the cheese, and half the remaining sauce.

Next, layer on the rest of the noodles, the remaining sauce, and the remaining 1 cup of cheese.

Cover and bake 40 to 50 minutes. Uncover and bake 15 minutes longer. Let stand 10 minutes before cutting and serving.

LASAGNE WITH BEAN SAUCE

SERVES 6

.33 GRAMS FAT
PER SERVING

Prep :30
Cook 1:30
Stand :10
Total 2:10

Sauce:
1 onion, chopped fine
2 teaspoons garlic, chopped fine
2 cups cooked beans (red or brown, canned or home cooked), drained and
   coarsely chopped
4 cups tomato purée, or 2 cups tomato sauce plus 2 cups purée
1 teaspoon oregano
1 teaspoon dried basil
Pepper to taste

¾ pound uncooked lasagne noodles
2 cups skim milk or fat-free ricotta cheese
8 ounces fat-free mozzarella cheese, sliced thin
¼ cup grated fat-free Parmesan cheese

Prepare the sauce: Sauté the onion in 2 tablespoons of water for a minute. Add garlic the last 10 seconds (be careful not to burn garlic—it's terrible!). Add the chopped beans. Cook this mixture, stirring, for several minutes longer. Add the tomato purée, oregano, basil, and pepper. Bring the sauce to a boil and simmer for 5 minutes. Meantime, heat the oven to 350 degrees.

To assemble the lasagne: Spread a thin layer of bean sauce on the bottom of a 9 x 13 x 2-inch baking dish. Arrange a layer of noodles to cover the bottom of the dish so they are touching but do not overlap. You should use about one third of the noodles. Cover the noodle layer with half the ricotta, half the mozzarella, and one third of the remaining sauce. Repeat with a layer of noodles, the remaining ricotta and mozzarella, and another third of the sauce.

Finish off with layers of remaining noodles and sauce. Sprinkle the Parmesan on top.

Cover the pan tightly with foil. Bake lasagne in the preheated oven for about 1 hour, or until the pasta is cooked. If there is too much liquid remaining in pan, remove the foil and bake for another 10 to 15 minutes. Let stand 10 minutes before serving.

SPAGHETTI SAUCE

1 large onion, chopped
1 medium green bell pepper, seeded and chopped
2 cloves garlic, chopped fine
1 (14-ounce) can Italian tomatoes with their juice
1 (8-ounce) can sliced mushrooms (optional)
1 (8-ounce) can tomato sauce
Pinch of oregano
Pinch of basil
Dash of salt and pepper
2 tablespoons cornstarch

SERVES 2

0 GRAMS FAT

Prep :10
Cook :30
Stand :00
Total :40

In a large skillet, sauté the onion, green pepper, and garlic in ¼ cup of water for 3 to 5 minutes, or until crisp-tender. Add the tomatoes, mushrooms if using, tomato sauce, oregano, basil, salt, and pepper. Simmer for 20 to 30 minutes.

To thicken, mix the cornstarch with ¼ cup cold water; gradually stir into sauce, and cook 3 minutes longer.

SPAGHETTI PIZZA

½ cup skim milk
¼ cup egg substitute
4 cups cooked spaghetti
½ pound ground lean turkey
1 cup chopped onion
1 cup chopped green bell pepper
2 cloves garlic, minced
1 (15-ounce) can tomato sauce
1 teaspoon Italian seasoning
1 teaspoon salt-free herb seasoning
¼ teaspoon pepper
1 cup sliced mushrooms
2 cups shredded fat-free Cheddar and mozzarella cheese mixed

SERVES 8

2 GRAMS FAT
PER SERVING

Prep :25
Cook :40
Stand :05
Total 1:10

(continued)

Pasta and Pizza ■ **239**

Preheat the oven to 350 degrees. Lightly spray a 15 x 10-inch jelly roll pan with vegetable oil cooking spray.

In a medium-size mixing bowl, blend the milk and egg substitute. Add the cooked spaghetti and toss to coat. Spread the spaghetti mixture evenly in the prepared pan. Set aside.

In a large nonstick skillet, cook the turkey, onion, green pepper, and garlic until the turkey is done. Add the tomato sauce and seasonings; simmer 5 minutes. Spoon the meat mixture evenly over the spaghetti. Top with mushrooms and cheese. Bake uncovered 20 to 25 minutes. Let stand 5 minutes before cutting.

Variation: Use lean ground pork or beef in place of the ground turkey.

Pizza

PIZZA CRUST

Have fun seeing how low-fat you can make your pizza, and how good. Your friends will not believe you when you tell them how low in fat it is. Use 98% fat-free ham or Canadian bacon, shredded, along with your vegetables and cheeses.

1 package active dry yeast
1½ cups warm (not hot) water
1 teaspoon salt
2 tablespoons canola oil
4½ cups all-purpose flour, approximately

MAKES
TWO 12-
INCH
CRUSTS

1.05 GRAMS
FAT PER
SERVING

Prep :25
Cook :15
Stand 1:30
Total 2:10

In a large bowl, sprinkle the yeast over the warm water and allow to soften for 5 to 10 minutes. Add the salt and oil and 3 cups of the flour; mix well. Add more flour, ½ cup at a time, beating with a wooden spoon, until you have a soft dough that is no longer sticky. Turn the dough into a bowl sprayed with vegetable oil cooking spray; spray the top lightly. Cover with a damp kitchen towel and allow to rise for 1 to 1½ hours, or until doubled in bulk.

Punch the dough down, divide in half, and allow to rest for 15 minutes. Roll out on a floured surface as thick or thin as desired.

To prebake, place the rolled-out dough on a cookie sheet sprayed with cooking spray. Bake in a 450 degree oven for 15 to 20 minutes, until golden.

Note: Remember to stay in the fat-free cheeses and toppings. If you are in a hurry you can use Healthy Choice spaghetti sauce.

VEGGIE PIZZA

MAKES TWO 12-INCH PIZZAS

3 GRAMS FAT

Prep :10
Cook :45
Stand :00
Total :55

1 recipe Pizza Crust (page 241), unbaked

Pizza Sauce:
½ cup chopped green pepper
1½ cups tomato sauce
2 tablespoons chopped garlic
1 teaspoon sugar
Pinch of salt
1 teaspoon oregano
2 teaspoons dried basil

Pizza Toppings:
Chopped green bell peppers
Chopped onion (or thinly sliced onion rings)
Sliced fresh or canned mushrooms
Sliced olives
Fat-free mozzarella cheese, shredded
Fat-free Parmesan cheese, grated

Place the rolled-out pizza dough on baking sheets that have been sprayed with vegetable oil cooking spray.

Mix the sauce ingredients with 1 cup of water and simmer for short time. Pour on crust. Top with any or all desired toppings. (Add turkey sausage, cooked and drained, or 98% fat-free ham, shredded, if desired.)

Bake in a 400 degree oven about 45 minutes, or until veggies and crust are done.

CORNMEAL-CRUST PIZZA

1½ cups yellow cornmeal
½ teaspoon salt (optional)
1 to 1½ cups boiling water
2 tablespoons grated fat-free Parmesan cheese
1 (26-ounce) jar fat-free pizza sauce
2 cups shredded fat-free mozzarella cheese
Chopped onion, chopped green pepper, drained canned sliced mushrooms, drained
     canned beans, or other desired toppings
Crumbled dried basil (optional)
Dried oregano (optional)

SERVES 4

0 GRAMS FAT

Prep :20
Cook :50
Stand :00
Total 1:10

Preheat the oven to 350 degrees.

In a medium mixing bowl, combine the cornmeal and salt, if desired. Gradually add the boiling water, stirring with a fork, until it is thick and forms a soft ball (not mushy). Add the Parmesan cheese; mix well.

With wet hands, pat the cornmeal mixture evenly into a 23-inch pizza pan or baking sheet lightly sprayed with vegetable oil cooking spray.

Bake the crust uncovered for 15 minutes or until just golden.

Spread the sauce evenly over the crust and sprinkle with half the mozzarella. Add your choice of vegetables and toppings, and additional sauce if desired; sprinkle with herbs and top with the remaining cheese.

Bake uncovered 10 to 15 minutes or until the cheese has melted. Cut into wedges.

Note: If you like your vegetables a little softer, sauté them in a nonstick skillet for a few minutes; you may want to add about ⅛ cup water, but usually the onion and pepper have enough water in them to do the job.

PIZZA MEXICANA

SERVES 2

2 GRAMS FAT

Prep :10
Cook :07
Stand :00
Total :17

1 (16-ounce) can refried beans, fat-free
1 (12-inch) pizza crust (page 241), prebaked
¾ cup salsa, chunky mild or medium
¼ cup shredded fat-free Monterey Jack cheese
¼ cup shredded fat-free Cheddar cheese
1 cup assorted fresh vegetables (sliced peppers, mushrooms, etc.)
¼ cup sliced green onions
1 (2-ounce) can black olives, drained and sliced
1 tablespoon minced cilantro (optional)

Preheat the oven to 450 degrees.

Spread the beans evenly over the cooked pizza crust, then spread with the salsa. Mix the cheeses together. Sprinkle over the salsa.

Top with the vegetables, green onions, and olives.

Bake for 7 to 10 minutes, or until the cheese is melted. Garnish with cilantro if desired.

STOVE TOP PIZZA

SERVES 2

2 GRAMS FAT

Prep :10
Cook :20
Stand :00
Total :30

2 cups Stove Top stuffing, any flavor
2 tablespoons Butter Buds liquid
⅔ cup hot water
Spaghetti sauce
Sliced or chopped vegetables
Fat-free mozzarella cheese, shredded

Mix the stuffing, Butter Buds, and water and stir until moistened. Spread evenly in 9-inch round pan, pressing lightly to form shape of pan.

Pour low-fat spaghetti sauce over evenly. Top with any desired veggies, sautéed in water until tender.

Bake at 350 degrees for 15 minutes before topping with fat-free mozzarella cheese. Bake about 5 minutes longer to melt cheese.

Variation: Double the amount of Butter Buds and stuffing, and use a 9 x 13 x 2-inch dish for serving 6.

GREEN BEAN CASSEROLE

SERVES 6

4 GRAMS FAT
ENTIRE DISH

Prep :15
Cook :45
Stand :00
Total 1:00

1 (10¾-ounce) can Healthy Request cream of mushroom soup
1¼ cups skim milk
2 (14-ounce) cans green beans, drained
2 medium onions, chopped
1 medium bell pepper, chopped
Salt and pepper to taste (optional)
¼ cup fine dry bread crumbs
1 teaspoon grated fat-free Parmesan cheese

Preheat the oven to 350 degrees.

Mix soup and milk. Mix drained green beans with chopped onion and bell pepper. Place in a baking dish lightly sprayed with vegetable oil cooking spray. Pour the soup mixture over. Add salt and pepper if desired. Top with bread crumbs and Parmesan cheese. Bake for 40 to 45 minutes or until nice and bubbly and lightly browned.

GREEN BEANS ITALIANO

SERVES 4

0 GRAMS FAT

Prep :10
Cook :10
Stand :00
Total :20

1 quart green beans, or 1 (10-ounce) package frozen may be used (I can my own)
1 (14-ounce) can Italian tomatoes, drained and chopped
¼ cup chopped onion
1 clove garlic, chopped fine
½ teaspoon dried oregano leaves (1 teaspoon fresh)
½ teaspoon dried basil leaves (1 teaspoon fresh)
⅛ teaspoon pepper

Combine all the ingredients in a saucepan and heat to boiling; reduce heat. Cover and simmer 8 to 10 minutes, or until the beans are crisp-tender. (Some of you like your green beans softer, so cook according to your desired taste.)

BROCCOLI CASSEROLE

½ cup chopped onion
½ cup chopped celery
1 (16-ounce) package frozen broccoli, thawed
1 (10¾-ounce) can Healthy Request cream of chicken soup
¾ cup skim milk
1 cup uncooked instant rice, or more if desired
3 cups shredded fat-free Cheddar cheese

SERVES 6

4 GRAMS FAT
ENTIRE DISH

Prep :15
Cook :45
Stand :00
Total 1:00

Preheat the oven to 350 degrees. Spray a casserole or a 13 x 9-inch baking dish lightly with vegetable oil cooking spray.

Sauté the onion and celery in ¼ cup of water in a medium saucepan until hot and bubbly. Add 1 cup of water; bring to a boil and add broccoli. Cover and let cook for about 10 minutes over low heat.

Stir in the soup, milk, and rice (adding more liquid if you use additional rice). Bring to a boil. Transfer to the prepared casserole and top with the cheese. Bake uncovered for 20 to 30 minutes, until the cheese is golden brown.

SCALLOPED BROCCOLI AND CORN

1 (10-ounce) package frozen chopped broccoli, defrosted
1 (16-ounce) can cream-style corn
½ cup crushed fat-free crackers, divided
¼ cup egg substitute
1 tablespoon instant minced onion
½ teaspoon salt
Dash of pepper
4 tablespoons Butter Buds, divided

SERVES 2

0 GRAMS FAT

Prep :15
Cook :45
Stand :00
Total 1:00

Heat the oven to 350 degrees. Spray a 1-quart casserole dish with vegetable oil cooking spray.

Combine the broccoli and corn with ¼ cup of the cracker

(continued)

crumbs, the egg substitute, minced onion, salt, pepper, and 2 tablespoons of the Butter Buds. Turn into the prepared casserole.

Mix the remaining ¼ cup cracker crumbs and 2 tablespoons Butter Buds. Sprinkle on top. Bake for 45 minutes.

QUICK BROCCOLI AND RICE

SERVES 2

**1 GRAM FAT
PER SERVING**

Prep :20
Cook 1:00
Stand :00
Total 1:20

1 (16-ounce) package frozen broccoli
½ cup uncooked instant rice
½ cup skim milk
1 cup cubed cooked chicken breast
2 tablespoons fat-free Parmesan cheese

Preheat the oven to 350 degrees. Lightly spray a 2-quart baking dish with vegetable oil cooking spray.

In a saucepan, cook the broccoli according to package directions. Drain.

Prepare the rice according to package directions, leaving out the butter or margarine and salt.

In a mixing bowl, combine the milk, broccoli, chicken, rice, and Parmesan cheese.

Pour into the prepared baking dish and bake uncovered for 25 to 30 minutes.

BROCCOLI SAUSAGE CASSEROLE

Serve this with a nice green salad and hot low-fat bread (no butter) and maybe corn for a side vegetable if desired.

1 pound low-fat sage sausage (3 grams per patty), crumbled
½ cup chopped onion
½ cup chopped green pepper
1 (16-ounce) package chopped frozen broccoli, cooked until crisp-tender, drained
2 cups instant rice, prepared according to package directions, leaving out the butter or margarine and salt
2 (10¾-ounce) cans Healthy Request cream of broccoli soup
1 cup shredded fat-free Cheddar cheese
Pepper to taste

SERVES 8

1.5 GRAMS FAT
PER 1-CUP
SERVING

Prep :20
Cook :55
Stand :00
Total 1:15

Preheat the oven to 350 degrees. Lightly spray a medium-size casserole with vegetable oil cooking spray.

Dry-fry the sausage in a large nonstick skillet, stirring to break up lumps, until browned and almost tender. Add the onion and green pepper when meat is about half cooked; sauté 5 minutes, stirring occasionally. Drain into a colander and rinse with hot water to remove any remaining fat. Blot with paper towels, return to the skillet, and add the broccoli, rice, soup, and ¾ soup can of water.

Bring to a simmer and stir in ¾ cup of the cheese. Transfer to the prepared casserole and sprinkle the remaining ¼ cup of cheese on top. Bake uncovered for 35 to 45 minutes, until lightly browned.

FRIED CABBAGE

Remember, this looks like a lot, but cabbage cooks down to about half or less.

SERVES 4

0 GRAMS FAT

Prep :10
Cook :10
Stand :00
Total :20

4 to 6 scallions, sliced
1 medium bell pepper, chopped
4 cups chopped cabbage

In a large nonstick skillet sprayed lightly with vegetable oil cooking spray, stir-fry the scallions and pepper for a couple of minutes, just until they begin to soften. Add the cabbage and stir-fry until crisp-tender and lightly browned on the edges.

MEXICAN CABBAGE

SERVES 2

0 GRAMS FAT

Prep :10
Cook :06
Stand :00
Total :16

1 large onion, sliced thin
1 large head cabbage, trimmed of large outer leaves and cored
1 can Rotel tomatoes and green chiles
¾ teaspoon salt
2 tablespoons vinegar (optional)

Place onions in the bottom of a microwave-safe serving bowl. Quarter the cabbage and place over the onions. Pour the tomatoes and green chiles on top of the cabbage. Sprinkle salt and vinegar over all.

Cover and bake in the microwave on medium heat for 3 minutes. Stir and cook 3 more minutes. (Time may vary according to your microwave oven.) Serve hot.

Cooking cabbage can be pretty smelly. Next time put a heel of bread on top of the cabbage before putting the lid on. When all is done (throw away the cabbage and eat the bread. Ha! Ha! I was only teasing), throw away the bread and the smell at the same time. This also works for broccoli and brussels sprouts. (My mom used to say to cook wild duck, place an apple and an onion in the pot with the duck to cook; when done, throw away the duck and eat the apple and the onion. The cabbage tease reminded me of this.)

BAKED CAJUN CABBAGE

1 large head cabbage

Cheese Sauce:
1 cup chopped onion
1 cup chopped celery
1 cup chopped green pepper
Salt
Cayenne pepper
1½ cups skim milk
3 tablespoons cornstarch
½ pound fat-free Cheddar cheese, shredded (2 cups)

Topping:
1 cup chopped green onions
¼ cup seasoned Italian bread crumbs

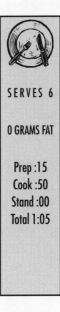

SERVES 6

0 GRAMS FAT

Prep :15
Cook :50
Stand :00
Total 1:05

Heat the oven to 350 degrees.

Remove the outer leaves and core from the cabbage. Cut into bite-size sections. Cook uncovered in a large pot of boiling water about 10 minutes or until tender crisp. Drain in a colander.

Make the cheese sauce: In a separate saucepan, sauté the onions, celery, and green pepper in ¼ cup water. Add the salt and cayenne pepper and sauté for about 10 minutes. Add the milk,

(continued)

blending well. Mix the cornstarch with ½ cup of cold water; add to the saucepan and stir in until creamy. Add the cheese. Stir until smooth.

Place the cabbage in a 2-quart casserole. Top with the cheese sauce. Sprinkle with the green onions and bread crumbs. Bake for about 30 minutes.

> When cooking cauliflower, squirt in a little lemon juice to keep it from turning dark.

SLOAN CORN

I hope you don't go to the store and try to find a variety of corn called Sloan corn. This is only a name for sweet corn that my dad tacked onto the corn grown here by my brother and his three children, which is now very well known, statewide.

When my brother's children were about six, eight, and ten years old, he put them in charge of about two acres of sweet corn, in a project to earn money. Now, you already know that the children's dad had to do all the machinery work, planting, and so forth, but he let them manage this project, and sell the corn from the back of the pickup truck under a big shade tree down on the corner, here in Gore. My dad did a good job of training my brother to be a farmer—the corn was big, juicy, tender, and free of worms. (Yes, worms. You have to really spray and watch your corn crops to keep them free of pests such as weevils and worms. Sometimes when you buy corn at a local farm stand or vegetable stand it is just terrible, with worms in the ends of each ear. You might find one or two in an entire bushel of our corn, but more likely you'll find none. They are the largest, prettiest ears of corn imaginable.)

People would be standing in line at daylight waiting for our corn harvest. The corn has to be picked at night while it is cooler so that it will keep better. If you picked it during the hot summer daytime hours, it would cook, from all the heat in the corn and from the sun, in the bottom of the trailer before you got the corn unloaded.

Here in the country we put vegetables in the freezer and can them, for the sake of economy as well as taste. Satisfaction also plays a large part in canning and freezing. I believe I mentioned in an earlier story or book that since Simon & Schuster got hold of me I don't have time to can anymore. My pressure cooker has been retired. I wish you could have seen us putting up corn. We usually did it outside under a tree. We had large lobster-type pots that we heated our water in, over a camp stove or Cajun-style burner. We shucked and washed our corn outside on the patio, and used regular old-fashioned washtubs for this process.

Sometimes we would put up as much as 20 or 30 bushels of corn in one day. The entire family would be out under the tree, shucking, brushing silks, dropping corn into the blanch pot, cooling corn, draining corn; and the big job was cutting it off the ears, bagging it, labeling, carrying to the freezer, and stacking. There is a job for everyone no matter how old or young. If you cut the corn off the cob outdoors, the splatters don't have to be scraped off the walls in the kitchen. (By the time I finish with this story you will really be glad to buy your corn in the supermarket.)

I want to tell you about the process of harvesting the corn when it is finally ready. They wait until the just-right stage, so you never know what day it will be ready. You can't say, "Well, I think I will can corn on Tuesday." It is sometimes Sunday or Saturday; just depends on Mr. Sunshine. I like to go to the field and pull an ear, shuck it, and eat it right there on the spot, raw. Now, do I like vegetables my brother grows or what??? All the Sloan family loves corn. One way you test the corn to see when it is just-right is to shuck it and pierce a kernel with your fingernail. If it squirts real healthy like, it is ready.

After the corn project started, these two acres they began with grew in popularity and demand until they were raising forty acres at peak project time, and it all had to be picked by hand. You got it—picked by hand. And then they had to pick very early in the morning because they couldn't see to pick at night, of course. They would drive a pickup truck or wagon (pulled by a tractor; it wasn't that long ago) down between two rows with kids on both sides pulling and throwing the ears into the bed of the trailer or truck. It looked like it was raining corn because they would pick two or three rows at a time on each side of the truck. These three kids did *not* do all this picking themselves. They proceeded to hire other young people in our small town who wanted to make some extra summer money, as most kids do. My niece and nephews would buy cases of pop and boxes of candy bars to give their workers a break. I thought that was nice.

They would walk up and down the length of these fields until the entire crop was harvested—not in one day by any means; this would go on for several days until the corn was all picked. But they did have to concentrate on doing a pretty large area at a time or per day, because once corn is ready and stays in the field for a few days the kernels start to get hard. When this happens it means you have lost your crop—no one wants corn that is tough and hard.

When the demand got so large, my brother invested in a one-row corn picker. This machine is pulled by a tractor and has a trailer following the picker. The picker has a chute on the back where the corn is ejected after it has been picked from the stalks. Several kids ride back there and cull out the little nubbins and stalks that slip through the machine. They have a big floodlight hooked onto the machine. Remember, this all takes place from first dark in the evening to daybreak the next morning.

There are peddlers who bring their trucks, trailers, wagons, or whatever they are hauling their corn in, and park them at the end of the field and sometime during the night the Corn Fairy fills up their carrier. Really what happens is there are big pitchfork-type shovels that transfer the corn onto the peddlers' vehicles. Yes, they still buy pop and candy for their midnight treats. Do you suppose I could talk those young teenagers into eating fat-free candy and diet pop? *Not!*

My dad always loved corn cooked any way you would cook it. We would put up several dozen ears on the cob for the big visits and cookouts involving the aunts. Dad would always say, "Must be Sloan corn!" I don't care if it was Jolly Green Giant, cream style, or whatever, he would say that anyway—but he always knew what was really Sloan corn. We rarely had anything else on any of our tables. I still serve it, but without the butter.

Corn is almost always ready on or near the Fourth of July in this part of the country. We could count on having to do corn on the Fourth about nine times out of ten. There is still the farm stand on the corner, and many people who come to the lake (we live just below Lake Tenkiler here in Oklahoma) have been buying corn from these kids for thirty years. The three kids, who are now adults, also have sideline occupations other than their corn adventure, but it will carry on. Their occupations? One is a doctor, one is a schoolteacher, and the third—you guessed it—is a farmer. He was the one who always would "ramrod" the corn adventures.

Corn played a welcome part in the education of all three corn entrepreneurs. As I write this, it is late March and the tractors are rolling—preparations are under way for corn planting. Fourth of July will be here in a short while.

I bet you have something in your family that is as special as corn is to the Sloan family.

CORN ON THE COB

To boil: Husk the corn, remove the silk, and place the corn in a large pot of boiling water. Return to a boil and cook about 4 or 5 minutes, or until tender.

To microwave: Clean the corn as described above, wrap each ear in plastic wrap, leaving one end open to let steam escape, and microwave each ear about 3 to 4 minutes, until kernels are tender. Holding the corn with tongs or a towel, remove the plastic wrap. Be careful not to burn yourself with the steam.

To blanch corn: Have a large container of water boiling over high heat. Very carefully, drop the corn into the boiling water and permit it to stand for 1 minute. Remove and plunge into ice water until chilled through. Remember to leave in the water long enough to chill the cob too. Remove from the water and drain. Use as desired.

CORN AND LIMA BEANS

⅓ cup low-fat reduced-sodium chicken broth
1 cup frozen or canned baby lima beans
1 cup frozen or canned corn
¼ teaspoon sugar
⅛ teaspoon black pepper
2 tablespoons fat-free sour cream

SERVES 2

0 GRAMS FAT

Prep :05
Cook :15
Stand :00
Total :20

Bring the broth to a boil. Add the beans and corn, return to a boil, reduce the heat, and cover. Simmer for 8 to 10 minutes, or until vegetables are just tender. If canned vegetables are used, adjust the time.

Add the sugar and pepper. Simmer uncovered until the liquid is almost evaporated. Stir in the sour cream and serve.

SCALLOPED CORN

¼ cup chopped onion
¼ cup chopped green bell pepper
1 egg white, slightly beaten
½ cup crushed fat-free saltine crackers, divided
½ cup skim milk
⅛ teaspoon seasoned salt
⅛ teaspoon pepper
1 (8-ounce) can whole-kernel corn
1 (8-ounce) can cream-style corn
1 teaspoon fat-free margarine, melted

SERVES 4

0 GRAMS FAT

Prep :15
Cook :40
Stand :00
Total :55

Preheat the oven to 350 degrees. Coat a 1-quart casserole with vegetable oil cooking spray.

In a medium saucepan, sauté the onion and green pepper in a small amount of water until crisp-tender. Drain.

In a large mixing bowl, stir together the egg white, ¼ cup of the crackers crumbs, the milk, seasoned salt, and pepper. Add the

(continued)

cooked onion and peppers, the whole-kernel corn, and the cream-style corn. Mix thoroughly.

Pour the corn mixture into the prepared casserole. In a small bowl toss the remaining ¼ cup cracker crumbs with the melted margarine. Sprinkle over the corn mixture.

Bake for about 35 to 40 minutes, or until a knife inserted near the center comes out clean. Let stand for 5 to 10 minutes before serving.

> When peeling onions cut the root end off last and you won't be in tears so much. Soaking onions in ice water also takes out some of the strength.

CORN PUDDING

SERVES 4

0 GRAMS FAT

Prep :15
Cook 1:15
Stand :00
Total 1:30

1¼ cups egg substitute
1 egg white
1 cup skim milk
2 tablespoons flour
¼ teaspoon baking powder
⅛ teaspoon black pepper
1⅓ cups fresh or frozen whole-kernel corn
2 green onions, including tops, chopped
2 teaspoons fat-free Parmesan cheese

Preheat the oven to 350 degrees. Spray a 9-inch deep-dish pie pan with vegetable oil cooking spray.

In a large bowl, whisk together the egg substitute, egg white, milk, flour, baking powder, and pepper. Stir in the corn, green onions, and cheese.

Transfer the mixture to the prepared pan. Set the pie pan in a large shallow baking pan. Add enough water to the baking pan to come halfway up the sides of the pie pan.

Bake uncovered for 1 to 1¼ hours, or until a knife inserted halfway between the side and center comes out clean and the pudding is puffed and golden.

CORN TAMALE PIE

1 cup yellow cornmeal
⅓ cup sugar
1 tablespoon baking powder
½ teaspoon salt
1 (16-ounce) carton fat-free cottage cheese
1 (16-ounce) package frozen petite corn kernels, thawed, or 2 cups canned
   shoepeg corn, drained
3 green onions, chopped
4 egg whites, at room temperature
2 (14-ounce) cans Mexican-style stewed tomatoes

SERVES 4

0 GRAMS FAT

Prep :20
Cook 1:00
Stand :10
Total 1:30

Preheat the oven to 350 degrees. Spray an 8-inch square glass baking dish with vegetable oil cooking spray.

In a large bowl, combine the cornmeal, sugar, baking powder, and salt. Whisk to blend. Mix in the cottage cheese, then the corn and green onions.

In a separate bowl, beat the egg whites until stiff but not dry. Fold the whites into the cornmeal mixture in 2 additions.

Transfer the batter to the prepared dish. Bake until the top is golden and feels firm in the center, about 50 minutes. Let stand 10 minutes.

While the tamale pie is baking, make a tomato sauce: Boil the stewed tomatoes uncovered in a heavy saucepan until reduced to sauce consistency, about 10 minutes.

Cut the tamale pie into squares and leave in the baking dish. Spoon tomato sauce over and serve.

CORN AND BROCCOLI MEDLEY

SERVES 4

0 GRAMS FAT

Prep :10
Cook :12
Stand :00
Total :22

1 (10-ounce) package frozen broccoli cuts, thawed, or 1½ cups fresh broccoli florets
1 cup frozen whole-kernel corn, thawed
½ cup water
½ cup chopped onion
2 teaspoons chopped fresh basil or ½ teaspoon dried basil
½ teaspoon vegetable bouillon granules
1 clove garlic, chopped fine
1 (2-ounce) jar diced pimentos, drained

Heat all ingredients to boiling, reduce the heat, cover, and simmer for 4 to 5 minutes (10 to 12 minutes if using fresh broccoli), or until broccoli is crisp-tender.

EGGPLANT CASSEROLE

SERVES 6

0 GRAMS FAT

Prep :30
Cook 1:15
Stand :30
Total 2:15

1 medium eggplant, sliced into rounds ½ inch thick
1 teaspoon salt
1 cup uncooked rice
1 small onion, chopped
1 clove garlic, minced
2 cups sliced fresh mushrooms
1 (8-ounce) can tomato sauce
1 teaspoon dried oregano
½ teaspoon dried basil
2 cups fat-free cottage cheese
¼ cup skim milk
1 cup shredded fat-free mozzarella cheese

Spray a 2½-quart casserole or baking dish lightly with vegetable oil cooking spray.

Place the sliced eggplant in a bowl, add 1 teaspoon salt, then cover with water and soak about ½ hour. (This takes out the strong taste some eggplants have and helps prevent discoloring.)

Cook the rice in 2 cups water until tender; drain if necessary and set aside. Preheat the oven to 350 degrees.

Drain eggplant and steam until just tender. If you do not have a steamer, place ½ cup water in saucepan, add the eggplant, cover, and bring to a boil. Lower the heat and cook just until tender, with the lid on. Watch closely; the water might cook away and burn your eggplant.

In a nonstick skillet, sauté the onion, garlic, and mushrooms with ¼ cup water until they start to brown, stirring frequently. Add the tomato sauce, oregano, and basil.

In a small bowl, mix the cottage cheese and skim milk.

Assemble the casserole: Make a layer on the bottom with half the cooked rice. Top with half the eggplant, half the cottage cheese and milk mixture, half the mushroom tomato sauce, and half the mozzarella. Repeat, ending with the cheese.

Bake for 30 to 35 minutes or until bubbly and heated through.

BAKED HOMINY

SERVES 4

LESS THAN 1 GRAM FAT

Prep :10
Cook :30
Stand :00
Total :40

2 cans hominy, drained
1 (8-ounce) carton fat-free sour cream
1 (4-ounce) can chopped green chiles
¼ cup grated fat-free Parmesan cheese

Preheat the oven to 350 degrees. Lightly coat a baking dish with vegetable oil cooking spray.

In a large bowl, combine the hominy with the sour cream and chiles. Mix thoroughly and put in the baking dish. Sprinkle grated cheese over the top. Cover and bake for 30 minutes. Serve hot.

SPICY MUSHROOMS

SERVES 4

0 GRAMS FAT

Prep :05
Cook :00
Stand 4:00
Total 4:05

½ cup fat-free Italian dressing
1 teaspoon crushed dried basil
4 cups fresh mushrooms, sliced

Mix the dressing and basil in a glass bowl. Stir in the mushrooms. Cover and refrigerate at least 4 hours, stirring occasionally.

STEWED OKRA AND TOMATOES

2 cups okra, frozen sliced or fresh
½ cup chopped onion
½ cup chopped green bell pepper
2 (8-ounce) cans tomatoes
1 tablespoon lemon juice
1 teaspoon crushed oregano
¼ teaspoon salt
¼ teaspoon bottled hot pepper sauce, or to taste

SERVES 4

0 GRAMS FAT

Prep :10
Cook :17
Stand :00
Total :27

Remove tip and stem ends from fresh okra and cut into ¼-inch slices.

Sauté the onion and green pepper in ¼ cup water in a large skillet for about 2 minutes, stirring constantly. Add the okra, tomatoes, lemon juice, oregano, salt, and hot pepper sauce. Cover and cook over medium low heat 15 to 20 minutes, or until okra is tender.

BREADED OKRA AND TOMATOES

SERVES 1

LESS THAN 1 GRAM FAT ENTIRE DISH

Prep :15
Cook :40
Stand :00
Total :55

8 cups fresh okra, washed, stemmed, and cut into 1-inch pieces, or frozen sliced okra
1 tablespoon vinegar
¾ cup chopped onion
1 small green pepper, sliced into thin rounds
½ teaspoon dried oregano
¼ teaspoon dried basil
¼ teaspoon lemon pepper
2 (8-ounce) cans stewed tomatoes, undrained
½ cup fine dry bread crumbs

Preheat the oven to 350 degrees. Lightly coat a 9 x 9-inch glass baking dish with vegetable oil cooking spray.

In a large nonaluminum saucepan, cover the okra with water, add the vinegar, and bring to a boil. Cook 2 to 4 minutes, only until crisp-tender. (Adding the vinegar to the okra will keep it from being slimy.) Drain okra in a colander and rinse with warm water. All the slime went down the drain. If using frozen okra, prepare the same way.

Mix the okra, onions, green pepper, oregano, basil, and lemon pepper. Spoon into the prepared baking dish. Pour the tomatoes over, spreading evenly, and top with bread crumbs.

Bake for 30 to 35 minutes, until bubbly.

OVEN-FRIED ONION RINGS

1 cup fine dry bread crumbs
2 tablespoons Butter Buds, liquid form (see Note)
Salt and pepper to taste (optional)
½ cup egg substitute or egg whites
2 large onions, sliced ¼ inch thick, separated into rings

SERVES 4

0 GRAMS FAT

Prep :10
Cook :15
Stand :00
Total :25

Preheat oven to 450 degrees. Lightly spray a large baking sheet with vegetable oil cooking spray.

In a small mixing bowl, combine the bread crumbs and Butter Buds or liquid form margarine, along with the salt and pepper, if using. Mix well. Spread on a sheet of waxed paper on a separate cooking sheet.

Place the egg substitute or whites in a shallow dish. Dip the onion rings in the egg substitute, coating thoroughly, then in the bread crumb mixture. Place the coated onion rings in a single layer on the prepared baking sheet.

Bake for about 15 minutes or until the onions are tender and the coating is crisp and golden.

> *Note:* If you have trouble finding Butter Buds, use a liquid fat-free margarine, such as Fleischmann's.

PINEAPPLE-STUFFED ACORN SQUASH

SERVES 6

**0 GRAMS FAT
(2 GRAMS
EACH IF
PECANS USED)**

**Prep :15
Cook 1:00
Stand :00
Total 1:15**

3 medium acorn squash
1 (8-ounce) can crushed pineapple in juice
⅓ cup firmly packed brown sugar
¼ cup pecans, chopped (optional)
3 tablespoons Butter Buds
½ teaspoon ground cinnamon

Preheat the oven to 375 degrees.

Cut the squash in half lengthwise and remove the seeds. Set aside.

Combine the pineapple, brown sugar, pecans, Butter Buds, and cinnamon in a medium bowl. Mix well. Spoon some of the pineapple mixture into each squash half. Arrange in a 9 x 13 x 2-inch baking dish; pour ¾ cup of water into the dish. Cover with foil and bake for 50 minutes. Uncover and bake 10 minutes longer.

BUTTERNUT SQUASH

SERVES 2

**0 GRAMS FAT
WITHOUT
NUTS**

**Prep :05
Cook :15
Stand :00
Total :20**

1 butternut squash (about 2 pounds), or other winter squash
½ cup honey
½ cup coconut amaretto
¼ cup packed brown sugar

Pierce the squash several times with a fork and place on a microwave-safe dish. Microwave 4 to 5 minutes on high power, rotating the dish a half-turn after 2 minutes. Cut the squash in quarters lengthwise; discard seeds and membrane. Place squash cut side down in baking dish. Cover with microwave-safe plastic wrap and microwave an additional 4 minutes.

Remove the plastic wrap; drizzle the honey and amaretto over squash. Sprinkle with brown sugar. Replace the plastic wrap, return to the microwave, and cook an additional 2 to 4 minutes, or until very tender.

Serve right in the shell or scoop the pulp out into a serving dish and garnish with a tablespoon of chopped nuts.

BUTTERNUT SQUASH PUDDING

1 butternut squash (about 2 pounds)
1½ cups skim milk
¼ cup packed brown sugar
1 tablespoon cornstarch
¼ teaspoon cinnamon
⅛ teaspoon ground nutmeg
⅛ teaspoon ground allspice
¼ cup egg substitute

SERVES 2

0 GRAMS FAT
WITHOUT
NUTS AND
TOPPING

Prep :05
Cook :22
Stand :45
Total 1:12

Prepare the squash according to the directions above, eliminating the honey, amaretto, and brown sugar. Cook the squash until completely tender; remove plastic wrap. Scoop the pulp into mixing bowl or food processor and measure out 1 cup. Reserve the remaining squash for another purpose.

In a food processor or blender, combine the 1 cup of squash with the skim milk, brown sugar, cornstarch, and spices. Process or mix until smooth. Add the egg substitute and mix until smooth.

Pour into a large microwave-safe bowl; microwave on high 8 to 10 minutes or until thickened, stirring every 2 minutes with a wire whisk. Spoon into individual serving dishes, cover, and chill. Serve with a dollop of light whipped topping and a few sprinkles of chopped nuts.

SQUASH CASSEROLE

Cook one and freeze one for later. The squash are plentiful in the summertime, so you'll have a quick meal ready later when they are all gone.

1 package herb-seasoned stuffing mix
1 cup Butter Buds, liquid form
1 to 1½ pounds yellow squash, sliced
2 small onions, chopped
1 (10¾-ounce) can Healthy Request cream of chicken soup
1 pint fat-free sour cream.
1 (4-ounce) jar pimentos, drained and chopped
1 (4-ounce) can sliced water chestnuts, drained
2 cups grated fat-free Cheddar cheese

Preheat the oven to 350 degrees. Lightly spray two 1½-quart casserole dishes with vegetable oil cooking spray.

Toss the stuffing mix in a bowl with the Butter Buds. Line the bottoms of the casserole dishes with the dressing mixture. Save a cupful for topping.

In a large saucepan, combine the squash and onions with ¼ cup of water. Bring to a boil, stir, cover, and cook 10 to 12 minutes, or until the squash is tender. Turn into a colander and drain well.

Return the squash to the saucepan and add the soup, sour cream, pimentos, and water chestnuts, stirring to mix.

Pour the squash mixture over the dressing and sprinkle with grated cheese, then top with the remainder of the dressing mix. Bake for 30 to 40 minutes, or until browned and bubbling.

ZUCCHINI PATTIES

3½ cups grated zucchini (about 1 pound)
2 tablespoons grated onion
2 tablespoons chopped parsley
⅓ cup fat-free Parmesan cheese
1 cup soft fresh bread crumbs
¾ teaspoon salt
¼ teaspoon pepper
½ cup egg substitute
Fine dry bread crumbs (packaged)

SERVES 2

LESS THAN
1 GRAM FAT
EACH

Prep :20
Cook :30
Stand :00
Total :50

Heat the oven to 350 degrees. Spray a cookie sheet with vegetable oil cooking spray.

After grating the zucchini, squeeze out as much liquid as possible with your hands. Combine the zucchini, onion, parsley, cheese, and 1 cup of soft bread crumbs with the salt, pepper, and egg substitute. Shape into patties and coat with dry bread crumbs.

Place on the cookie sheet, then lightly spray the patties with cooking spray. Bake for 30 to 40 minutes, or until golden brown.

VEGETABLE-STUFFED PEPPERS

SERVES 2

1 GRAM FAT
PER SERVING

Prep :15
Cook :10
Stand :00
Total :25

½ cup whole-kernel corn, frozen or canned
¼ cup chopped onion
½ cup herbed tomato sauce
⅓ cup quick-cooking rice
Pinch of sugar
Pepper to taste
1 (8-ounce) can chili-flavored beans, drained
1 large bell pepper
1 tablespoon shredded fat-free Cheddar cheese

Combine the corn, onion, and 1 tablespoon of water in a nonstick skillet. Sauté for about 2 minutes; stir in the tomato sauce, uncooked rice, sugar, and pepper. Cook covered for 2 or 3 minutes or until bubbly, stirring after 1 minute. Stir in beans, cover, and set aside.

Cut the pepper in half lengthwise; remove seeds and membranes. Place the pepper cut side down in a microwave-safe dish, cover with plastic wrap, and microwave on high for 3 minutes or until nearly tender. Drain.

Turn the pepper halves cut side up. Fill with the rice mixture, cover, and microwave on high about 2 minutes or until the rice mixture is heated through and the peppers are tender. Sprinkle cheese over peppers before serving.

SPINACH STORY

My dad was a farmer and my brother and my nephew are farmers. That's right—I am a farmer's daughter. Spinach holds a special fondness in my memories. As well as being one of my favorite vegetables, it is very good for you. It is full of iron and vitamins and is a good cancer-fighting source. Besides, it makes you strong like Popeye.

During World War II my dad went down to the county courthouse to sign up to serve his country. I can remember the day so clearly. My mom, brother, and I sat on the lawn of the courthouse while he went in to take care of business. We were very sad. When he came out, he had wonderful news. The Army wanted him to raise spinach for them, so we would get to keep dad at home with us while he was serving his country. That was the beginning of the Spinach Impact in the Sloan family.

Dad planted large fields of spinach. When it was to be harvested, in those days, it had to be cut by hand. I am talking about getting down on your knees with a large sharp knife, holding the bunch of spinach (it grew in small bunches right on the ground) in one hand and cutting with the other. This very often resulted in cut fingers, sometimes serious cuts. You then put your spinach in a wooden bushel basket. They must have weighed 30 pounds per basket. You packed and smashed it down. Then you carried the basket to the truck where there was a scale you put it on to be weighed. If it didn't weigh what it was supposed to, you took it back and cut some more. You got paid 10 cents a basket. That was my job: I got to hand out the dimes. I was of course supervised by an adult, as I was only about six years old. The baskets of spinach were then thrown up onto the truck, dumped out, and tromped down. Dad then had to haul it to a town about 55 miles away. It was late in the day and sometimes night before he would return.

If he had a good crop he would sometimes buy us a little present before returning. One time I got a little red ring, my first ring. I was so proud of it, I thought I had a 3-carat diamond, but I dropped it in the chicken yard and my pet chicken ate it before I could grab it. Oh, well. Was great while it lasted. My chicken's name was Carter Red.

My brother and nephew now raise spinach, but it is much different in this day and time. They have large equipment and an improved hybrid seed that stands up higher off the ground and is much larger. It is quite a treat to go watch the "cutting of the spinach" and remember how it used to be. I had a picture of the old truck in my dad's field with my grandfather sitting on the running board. I had it enlarged and gave it to my brother.

They still dump the spinach into the trucks, but it is a semi truck that drives alongside the cutting machine, which is pulled by a huge tractor. They talk by remote phones to each other to stay in line. Then there are the trompers. Yes, they still tromp it to pack it down in order to get more on the truck. As you see, it is very light, and without tromping it you would have very little weight when you got to the canners. It is sold by the pound just as we buy it in the grocery stores.

My brother raises spinach for a company named—you guessed it—"Popeye" spinach. We always enjoy going over to the field, just standing and looking out across the beautiful green waves of luscious vegetation and of course filching a bit for the freezer. I also like to use spinach leaves on sandwiches instead of lettuce. It is wonderful.

You can see from the short story that spinach is very special to our family.

SPINACH POTATO CASSEROLE

6 to 8 potatoes
1 cup fat-free sour cream
1/4 cup fat-free margarine, at room temperature
2 teaspoons salt
1/4 teaspoon pepper
1/3 cup chopped scallions, tops and all
1 (10-ounce) package frozen chopped spinach, thawed and squeezed dry
1 cup shredded fat-free Cheddar cheese

SERVES 6

0 GRAMS FAT

Prep :20
Cook :50
Stand :00
Total 1:10

Peel and cube the potatoes, place in a medium-size saucepan, and cover with water. Boil until tender, 20 to 30 minutes.

While the potatoes are boiling, preheat the oven to 400 degrees. Lightly spray a 2-quart casserole with vegetable oil cooking spray.

Drain the potatoes, place in a large bowl, and crush, then mash, with a hand-held electric mixer. Beat in the sour cream, margarine, salt, and pepper. Add the scallions and spinach and stir until thoroughly mixed.

Spoon into the prepared casserole and bake uncovered for 15 minutes. Spread the shredded cheese evenly over the casserole and bake 5 or 6 minutes longer, or until the cheese is melted.

GREEN TOMATO CASSEROLE

4 white onions
5 green tomatoes
1 1/2 pounds fat-free sharp Cheddar cheese

SERVES 4

0 GRAMS FAT

Prep :15
Cook 1:00
Stand :00
Total 1:15

Preheat the oven to 350 degrees. Lightly spray a 13 x 9-inch glass baking dish with vegetable oil cooking spray.

Slice the onions and tomatoes very thin. Grate the cheese. (I usually buy it already grated.)

Layer tomatoes, onions, and cheese until all are used, ending with the cheese on top.

Bake for about 1 hour, or until the tomatoes and onions are tender.

> Lettuce leaves absorb fat. Place several on top of your stew pot or whatever you are cooking and watch the fat cling to them.

VEGETABLE GUMBO

Serve this on a bed of rice, or add cooked macaroni and serve with a salad and garlic toast.

SERVES 4

0 GRAMS FAT

Prep :10
Cook :33
Stand :00
Total :43

1 onion, chopped
1 clove garlic, chopped
1 (14½-ounce) can stewed Italian tomatoes, juice and all
1 (16-ounce) package vegetable gumbo mix
Salt and pepper to taste
Dash of cayenne pepper

Sauté onion and garlic in ¼ cup water for 2 or 3 minutes. Add tomatoes, vegetable mix, and ½ tomato can of water. Simmer 30 minutes, or until tender. Season with salt, pepper, and cayenne.

> Cabbage, kale, turnip, spinach, mustard greens, brussels sprouts, broccoli—all of these vegetables are good cancer fighters. Try to include at least one of them in your diet several times a week.

VEGETABLE SOUFFLÉ IN PEPPER CUPS

1 cup chopped broccoli
½ cup shredded carrot
¼ cup chopped onion
1 teaspoon diced basil leaves, or ⅓ teaspoon dried
½ teaspoon black pepper
2 tablespoons cornstarch
1¼ cups skim milk
1 (8-ounce) container egg substitute
3 large green peppers, cored and halved lengthwise

SERVES 6

0 GRAMS FAT

Prep :15
Cook :40
Stand :00
Total :55

Heat the oven to 375 degrees.

In a nonstick skillet sauté the broccoli, carrot, onion, basil, and black pepper in ¼ cup water until limp and brightly colored, 3 to 5 minutes. Dissolve the cornstarch in ¼ cup of the cold skim milk. Gradually add the remaining 1 cup of milk, stirring constantly over medium heat until thickened. Remove from heat; set aside.

In a medium bowl, with an electric mixer at high speed, beat the egg substitute until foamy. Gently fold into the broccoli mixture; spoon into the pepper halves. Place in a baking dish. Bake for 30 to 35 minutes, or until a knife inserted near the center comes out clean. Serve immediately with a nice green salad.

Vegetables are so good for you; try just cooking them plain with no seasoning. And try not to overcook them and lose so much of their flavor. Cook them crisp-tender. I have learned to appreciate the flavor of so many vegetables since I have cut out the fat, which was used for flavor. They have their very own special taste.

VEGETABLE SPECIAL

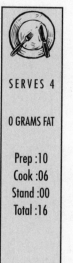

1 cup sliced yellow squash or any available summer squash
1 small bell pepper, cut into strips
⅓ cup sliced celery
⅓ cup 1-inch-long scallions slices, including tops
½ teaspoon canola oil
1 tablespoon lemon juice
¼ teaspoon lemon pepper
4 ounces Chinese pea pods, fresh, if available, or frozen

Cook the squash, bell pepper, celery, and scallions in oil in a non-stick skillet for about 2 minutes, stirring frequently, until tender-crisp. Stir in the remaining ingredients. Cook about 1 minute longer, until the pea pods are hot.

CHEESE SAUCE FOR VEGETABLES

2 tablespoons nonfat dry milk powder
1 tablespoon all-purpose flour
¾ cup skim milk
4 slices fat-free American cheese, torn into pieces

In a saucepan, combine milk powder and flour; stir in the skim milk until smooth. Cook over medium heat until bubbly. Lower the heat to low and continue cooking and stirring about 1 minute more or until the sauce starts to thicken slightly. Stir in the cheese pieces, cooking until cheese melts

Serve over steamed veggies.

Variation: White Sauce: Omit cheese and substitute ¼ cup butter-flavored sprinkles. Mix them with the dry milk and flour; continue recipe as directed.

HERB SAUCE FOR VEGETABLES

¾ cup plain nonfat yogurt
1 teaspoon honey
¾ teaspoon chopped fresh basil or ¼ teaspoon dried
¾ teaspoon chopped fresh tarragon leaves or ¼ teaspoon dried
¼ teaspoon salt
1 clove garlic, crushed
Pinch dried dill weed

SERVES 2

0 GRAMS FAT

Prep :05
Cook :00
Stand 2:00
Total 2:05

Mix all ingredients. Cover and refrigerate at least 2 hours but no longer than 24 hours.

Serve over steamed vegetables.

POTATO STORY

I have many fond memories of potato planting time and digging them with my dad. Planting is quite a job. You have to cut the potatoes into chunks with an eye on each chunk; that is what sprouts and makes them grow. The seed potatoes are covered with dirt, as they have never been cleaned or washed. (They are just going to go back into the dirt so why wash them? Well believe me it takes several days of scrubbing before your hands look like they are clean again.) You get the starchy juice from inside and the dirt from the outside mixed and now you have a dirt paste on your hands.

Your ground has to be hilled up and a hole dug in each hill. Then you go along carrying this heavy bucket full of potatoes you have cut, not to mention that you have several fingers bleeding by this time. You drop a potato in each hill, then you cover them with dirt. Now you wait for time to do its thing along with the fertilizer and watering and weeding.

You get the prettiest bushes of nice green that comes up and they start to spread out and pretty soon they are solid rows of nice greenery. Sometimes Dad's would be knee high. He was some kind of great farmer.

The time has come for the fun—you get to dig under the vines to find the potatoes. What you find is such fun, maybe a little tiny one, maybe a half dozen big ones, but early in the season you get to use the tiny ones for several things. My favorite is green (garden) peas and new potatoes with white gravy. This was always one of the first things you got to eat from the garden in the spring as the green peas are also early. My mom could make the best "peas and taters" in the world bar none.

Now is time for the work to strike again. You have to dig all the hills of potatoes now and pick them up. Carry the heavy buckets of big potatoes somewhere and spread them out so that they will not rot and can get air and dry. Dad always planted such a large garden that it took the whole family to pick potatoes. We would have home-grown potatoes all summer long and store some inside when it came time for the winter to set in so they wouldn't freeze.

I use potatoes in many of my recipes. I know that you will enjoy them, most of all because they are so good for you, but just think of how easy it was to go to the grocery store and "pick potatoes." I bet the price of potatoes doesn't bother you near as much as before you read my "Potato Story," does it? If you think that was bad I could raise the hair on the back of your neck with some pork tales.

MASHED POTATOES

6 to 8 medium potatoes
¾ cup buttermilk (skim or 1 gram fat per cup)
Salt and pepper to taste
2 teaspoons Butter Buds sprinkles, or ¼ cup liquid form

SERVES 6

**1 GRAM FAT
ENTIRE DISH**

Prep :20
Cook :30
Stand :00
Total :50

Peel and cube the potatoes into about 2-inch squares. Place the potatoes in a large saucepan and cover with 2 quarts of cold water (add more if needed to cover). Bring to a boil, lower the heat to medium, and slow-boil until tender, about 30 minutes. Drain, reserving about ¾ cup liquid.

Transfer the potatoes to a medium glass mixing bowl. Using a hand-held electric mixer, crush the potatoes with the mixer beaters up and down a little before you turn the mixer on, to get rid of lumps. Start the mixer and start mashing the potatoes. When about half mashed, start adding buttermilk, seasonings, and Butter Buds. Add a little of the liquid reserved from boiling to get them to the right fluffy consistency. Turn the mixer on high and very vigorously move the mixer in circles around the edge of the bowl as you continue to mix. This will fluff your potatoes. Serve hot.

Variation: Instead of buttermilk, use just plain skim milk and Butter Buds. If you use skim milk, it is nice to heat the milk; this will keep the potatoes hot longer.

MASHED POTATO CASSEROLE

SERVES 6

0 GRAMS FAT

Prep :20
Cook :60
Stand :00
Total 1:20

2 pounds baking potatoes
1 (8-ounce) package fat-free cream cheese, at room temperature
1 cup plain nonfat yogurt
½ teaspoon garlic powder
¼ teaspoon salt
2 tablespoons Butter Buds, liquid form
½ teaspoon paprika

Peel the potatoes and cut into 2-inch chunks. Place in a large saucepan, cover with cold water, and bring to a boil. Lower the heat to medium and continue to cook until very tender, about 30 minutes.

Meanwhile, preheat the oven to 350 degrees. Lightly coat an 11 x 7-inch baking dish with vegetable oil cooking spray.

Drain the potatoes and put in a mixing bowl. Add the cream cheese, yogurt, garlic powder, and salt. Beat at medium speed with an electric mixer until smooth.

Spoon into the prepared baking dish, drizzle with Butter Buds, and sprinkle with paprika. Bake uncovered for 30 minutes.

POTATO BOATS

2 baking potatoes
2 ounces fat-free cream cheese, softened
2 tablespoons minced chives
¼ teaspoon dried basil, crushed
⅛ teaspoon salt
Dash of pepper
3 to 4 tablespoons skim milk
Paprika

SERVES 4

0 GRAMS FAT

Prep :30
Cook 1:10
Stand :00
Total 1:40

Scrub potatoes and prick with a fork. Bake in a preheated 375 degree oven for about 45 to 50 minutes, depending on the size of potatoes, or until tender.

Cut potatoes in half lengthwise. Gently scoop out each potato half, leaving a thin shell. Set shells aside.

Place the pulp in mixing bowl, add softened and cubed cream cheese, chives, basil, salt, and pepper. Beat until smooth. Add milk a little at a time, beating until potato mixture is fluffy.

Spoon the mixture back into the potato shells. Sprinkle with paprika. Place on a baking sheet, cover loosely with foil, and bake for 10 minutes. Uncover and bake an additional 10 minutes.

Variations: You may choose many variations to these boats. Use sour cream instead of cream cheese. Use fat-free Cheddar cheese in and on top of the potatoes. Use your imagination and add your favorite toppings or herbs and spices. You can even make an entire meal with these by adding steamed broccoli, or one or more other vegetables.

Avoid green-skinned potatoes; they have been exposed to the light too long. They are actually "sunburned." You can peel the green away, but if it is halfway into the potato throw it away.

BROCCOLI-STUFFED POTATOES

SERVES 6

LESS THAN 1 GRAM FAT IN ALL

Prep :10
Cook 1:19
Stand :00
Total 1:29

6 medium-size baking potatoes, scrubbed
1 teaspoon Butter Buds, liquid form
3 stalks broccoli (about 1 pound), stems peeled
1 cup shredded fat-free Cheddar cheese
1$\frac{1}{4}$ cups skim milk
1 teaspoon salt
$\frac{1}{8}$ teaspoon black pepper

Preheat the oven to 400 degrees. Brush the skins of potatoes with Butter Buds and score them down the middle lengthwise. Bake for 45 to 60 minutes, or until tender.

Steam the broccoli for 6 to 8 minutes, or until just tender. Chop fine. Carefully slice the potatoes in half lengthwise and scoop the flesh into a bowl. Reserve the skins. Add the broccoli, $\frac{1}{2}$ cup of the cheese, the milk, salt, and pepper to the potato. Mash until the mixture is pale green with dark flecks.

Spoon the mixture into the potato skins and sprinkle with the remaining cheese. Place on a baking sheet and bake for 10 minutes longer. Heat the broiler and broil the potatoes for 1 minutes, or until the tops are golden brown.

BAKED POTATO TOPPING

½ cup fat-free sour cream
½ cup plain nonfat yogurt
¼ cup chopped fresh scallions or chives
2 tablespoons chopped fresh parsley
1 tablespoon Dijon mustard
Salt and pepper to taste

In a small bowl, combine all ingredients. Spoon some of the mixture over a split hot baked potato and serve.

> *Note:* This makes about 1 cup, enough for 4, but at our house I make a double batch because we like lots of topping on our potatoes.

SERVES 4

0 GRAMS FAT

Prep :05
Cook :00
Stand :00
Total :05

COMPANY TATERS

5 to 6 medium baking potatoes
2 cups fat-free sour cream
1 teaspoon cornstarch
¾ cup chopped green onions
1½ cups shredded fat-free Cheddar cheese
1½ teaspoons salt
1 teaspoon pepper
Paprika

SERVES 8

0 GRAMS FAT

Prep :20
Cook 1:30
Stand 4:00
Total 5:50

Preheat the oven to 350 degrees.

Boil the potatoes, jackets on, in water to cover, for 35 minutes or until tender. Cool. Peel and grate.

In a medium bowl, combine the sour cream, cornstarch, green onions, Cheddar cheese, salt, and pepper. Mix well. Add the grated potatoes and spoon the mixture into a 9 x 13 x 2-inch baking dish. Cover and refrigerate for 3 to 4 hours or overnight.

Bake uncovered for 40 to 50 minutes. Sprinkle with paprika and serve.

Potatoes were one of the first things that we thought we had to give up years ago when we thought of losing weight or going on a diet. The potato is not what is fattening—it is the way it is prepared and the things that we put on the potato: sour cream and butter. Nowadays, the facts are out and we can start with the potato and build a meal around it.

HASH BROWN BREAKFAST CASSEROLE

1 (10-ounce) package fat-free frozen hash brown potatoes
¼ cup chopped onion
¼ cup chopped bell pepper
½ cup shredded fat-free cheese
1 cup plain nonfat yogurt
1 cup fat-free sour cream
½ cup chopped green chiles (optional)
Salt and pepper to taste

SERVES 8

0 GRAMS FAT

Prep :10
Cook :45
Stand :00
Total :55

Preheat the oven to 350 degrees. Lightly spray a 9 x 9-inch baking dish with vegetable oil cooking spray.

Combine the potatoes, onions, bell peppers, cheese, yogurt, and sour cream. (If desired include green chiles, especially if you are serving a Western theme breakfast, or breakfast on the patio or deck.) Season to taste with salt and pepper. Mix well and spoon into the prepared baking dish.

Bake uncovered for 40 to 50 minutes or until golden brown.

Note: The casserole may be mixed a day ahead, covered with plastic wrap, and refrigerated until time to cook.

CONFETTI POTATOES

SERVES 6

VERY LOW-FAT

Prep :15
Cook :40
Stand :00
Total :55

½ cup chopped onion
1 (16-ounce) package frozen hash brown potatoes
1 (10-ounce) can Healthy Request cream of mushroom soup
1 soup can skim milk
1 cup shredded fat-free Cheddar cheese
1 small green pepper, cored and chopped
2 tablespoons chopped pimiento
1 cup cheese-cracker crumbs (I use Cheese Nips, which have less fat)

Preheat the oven to 375 degrees.

In a nonstick skillet sauté the onion in about ¼ cup water for 3 to 5 minutes, until tender. Stir in the potatoes, soup, and milk. Add the cheese, green pepper, and pimiento and ½ cup of the cheese crackers.

Pour into shallow casserole and top with the remaining cracker crumbs.

Bake uncovered for 35 to 40 minutes, until bubbly.

POTATO CONFETTI CASSEROLE

A good do-ahead dish.

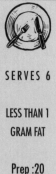

SERVES 6

LESS THAN 1
GRAM FAT

Prep :20
Cook 1:00
Stand :30
Total 1:50

3 pounds medium potatoes, peeled and quartered
½ cup Butter Buds liquid
2 (3-ounce) packages fat-free cream cheese, softened
1 cup shredded fat-free Cheddar cheese
1 (2-ounce) jar diced pimientos, drained
1 small green pepper, chopped fine
1 bunch green onions, chopped fine
½ cup grated fat-free Parmesan cheese
¼ cup skim milk
1 teaspoon salt

Cook potatoes in boiling water to cover for 15 to 20 minutes, or until tender. Drain and mash. Add Butter Buds and cream cheese. Beat with an electric mixer until smooth. Stir in ½ cup of the Cheddar cheese, the pimientos, green pepper, onions, Parmesan, milk, and salt. Spoon into a baking dish (11 x 7 x 1½) that has been lightly sprayed with vegetable oil cooking spray. Cover and chill if desired.

The next day, or when you are ready to bake the casserole, remove it from the refrigerator and let stand 30 minutes. Bake uncovered in a preheated 350 degree oven for 40 minutes, or until thoroughly heated. Sprinkle with the remaining ½ cup of Cheddar cheese. Bake 5 minutes longer, or until the cheese melts.

CORN AND POTATO CASSEROLE

1 medium onion, chopped
¼ cup chopped green pepper
1 (32-ounce) package fat-free frozen hash brown potatoes
2 cups frozen whole corn kernels
1 (16-ounce) container fat-free sour cream
1 (10¾-ounce) can Healthy Request cream of celery soup
1 cup shredded fat-free Cheddar cheese
2 cups cornflake crumbs

SERVES 6

4.75 GRAMS FAT ENTIRE DISH

Prep :10
Cook 1:05
Stand :00
Total 1:15

Preheat the oven to 350 degrees. Spray an 11 x 7-inch baking dish lightly with vegetable oil cooking spray.

In a nonstick skillet, sauté the onion and green pepper in a couple of tablespoons of water until tender, about 5 minutes

Combine the hash brown potatoes, corn, onion and pepper, sour cream, soup, and cheese in a large bowl. Stir well. Spoon into the prepared baking dish and top with cornflake crumbs.

Bake uncovered for 1 hour or until golden brown.

Note: If making ahead, after assembling in the baking dish, cover with plastic wrap and store in the refrigerator. Set out at room temperature about 15 minutes before baking time. Do not add cornflake crumbs until baking time.

FAKE FRENCH FRIES

Serve these potatoes right away since they lose their crispness quickly.

SERVES
2 TO 4

LESS THAN 1
GRAM FAT PER
SERVING

Prep :10
Cook :25
Stand :00
Total :35

3 large unpeeled potatoes, scrubbed and patted dry
1 tablespoon canola oil
½ teaspoon salt

Preheat the oven to 400 degrees. Cut the potatoes into sticks about the size of french fries. Put them in a bowl with the oil and salt. Toss them well. Spread them on a baking sheet and bake until golden brown and tender, about 25 minutes.

Low-Fat Pan Fries
For pan fries without all the fat try using steamed or baked potatoes, sliced thin. Spray a nonstick skillet and dry fry at a medium high heat. Spray the tops of the potatoes a couple of times after stirring them. This will satisfy your fry craving and your figure.

Keep potatoes cool but not cold and in a dark place. Refrigeration converts the potato starch into sugar, creating a sweet taste and causing potatoes to darken prematurely while cooking.

HASH BROWN CASSEROLE

1½ cups chopped onion
3 tablespoons flour
½ teaspoon dry mustard
¼ teaspoon salt
1½ cups skim milk
½ cup low-sodium chicken broth
1½ cups shredded fat-free Cheddar cheese
¾ cup fat-free shredded Swiss cheese
½ teaspoon pepper
1 cup fat-free sour cream
1 (32-ounce) package frozen Southern-style hash brown potatoes, thawed
Paprika

SERVES 8

LESS THAN 1
GRAM FAT

Prep :14
Cook 1:16
Stand :00
Total 1:30

Preheat the oven to 350 degrees. Spray a 9 x 13 x 2-inch baking dish with vegetable oil cooking spray. Set aside.

Coat a medium saucepan with vegetable oil cooking spray. Add the onion and sauté 3 to 5 minutes, until tender. Add the flour, mustard, and salt; stir well and cook 1 minute. Remove from the heat. Gradually add the milk and broth, stirring with a wire whisk until blended. Cook until thickened, stirring constantly. Remove from the heat; add the cheeses and pepper, stirring until cheeses melt. Stir in the sour cream.

Combine the cheese mixture and potatoes. Stir well. Spoon into the prepared baking dish. Sprinkle with paprika. Cover with foil and bake 35 minutes. Uncover and bake an additional 35 to 40 minutes.

> To bring out the true flavor of a potato, bake it in its own skin. Foil locks in the moisture and gives you a boiled flavor. Pierce the skin before baking—have you ever cleaned an oven after one explodes? You won't ever forget to pierce one again. I had an all-chrome-inside oven when mine exploded the only time in my life that I failed to pierce one.

SCALLOPED POTATOES

SERVES 10

**2.9 GRAMS FAT
PER 1-CUP
SERVING**

**Prep :15
Cook 1:16
Stand :00
Total 1:31**

¼ cup nonfat dry milk powder
2 cups skim milk
2 tablespoons light margarine
¼ cup all-purpose flour
½ teaspoon salt
½ teaspoon pepper
1¾ pounds potatoes, pared and cut into ¼-inch-thick slices (about 4 potatoes)
1½ cups thinly sliced onions
¾ cup shredded fat-free Cheddar cheese
¼ cup soft bread crumbs

Coat a 12 x 8-inch casserole with vegetable oil cooking spray. Preheat the oven to 375 degrees.

Dissolve the milk powder in the skim milk and set aside. Melt the margarine in a heavy pan; add the flour and stir well. Cook over medium heat for 1 minute; it will be lumpy. Gradually add the milk, stirring constantly with a wire whisk until thickened. Add the salt and pepper. Remove the sauce from the heat.

Spread ¼ cup of the sauce in the prepared baking dish; add half each of the potatoes, onions, and cheese, and spread with a layer of sauce. Repeat except for cheese. Cover and bake for 1 hour, or until the potatoes are tender. Uncover and sprinkle with the remaining cheese and bread crumbs. Coat lightly with cooking spray. Bake an additional 5 minutes.

Potatoes are good for you. They are loaded with vitamins B and C, have no fat or cholesterol, and are an excellent source of potassium, a medium potato containing $1\frac{1}{2}$ times as much as a banana or cup of orange juice.

BUTTERMILK SCALLOPED POTATOES

The buttermilk bakes into a remarkably cheesy tasting sauce. Very simple to make.

SERVES 4

LESS THAN 3
GRAMS FAT

Prep :15
Cook 1:15
Stand :00
Total 1:30

¼ cup whole wheat flour
1 teaspoon salt
⅛ teaspoon pepper
2 large baking potatoes, peeled and sliced thin
2 tablespoons Butter Buds
1 medium onion, chopped
2 cups skim buttermilk (check the label; buy the 1 gram per cup)
Pinch of paprika

Preheat the oven to 350 degrees.

In a shallow dish combine the flour, salt, and pepper. Dredge the potatoes in the flour mixture and place them in a shallow 2-quart baking dish.

In a small skillet sprayed with vegetable oil cooking spray, sauté the onion for about 5 minutes, or until tender. Spoon the onion over the potatoes and pour buttermilk over top. Sprinkle paprika over potatoes and bake uncovered for 1 to 1¼ hours, or until the potatoes are tender.

WORKING WOMAN'S
SCALLOPED POTATOES

SERVES 6

1 GRAM FAT
PER SERVING

Prep :05
Cook :40
Stand :00
Total :45

1 package scalloped potato mix
⅓ cup chopped green onions
½ to 1 teaspoon Italian seasoning
1½ cups boiling water
1¼ cups skim milk

Combine the dried potatoes, sauce mix, onions, and seasoning. Stir in the boiling water and milk; mix well. Turn into a casserole and bake at 375 to 400 degrees for 30 to 40 minutes.

POTATO SPEARS

Serve with oven-fried fish or as appetizers with a fat-free sour cream.

SERVES 2
TO 4

LESS THAN 1
GRAM FAT IN
ALL

Prep :10
Cook :30
Stand :00
Total :40

3 to 4 large unpeeled baking potatoes, scrubbed and cut lengthwise into 8 wedges each
1 package onion soup mix (see Note)

Preheat the oven to 400 degrees.

Lightly spray the potato wedges with vegetable oil cooking spray. Put into a large plastic bag or bowl. Add the onion soup mix. Shake to coat potatoes. Arrange on a cookie sheet sprayed with cooking spray and bake until golden, 30 to 45 minutes.

Note: Read your labels. On the soup mix one has fat, one does not.

SWEET POTATOES

3 medium sweet potatoes
2 tablespoons orange juice
½ cup honey
¼ cup packed brown sugar
¾ cup coconut amaretto

SERVES 4

0 GRAMS FAT

Prep :10
Cook :50
Stand :00
Total 1:00

Preheat the oven to 350 degrees. Lightly spray a 3-quart baking dish with vegetable oil cooking spray.

Peel the sweet potatoes and cut into 1½-inch chunks. Place in the prepared baking dish. Sprinkle orange juice over evenly. Stream honey evenly over all, sprinkle brown sugar over the honey, and pour amaretto over evenly. Really doesn't matter how you pour these four ingredients over these potatoes, they are going to be so good.

Bake uncovered for 45 to 50 minutes or until tender and bubbly.

Tip: If you are in a hurry you can boil the potatoes until they start to get tender. Peel and cube them, place in the baking dish, and continue with the directions.

SWEET POTATO CRISP

Make ahead for the holidays.

SERVES 16

0 GRAMS FAT
(NUTS OMIT-
TED)

Prep :35
Cook 1:20
Stand :00
Total 1:55

3½ pounds medium sweet potatoes
⅓ cup packed brown sugar
⅓ cup orange juice
½ cup egg substitute
3 tablespoons Kahlúa
1½ teaspoons pumpkin pie spice
1 tablespoon Butter Buds, liquid form

Topping:
¼ cup finely chopped pecans, toasted
3 tablespoons all-purpose or whole-wheat flour
¼ cup packed brown sugar
1 teaspoon ground cinnamon
1 tablespoon Butter Buds, liquid form

Wash the potatoes, place in a deep stockpot, cover with water, and cook 35 to 40 minutes, or until tender. Drain and cool. When cool enough to handle, peel potatoes and place in a large mixing bowl. Mash until smooth.

Preheat the oven to 350 degrees. Lightly spray a 2-quart baking dish with vegetable oil cooking spray.

Stir the ⅓ cup brown sugar, orange juice, egg substitute, Kahlúa, pie spice, and Butter Buds into the mashed sweet potatoes. Transfer to the prepared baking dish.

Make the topping: Combine the pecans, flour, ¼ cup brown sugar, cinnamon, and 1 tablespoon Butter Buds in a small bowl and mix with a fork. Sprinkle over the sweet potatoes. Bake uncovered for 40 minutes.

OVEN-FRIED SWEET POTATOES

3 large sweet potatoes
½ cup skim milk
¾ to 1 cup fine, dry bread crumbs

Preheat the oven to 350 degrees. Lightly spray a baking sheet with vegetable oil cooking spray.

Scrub the potatoes, but do not peel. Cut them crosswise into the thickness you desire. Dip in skim milk and coat with bread crumbs. Place the sweet potato slices on the prepared baking sheet and spray the top of each piece lightly with cooking spray.

Bake uncovered for 15 to 20 minutes. Turn the potatoes and bake 15 to 20 minutes more, depending on the thickness, until tender.

SERVES 4

SLIGHT TRACE OF FAT PER SERVING

Prep :15
Cook :40
Stand :00
Total :55

SWEET POTATO FLUFF

3 medium sweet potatoes
2 tablespoons orange juice
1⅓ teaspoons cinnamon
½ cup packed brown sugar
¼ cup coconut amaretto

Peel the potatoes and cut them into 2-inch chunks. Place them in a medium saucepan, cover with water, and boil gently until tender, about 15 to 20 minutes.

Drain the potatoes and put in a mixing bowl. Add the orange juice, cinnamon, brown sugar, and half the amaretto. With an electric mixer, beat the potatoes until fluffy, adding amaretto as needed. You may need just a little more than ¼ cup, especially after you taste it.

SERVES 6

0 GRAMS FAT

Prep :15
Cook :20
Stand :00
Total :35

SWEET POTATO PUFF

SERVES 4

0.3 GRAM FAT

Prep :15
Cook :35
Stand :00
Total :50

3 cups sliced carrots
1 (16-ounce) can cut sweet potatoes in light syrup, drained
¼ cup firmly packed brown sugar
2 tablespoons unsweetened orange juice
½ teaspoon ground cinnamon
⅛ teaspoon salt
¼ teaspoon vanilla extract

Preheat the oven to 350 degrees. Spray a 9-inch square baking dish with vegetable oil cooking spray.

Cook the carrot slices in boiling water to cover for 15 minutes, or until very tender; drain.

Fit a food processor with the steel blade. Turn the carrots into the processor bowl along with the sweet potatoes, brown sugar, orange juice, cinnamon, salt, and vanilla. Process until smooth; scrape down sides as needed.

Spoon the sweet potato mixture into the prepared dish, spreading it evenly. Bake uncovered for 20 to 25 minutes.

Variation: Marshmallow creme may be dotted on top. Bake 5 minutes longer.

When storing carrots, be sure to take off the tops. They drain out all the moisture from them and make them limp. You can revive them sometimes by soaking in very cold water.

Breads

APPLE WHEAT MUFFINS

SERVES 12

LESS THAN 1 GRAM FAT EACH

Prep :15
Cook :20
Stand :05
Total :40

1 cup low-fat buttermilk
2 cups Wheaties cereal
½ cup finely chopped pared apple (about half a medium apple)
¼ cup unsweetened apple juice
¼ cup molasses
¼ cup egg substitute
1 cup whole wheat flour
¾ teaspoon baking soda
¼ teaspoon salt
¼ teaspoon cinnamon

Preheat the oven to 400 degrees. Line 12 muffin cups with paper baking cups. Spray with vegetable oil cooking spray.

Pour the buttermilk over the cereal in a medium bowl. Let stand 5 minutes, or until the cereal is soft. Add the chopped apple, the apple juice, molasses, and egg substitute; stir to combine.

In a small bowl, whisk together the flour, baking soda, salt, and cinnamon. Add the dry ingredients all at once to the cereal mixture; stir just until flour is moistened. The batter should be lumpy. Fill the muffin cups ¾ full.

Bake 20 minutes, or until a toothpick inserted in the center comes out *almost* clean. Immediately remove from pan.

BANANA BREAD

MAKES 1
LOAF (18
SLICES)

1 GRAM FAT
PER SLICE

Prep :15
Cook 1:00
Stand :05
Total 1:20

⅔ cup sugar
¼ cup reduced-fat margarine, softened
¾ cup egg substitute
1 cup mashed ripe bananas (about 2 large bananas)
1⅔ cups flour
1 teaspoon baking soda
¼ teaspoon baking powder
½ teaspoon salt

Preheat the oven to 350 degrees. Spray an 8- or 9-inch loaf pan with vegetable oil cooking spray.

Beat the sugar and margarine in a medium bowl with an electric mixer until light and fluffy. And the egg substitute, bananas, and ¼ cup of water. Beat on low speed until well blended.

Mix together the flour, baking soda, baking powder, and salt. Stir into the banana mixture just until moistened. Pour and scrape into the loaf pan.

Bake the 8-inch loaf for 60 minutes, the 9-inch for 45 to 50 minutes, or until a toothpick inserted in the center comes out clean.

Cool 5 minutes. Loosen sides of loaf from pan. Remove from pan and cool completely on a rack before slicing—if you can resist.

Everyone probably knows that you ripen bananas by putting them in a paper sack, and that wrapping them in a wet towel will make them ripen even faster. But how in the world do you keep them from ripening so fast?

HOMEMADE BISCUITS

MAKES 8
THICK OR
12 THIN
BISCUITS

1 GRAM FAT
EACH

Prep :10
Cook :35
Stand :00
Total :45

3 cups self-rising flour
1 to 1½ cups skim milk, or enough to make a sticky dough

Preheat the oven to 400 degrees. Spray a baking sheet with vegetable oil cooking spray.

Put the flour in a bowl and add enough milk to make a sticky consistency (the stickier you can handle the dough the lighter the biscuits).

Turn out on a floured surface and knead just enough to make the dough workable. Pat out with fingers until thickness desired. (You can use a rolling pin but then you just have to clean it.) Cut out biscuits. Put in the sprayed pan. Spray the tops of the biscuits lightly; this will make them brown nice.

Bake thin biscuits for 12 to 15 minutes, or until golden brown. Thicker biscuits will take 35 to 40 minutes.

ALMOND SHORTCAKE BISCUITS

Serve with fresh strawberries.

MAKES 8
BISCUITS

7 GRAMS FAT
EACH

Prep :15
Cook :15
Stand :00
Total :30

2¼ cups all-purpose flour
⅓ cup sugar, plus 1 tablespoon for sprinkling over top
1½ teaspoons baking powder
¾ teaspoon baking soda
¼ teaspoon salt
2 tablespoons light margarine, cold, cut into small pieces
¾ to 1 cup low-fat buttermilk (1 gram fat per cup)
1 tablespoon canola oil
½ teaspoon vanilla extract
⅛ teaspoon almond extract
1 tablespoon skim milk
¼ cup sliced almonds

Heat the oven to 400 degrees. Spray a baking sheet with vegetable oil cooking spray; set aside.

Mix the flour, ⅓ cup of sugar, the baking powder, soda, and salt. Cut in the margarine until crumbly.

In a small bowl, combine ¾ cup of buttermilk, the oil, and the vanilla and almond extracts. Make a well in the center of the flour mixture. Add the buttermilk mixture. With a fork, stir just until combined, adding extra buttermilk if necessary to form a slightly sticky dough. Do *not* overmix.

Place the dough on a lightly floured surface and sprinkle with flour. Gently pat with fingertips to 1-inch thickness. Cut with a biscuit cutter. Place on the baking sheet. Brush with milk and sprinkle with the remaining tablespoon of sugar and the almonds. Bake for 10 to 15 minutes, until golden.

APPLE COFFEE CAKE

1 cup all-purpose flour
1½ teaspoons baking powder
½ teaspoon salt
¾ cup granulated sugar
⅓ cup skim milk
2 egg whites
⅓ cup light or dark corn syrup
2 medium apples, peeled and cut into ½-inch wedges
2 tablespoons cinnamon sugar

SERVES 4

FAT-FREE

Prep :15
Cook :50
Stand :00
Total 1:05

Spray a 9-inch round baking pan with vegetable oil cooking spray. Preheat the oven to 350 degrees.

In a large bowl, combine the flour, baking powder, and salt. In a medium bowl, using a wire whisk or fork, mix the granulated sugar and milk. Whisk in the egg whites and corn syrup. Gradually stir into the dry ingredients until smooth. Pour into the prepared pan.

Arrange the apples over the top, overlapping to cover. Sprinkle with cinnamon sugar. Bake for 50 minutes, or until a toothpick inserted in center comes out clean. Cool on a wire rack.

OVERNIGHT COFFEE CAKE
(DO AHEAD)

SERVES 8

1 GRAM FAT
PER CAKE, IF
NUTS OMITTED

Prep :10
Cook :35
Stand 8:00
Total 8:45

2 cups all-purpose flour
1 cup granulated sugar
1 cup firmly packed brown sugar, divided
1 teaspoon baking soda
1 teaspoon baking powder
½ teaspoon salt
2 teaspoons cinnamon, divided
1 cup low-fat buttermilk (1 gram fat per cup)
⅔ cup Butter Buds liquid
½ cup egg substitute
½ cup pecans, chopped (optional)

Preheat the oven to 350 degrees.

In a mixing bowl, combine the flour, granulated sugar, ½ cup of the brown sugar, the baking soda, baking powder, salt, and 1 teaspoon of cinnamon. Add the buttermilk, Butter Buds, and egg substitute. Beat on low speed until the mixture is moistened, then beat on medium speed for 3 minutes.

Spoon into an oil-sprayed and floured 9 x 13 x 2-inch baking pan. Combine the remaining ½ cup of brown sugar, the pecans, and 1 teaspoon of cinnamon. Sprinkle over the batter. Cover and refrigerate 8 to 12 hours.

Uncover and bake for 30 to 35 minutes, or until a toothpick inserted in the center comes out clean. Serve warm.

CHERRY-DATE QUICK BREAD

A good make-ahead recipe. You may freeze the loaf and store it for up to 3 months.

All-purpose flour
1 cup boiling water
¾ cup quick-cooking rolled oats
⅓ cup candied cherries
1 (16-ounce) package date bread mix
½ teaspoon grated nutmeg
¼ cup egg substitute

SERVES 10

1 GRAM FAT
PER SLICE

Prep :15
Cook :40
Stand :10
Total 1:05

Heat the oven to 375 degrees. Spray an 8 x 4-inch or 9 x 5-inch loaf pan with vegetable oil cooking spray. Sprinkle in a little flour to coat the pan, then tap out the excess flour.

Pour the boiling water over the oats and let stand 5 minutes. Chop the cherries and sprinkle with ½ teaspoon of flour; toss to coat.

Combine the bread mix, nutmeg, and egg substitute with ½ cup water. Add the oat mixture and the chopped cherries. Stir just until the dry ingredients are moistened. Pour into the greased and floured pan.

Bake for 35 to 40 minutes, or until the top of the loaf is deep golden brown. Cool 5 minutes before removing from pan. Turn out on a rack and cool completely.

CRANBERRY BREAD

SERVES 12

0 GRAMS FAT

Prep :15
Cook 1:10
Stand :10
Total 1:35

2½ cups all-purpose flour
¾ cup sugar
2 tablespoons poppy seeds
1 tablespoon baking powder
1 cup skim milk
⅓ cup (5 tablespoons plus 1 teaspoon) fat-free margarine, melted
¼ cup egg substitute
1 teaspoon vanilla extract
2 teaspoons grated lemon rind
1 cup fresh or frozen cranberries, chopped
Powdered Sugar Glaze (optional) (page 308)

Heat the oven to 350 degrees. Spray the bottom of an 8½ x 4½ x 2½-inch loaf pan with vegetable oil cooking spray.

In large a bowl, mix the flour, sugar, poppy seeds, and baking powder. Mix the milk, margarine, egg substitute, vanilla, and lemon rind. Stir into the flour mixture just until moistened. Stir in cranberries; spoon into the prepared pan and smooth the top.

Bake for 60 to 70 minutes, or until a toothpick inserted near the center comes out clean. Cool in the pan for 10 minutes; then turn out on a wire rack and cool completely.

Cranberries: If you have trouble finding cranberries in your area other than at Thanksgiving and Christmastime, buy extra during the holidays and freeze them. You don't have to do anything except set them in the freezer in the bag you buy them in. They will keep for up to 6 months.

CRANBERRY NUT BREAD

3 cups all-purpose flour
1 cup sugar
1 tablespoon baking powder
¼ teaspoon baking soda
¼ teaspoon salt (optional)
¼ cup egg substitute
1⅔ cups skim milk
¼ cup applesauce
2 teaspoons finely shredded orange zest
1 cup coarsely chopped cranberries
¼ cup chopped English walnuts or pecans
Powdered Sugar Glaze (see next page) (optional)

MAKES 1
LARGE OR
2 SMALL
LOAVES;
SERVES 4

2 GRAMS FAT
PER SERVING

Prep :20
Cook 1:15
Stand :10
Total 1:45

Preheat the oven to 350 degrees. Lightly spray one 9 x 5 x 3-inch loaf pan or two 7½ x 3½ x 2-inch loaf pans with vegetable oil cooking spray.

Stir together in a large mixing bowl the flour, sugar, baking powder, baking soda, and salt, if desired. In a smaller mixing bowl, stir together the egg substitute, milk, applesauce, and orange zest. Add to the flour mixture, stirring just until combined. Stir in the cranberries and walnuts. Pour the batter into the prepared pans.

Bake for 1 to 1¼ hours for the 9-inch pan, 45 minutes for the 7-inch pans, or until a toothpick inserted near the center comes out clean.

Cool the bread in the pan on a wire rack for 10 minutes. Remove the bread from the pan and cool completely on the rack. Wrap and store overnight for the best slicing consistency. Drizzle with powdered sugar glaze if desired.

(continued)

Powdered Sugar Glaze

0 GRAMS FAT

Prep :05
Cook :00
Stand :00
Total :05

1½ cups powdered sugar
½ teaspoon vanilla extract
2 tablespoons skim milk

Mix all above ingredients together until smooth. If necessary, add more or less milk, to get the consistency desired.

FAT-FREE PANCAKES

SERVES 8

0 GRAMS FAT

Prep :10
Cook :10
Stand :00
Total :20

1¼ cups all-purpose flour
2½ teaspoons baking powder
½ teaspoon salt
¼ cup egg substitute
1¼ cups skim milk

In a mixing bowl, combine the flour, baking powder, and salt. Mix well. In a small bowl, mix together the egg substitute and milk. Stir into the flour mixture just until moistened. (Batter will be lumpy.)

Spray a nonstick skillet lightly with vegetable oil cooking spray. Heat to medium hot. Spoon the batter into hot skillet to make pancakes about 4 inches in diameter.

Cook until bubbles form on the surface, turn with a spatula, and continue to cook until the bottom is golden brown. Serve with hot or warm syrup.

Tip: While you are mixing and cooking your pancakes, place your syrup bottle in a bowl or pan full of very hot water. By the time you are ready the syrup will be nice and warm.

Variation: Whole-Wheat Pancakes: Follow directions above, substituting an equal quantity of whole-wheat flour for the all-purpose flour (or use a mixture of whole-wheat and white). Increase the milk to 1½ cups.

DE "LITE" FUL ZERO-FAT PANCAKES

½ cup egg substitute
1 cup fat-free cottage cheese
⅔ cup skim milk
½ teaspoon vanilla extract
1 cup all-purpose flour
½ teaspoon baking soda
Pinch of salt (optional)

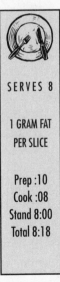

SERVES 4

0 GRAMS FAT

Prep :10
Cook :10
Stand :00
Total :20

In a blender or the bowl of an electric mixer, combine the egg substitute, cottage cheese, milk, and vanilla. Mix until smooth. Add the flour, baking soda, and salt, if desired. On low speed, continue just until mixed.

Lightly spray a large nonstick skillet or griddle with vegetable oil cooking spray; heat over medium heat. Ladle the batter onto the skillet to form 4-inch pancakes. Cook until bubbles form on surface. Turn; cook the other side until golden brown. Serve with warm syrup.

OVERNIGHT FRENCH TOAST

8 slices (¾ inch thick) French bread
1 cup egg substitute (equal to 4 eggs)
1 cup skim milk
1 tablespoon sugar
½ teaspoon vanilla extract
¼ teaspoon cinnamon

SERVES 8

1 GRAM FAT
PER SLICE

Prep :10
Cook :08
Stand 8:00
Total 8:18

Place bread in one layer in a 9 x 13 x 2-inch baking dish. Combine the egg substitute, milk, sugar, vanilla, and cinnamon. Beat well. Pour over the bread; turn each slice of bread to coat evenly. Cover and refrigerate up to 8 hours.

To serve: Heat a nonstick skillet and dry-fry the bread on both sides. Serve with hot syrup (light).

MAPLE FRENCH TOAST

SERVES 4

1 GRAM FAT
PER SLICE

Prep :10
Cook :12
Stand :00
Total :22

2 large egg whites, lightly beaten
⅔ cup skim milk
1 teaspoon maple extract
8 slices whole-wheat bread

Preheat the oven to 200 degrees.

In a shallow bowl or pie pan, whisk together the egg whites, milk, and maple flavoring until just blended. Spray a nonstick skillet lightly with vegetable oil cooking spray; heat to medium heat.

Quickly dip bread slices in the egg mixture, turning to coat both sides. Place in the skillet and cook about 3 minutes on each side, or until golden brown. (Just dip the number of slices that will fit in your skillet; don't do them all at once—they get too mushy.) As the slices are cooked, place on a platter in the oven to keep warm until serving time.

Serve with hot syrup.

Variation: Substitute 1 teaspoon ground cinnamon, ¼ teaspoon grated nutmeg, and ½ teaspoon vanilla extract for the maple flavoring. This makes a nice spicy toast.

CHRISTMAS MORNING
FRENCH TOAST

1 cup packed brown sugar
2 tablespoons light maple syrup
2 large tart apples, peeled and sliced ¼ inch thick
¾ cup egg substitute
1 cup skim milk
1 teaspoon vanilla extract
8 (¾-inch) slices day-old French bread

Syrup:
1 cup applesauce
1 (10-ounce) jar apple jelly
½ teaspoon ground cinnamon
⅛ teaspoon ground cloves

SERVES 8

ABOUT 1 TO
1.5 GRAMS FAT
PER SLICE

Prep :20
Cook :40
Stand 8:30
Total 9:30

Preheat the oven to 350 degrees.

In a small saucepan, boil together the brown sugar, maple syrup, and ½ cup of water until slightly thick. Pour into an ungreased 9 x 13-inch baking dish; arrange the apples on top.

In a mixing bowl, lightly beat the egg substitute, milk, and vanilla. Dip the bread slices into the egg mixture for 1 minute; place over apples. Cover and refrigerate overnight. Remove from the refrigerator 30 minutes before baking.

Bake, uncovered, for 35 to 40 minutes, or until puffy and golden brown.

Syrup

Combine the applesauce, jelly, cinnamon, and cloves in a medium saucepan; cook and stir until hot. May be made the day ahead as is the toast; just warm it while the toast cooks. Pour the warm syrup into a gravy boat and pass at the table.

BLUEBERRY BREAKFAST BAKE

Great do-ahead for holiday entertaining.

SERVES 6

LESS THAN 1 GRAM FAT PER SERVING

Prep :15
Cook :40
Stand 1:00
Total 1:55

¼ cup egg substitute
⅓ cup packed brown sugar
1 cup skim milk
1 teaspoon ground cinnamon
1 teaspoon grated lemon rind
Pinch of ground nutmeg
1 teaspoon vanilla extract
6 slices whole-wheat bread
2 cups frozen dry-pack or fresh blueberries, sorted and stemmed

In a large bowl, beat the egg substitute and sugar together with a fork until well blended. Stir in the milk, cinnamon, lemon rind, nutmeg, and vanilla. Tear the bread into ½-inch pieces and stir into the mixture. Cover and refrigerate at least 1 hour or overnight.

Preheat the oven to 375 degrees. Lightly coat an 8 x 8-inch baking dish with vegetable oil cooking spray. Stir the blueberries into the bread mixture and spoon into the pan, spreading evenly.

Bake for 40 to 45 minutes, until firm. Serve warm. Sprinkle with a little powdered sugar for garnish.

COFFEE CAKE

Make this the night before and bake while the family is getting up. Nice for the holidays or for brunch.

1½ cups all-purpose flour
1 teaspoon baking powder
½ teaspoon baking soda
½ teaspoon salt (optional)
1½ cups bran flakes cereal with raisins
½ cup sugar or sugar substitute
1 cup low-fat buttermilk (1 gram per cup)
¼ cup Butter Buds, liquid form
¼ cup egg substitute

Topping:
2 tablespoons sugar or sugar substitute
½ teaspoon cinnamon

MAKES 9
SERVINGS

1 GRAM FAT
PER SERVING

Prep :10
Cook :40
Stand :00
Total :50

Preheat the oven to 400 degrees. Lightly spray an 8-inch-square pan with vegetable oil cooking spray.

In a large bowl, combine the flour, baking powder, baking soda, and salt, if desired. Stir with a wire whisk to blend. Mix in the bran flakes, sugar, buttermilk, Butter Buds, and egg substitute, stirring just until moistened. Spread the batter in the prepared pan.

Combine topping ingredients; sprinkle over the batter. Bake 30 to 40 minutes or until a toothpick inserted in the center comes out clean. Serve warm.

> *Note:* If making ahead, cover with plastic wrap after adding the topping and refrigerate until baking time.

YEASTED PUMPKIN BREAD

MAKES 1 LOAF

0 GRAMS FAT

Prep :15
Cook :40
Stand 2:15
Total 3:10

2 tablespoons Butter Buds, liquid form
1 envelope (¼ ounce) active dry yeast
⅓ cup warm water
2 tablespoons packed light brown sugar
¼ cup egg substitute
1 teaspoon grated orange zest
½ teaspoon ground cinnamon
¼ teaspoon salt
⅛ teaspoon ground cloves
½ cup mashed cooked pumpkin, or acorn or butternut squash
2¾ cups all-purpose flour
1 large egg white, lightly beaten

Lightly coat a 9 x 5 x 3-inch loaf pan with vegetable oil cooking spray.

Set Butter Buds out of the refrigerator to warm to room temperature.

Rinse a large mixing bowl with hot water to take the chill off; dry well. In this bowl, combine the yeast, water, and 1 tablespoon of sugar. Let stand about 5 minutes or until bubbly; stir until yeast is dissolved. To the yeast mixture, add the egg substitute, orange zest, cinnamon, salt, cloves, and pumpkin or squash, along with the Butter Buds. Stir until thoroughly mixed. Add the flour, 1 cup at a time, to make a firm but not dry dough.

Turn the dough out onto a floured surface and knead vigorously for 6 to 8 minutes. Coat a large bowl with cooking spray, shape the dough into a ball, place in the bowl, and turn so that the dough is coated on all sides. Cover with a clean dish towel and let rise in a warm draft-free place until doubled in bulk, about 1½ hours.

Punch down the dough, knead for 1 or 2 minutes, shape into a loaf, and place in the prepared pan, seam side down. Cover with the towel and let the loaf rise to 1 inch above the rim of the pan, about 45 minutes. Shortly before the end of rising time, preheat the oven to 375 degrees.

Brush the top of the loaf with the egg white and bake for 35 to 40 minutes or until the top is golden and the loaf sounds hollow when tapped.

Variation: Drizzle with a sugar glaze or serve plain. The bread can be made when squash or pumpkins are in season and frozen for the holidays. Makes a great gift also: wrap in a pretty colored plastic wrap and tie a bow around the loaf.

"CORNMEAL MANIA"

I know you can buy cornmeal in the store for a very low price, but let me tell you how I come by my cornmeal.

First you have to harvest the ears of corn, usually the last of August in about 100-degree weather. You guessed it—filching off brother again. He grows both sweet and field corn, and for cornmeal we use field corn.

The stalks are usually about 8 to 9 feet tall. Now, I am only 5'3", so I am talking away above my head. (Bob is 6'4" and I am still talking way above.)

Let me set the mood here for you. It is August, 100 degrees, stalks 9 feet tall and about 30 inches apart, which means they are touching stalk leaves all along the way. The leaves are flat and thin and sharp on the edge, so you have to be real careful or they will give you a paperlike cut if you brush through them too fast.

Have I got your attention, and are you really feeling like you would love to go out and pick some corn? Here we go! We have five-gallon buckets. The corn is dry so it is pretty easy to pick, but you also have to shuck it and the shucks are hard to get off, because they aren't dry enough to turn loose easy. When your bucket is full, pack it back to the (you thought for sure I was going to say *wagon*) truck. Hot deluxe by now. We always take towels to dry up the— down here in Oklahoma we call it sweat—and ice water to drink. Of course you know the more you drink the more you . . . Yep, down in the corn row I go. Carter Red should see me now.

Get our corn home and we have to store it for several weeks until it gets really dry. Then we have to prepare it for going to the corn-mill. You nub your corn; that is, hit it on the concrete floor or a rock to knock off any bad kernels on the very tip end. Then we have a corn sheller that was my grandfather's; you just drop your ear of corn in, turn the handle, and it shells the corn and spits out the cob on the side. It just tickles me to death to watch it work. I love it. There is a wooden box that the sheller sits on and the kernels drop into it. When finished shelling you then have to clean the corn.

We do this cleaning job by setting up an electric fan—yes, we do have electricity—then we pour the corn from one container to another in front of the fan; it blows out all the husk and silks. After about four passes by the fan the corn is clean enough to go to the mill.

Going to the mill is always a treat for Bob and me. It is about a forty-minute drive and way out in the country. The man who has this operation has updated and modernized somewhat. He has an electric mill, powered by a tractor that has a big pulley belt hooked up to it. It is loud and the meal dust is flying. We look like we have been in a cornmeal dust storm when it is finished. But it is too good to not stand right there and watch. The meal is hot when it is put into the containers, usually brown paper bags. It costs us five cents a pound to have it ground. Is that great or what?

The meal is a little heavier than store bought and a wonderful yellow color. It is absolutely the best thing ever to coat fish with. We bag up meal and give it for Christmas gifts. All our city friends love it, and so do our country friends.

The mill owner has sweet potatoes and apples that he grows, harvests, and sells in the fall. A trip to the mill is always one of my favorite fall activities. Makes you forget about that hot harvest. This meal sure makes good corn bread too. It is a little heavier than that made from the store-bought meal. I love it. I don't slow down long enough to make it very much anymore. But I do make it fat-free now.

CORN BREAD

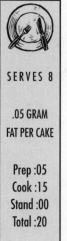

SERVES 6

.05 GRAM
FAT PER
SERVING

Prep :10
Cook :35
Stand :00
Total :45

2 cups self-rising cornmeal (read the label—choose the 0-fat one)
½ cup egg substitute
1 cup skim milk, or enough to make a fairly stiff dough

Preheat the oven to 350 degrees. Spray an 8-inch baking pan or your cast-iron skillet with vegetable oil cooking spray.

Put the cornmeal in a bowl and make a well in the center. Beat the egg substitute and milk together; pour into the cornmeal and stir until well mixed. Pour the batter into the prepared pan and bake until set in the middle. Spray the top of the corn bread with vegetable oil cooking spray. Continue to bake until golden brown and firm, about 35 minutes in all.

DRY-FRIED CORN BREAD CAKES

Quick and excellent.

SERVES 8

.05 GRAM
FAT PER CAKE

Prep :05
Cook :15
Stand :00
Total :20

2 cups self-rising cornmeal
½ cup egg substitute
Skim milk (enough to make a fairly heavy dough)

Mix all the above ingredients. Drop by large spoonfuls on a hot nonstick skillet, like cooking pancakes. Turn when bubbles show on the top; cook until the other side is golden brown.

BUTTERMILK CORN BREAD

1½ cups cornmeal
¾ cup all-purpose flour
1 teaspoon baking powder
½ teaspoon salt
1 teaspoon baking soda
½ cup egg substitute
1 cup skim buttermilk (1 gram fat per cup)
1 tablespoon canola oil

SERVES 8

**I GRAM FAT
PER SERVING**

Prep :20
Cook :35
Stand :00
Total :55

Preheat the oven to 400 degrees. Lightly spray a 9 x 9-inch baking pan with vegetable oil cooking spray. Or preheat a medium-size cast-iron skillet in the oven; then coat with cooking spray just before adding the batter.

In a mixing bowl, combine the cornmeal, flour, baking powder, salt, and baking soda. Stir to mix all ingredients. Make a well in the middle; add the egg substitute, buttermilk, and oil. Stir these three ingredients and gradually start mixing the meal mixture into the buttermilk mixture. You may need to add a little water; stir in about 2 tablespoons at a time until all the dry ingredients are moistened.

Turn the batter into the prepared pan and bake for 35 to 45 minutes, or until the corn bread is lightly browned and springy to the touch.

MEXICAN CORN BREAD

SERVES 8

0.05 GRAM FAT
PER 4-INCH-
SQUARE
SERVING

Prep :10
Cook :40
Stand :00
Total :50

2 cups fat-free self-rising cornmeal mix
1½ cups skim milk
½ cup egg substitute
½ cup whole-kernel corn
¼ cup finely chopped onion
¼ cup finely chopped pimento
6 jalapeño pepper rings, chopped fine

Preheat the oven to 400 degrees. Lightly coat a 9 x 9-inch baking pan with vegetable oil cooking spray.

In a medium-size mixing bowl, mix all of the above ingredients. You may need to add a little water or a little more milk to get the consistency you desire. Pour into the prepared pan and smooth out level. Bake for about 30 to 40 minutes or until lightly browned.

PICANTE CORN BREAD

SERVES 8

0 GRAMS FAT

Prep :10
Cook :40
Stand :00
Total :50

2 cups fat-free self-rising cornmeal mix
½ cup egg substitute
1 cup skim milk
⅓ cup picante sauce

Preheat the oven to 400 degrees. Lightly spray an 8 x 8-inch baking pan or medium cast-iron skillet with vegetable oil cooking spray.

Mix the cornmeal, egg substitute, and milk. When thoroughly moistened, add the picante sauce. Continue mixing, adding a little water if necessary, to get a medium heavy batter.

Pour the batter into the prepared pan and bake for about 35 to 40 minutes, or until done to the touch in the middle and golden brown on top.

Variation: Fried Mexican Corn Bread: This batter may be cooked like pancakes. I call it dry-fry. This is a good way to fix corn bread in the summer without heating up your kitchen and also a way to cook in a hurry. Just use a nonstick skillet and spray it lightly with cooking spray. Spoon in batter just as you would a pancake, about ¼ cup to a cake. Turn when bubbles appear on the surface and cook on the flip side until brown. Ummm, good!!!

TEX-MEX MUFFINS

1½ cups yellow cornmeal
1 teaspoon baking soda
½ teaspoon salt
1 (2-ounce) jar diced pimentos, drained
1 cup shredded fat-free Cheddar cheese
½ cup finely chopped onion
¼ cup chopped green chiles, undrained
½ cup egg substitute
1 cup skim milk
1 (8-ounce) can yellow cream-style corn

MAKES ABOUT 18 MUFFINS, 2 MUFFINS PER SERVING

ONLY A SLIGHT TRACE OF FAT PER MUFFIN

Prep :10
Cook :30
Stand :00
Total :40

Preheat the oven to 400 degrees. Lightly spray two muffin pans with vegetable oil cooking spray.

In a mixing bowl, combine the cornmeal, baking soda, and salt; stir in the pimentos, cheese, onion, and chiles. Make a well in the center. Combine the egg substitute, milk, and corn; add to the dry ingredients, stirring just until moistened. Spoon into the prepared muffin pans, filling the cups ¾ full. Bake for 30 minutes or until golden. Remove from the pans immediately.

Variation: Add 1 teaspoon jalapeño peppers, chopped fine, for a spicier Mexican flavor.

Cakes, Pies, Cookies, and Frostings

Cakes

A GOOD FRIEND CAKE

SERVES
EVERYONE

0 GRAMS FAT

Prep: many
hours
Cook: cen-
turies
Total: lifetime

1 cup Kindness
2 cups Courtesy
3 cups Truthfulness
2½ cups Dependability
1 cup Freedom
2 tablespoons Industry
4 cups Obedience
1½ cups Honesty
2 cups Modesty
3 cups Sharing
6½ cups Honor to Parents

Simmer all ingredients over a gentle fire of family love, for a life-time. Serve with smiles and heartfelt praise and good humor.

"THE BEST CAKE"

This is my number-one cake and best seller for the book. I hope you enjoy it just a tiny bit as much as I have.

SERVES 8

0 GRAMS FAT, IF NUTS OMITTED

Prep :15
Cook :40
Stand :10
Total 1:05

½ cup egg substitute
2 cups granulated sugar
2 cups all-purpose flour
2 teaspoons baking soda
1 (20-ounce) can crushed pineapple, juice and all (2½ cups)
1 teaspoon vanilla extract
1 cup nuts, chopped (optional)

Frosting:
1 (8-ounce) package fat-free cream cheese, softened
1½ cups confectioners' sugar
¼ teaspoon vanilla extract

Heat the oven to 350 degrees. Spray a 9 x 13 x 2-inch pan with vegetable oil cooking spray.

Beat the egg substitute and granulated sugar together in an electric mixer. Mix the flour and baking soda; beat into the egg mixture. Add the pineapple, juice and all, and continue to mix, with mixer, until blended. Stir in the vanilla and nuts, if using.

Pour and scrape the batter into the prepared pan. Bake for 40 minutes.

Meantime, mix the frosting ingredients: Stir the cream cheese with a wire whisk, not with a mixer (fat-free cream cheese gets thin if beaten with a mixer). Gradually beat in the sugar, then stir in the vanilla.

Cool the cake about 10 minutes and frost. If frosting is thin, pour on the cake anyway; it is OK. Hot cake takes care of that.

You may sprinkle with additional nuts.

APPLE CAKE

SERVES 8

1 GRAM FAT
PER SERVING
(WITHOUT
NUTS)

Prep :20
Cook :40
Stand :00
Total 1:00

1 cup sugar
¼ cup applesauce
¼ cup egg substitute
1 cup all-purpose flour
1 teaspoon baking soda
½ teaspoon ground cinnamon
¼ teaspoon salt (optional)
2 cups shredded peeled tart apples
¼ cup chopped walnuts (optional)
Vanilla Sauce (page 407)

Preheat the oven to 350 degrees. Spray an 8 x 8-inch baking pan with vegetable oil cooking spray.

In a mixing bowl, stir together the sugar and applesauce. Add the egg substitute and mix well. In a separate bowl, mix the flour, baking soda, cinnamon, and salt, if using. Beat together the wet ingredients and the flour mixture just until smooth. Fold in the apples and walnuts, if desired.

Spread the batter in the prepared baking dish. Bake for 35 to 40 minutes, or until the cake shrinks slightly from the sides of the pan and is springy to the touch. Remove to a rack and cool slightly in the pan. Serve the warm cake with warm vanilla sauce.

Sugar Tips: If you need to reduce your sugar, Sweet One granulated sugar substitute is very good. It is heat stable, which means it holds up well during cooking and baking without turning bitter.

In baked goods substitute a portion of the recipe's sugar with Sweet One; in recipes for sweetened beverages and sauces, you can replace all of the sugar with Sweet One.

APPLESAUCE CAKE

Good with powdered sugar frosting or plain
with frozen yogurt (fat-free of course).

½ cup Butter Buds liquid
1 cup sugar
¼ cup egg substitute
2 cups all-purpose flour
1 teaspoon salt
1 teaspoon baking soda
1 teaspoon baking powder
1 teaspoon ground cinnamon
½ teaspoon ground allspice
½ teaspoon ground nutmeg
¼ teaspoon ground cloves
1 cup applesauce
¾ cup chopped nuts (optional)

SERVES 4

0 GRAMS FAT
IN ENTIRE
DISH IF NUTS
OMITTED—8
GRAMS WITH
NUTS

Prep :15
Cook 1:00
Stand :05
Total 1:20

Preheat the oven to 350 degrees. Spray a 9-inch round cake pan with vegetable oil cooking spray.

Cream the Butter Buds and sugar until fluffy. Add the egg substitute and blend well. Whisk the dry ingredients together and add to the butter-sugar mixture in thirds, alternately with the applesauce. Fold in the nuts.

Pour into the prepared cake pan and bake for 50 to 60 minutes.

Cool in the pan for 5 minutes, then turn out of the pan and cool on a rack.

CHOCOLATE APPLESAUCE CAKE

SERVES 12

VERY LOW-FAT

Prep :15
Cook 1:00
Stand :10
Total 1:25

¾ cup Butter Buds liquid
1 cup firmly packed light brown sugar
½ cup granulated sugar
¾ cup egg substitute
1½ cups all-purpose flour
½ cup cocoa powder
1½ teaspoons baking soda
¼ teaspoon salt
1¾ cups unsweetened applesauce
¾ cup chopped walnuts (optional)
1 cup (8 ounces) glazed whole red cherries, cut in halves (see Note)
1 cup (8 ounces) green glazed pineapple wedges, diced or coarsely chopped
¼ cup (2 ounces) glazed diced orange peel, chopped

Glaze:
1½ cups confectioners' sugar
3 tablespoons skim milk

Heat the oven to 350 degrees. Spray a medium-size Bundt pan with vegetable oil spray and dust with flour.

Beat together the Butter Buds and sugars; add the egg substitute. In a separate bowl, mix together the flour, cocoa, baking soda, and salt. Beat into the butter-sugar mixture alternately with the applesauce, beginning and ending with dry ingredients. Stir in the walnuts, cherries, pineapple, and orange peel.

Pour the batter into the prepared pan and bake about 1 hour, until springy to the touch. Meantime, mix the ingredients for the glaze together. Cool the cake 10 minutes; remove from the pan. Cool. Drizzle with glaze and decorate with reserved cherries and pineapple pieces.

Note: Save a few cherries and pineapple pieces for decorating the top.

APPLICIOUS CARAMEL CAKE

1 (18-ounce) package caramel-flavor cake mix
1 (1-ounce) package sugar free butterscotch instant pudding mix
¾ cup egg substitute
¾ cup applesauce
⅓ cup fat-free mayonnaise or salad dressing, such as Miracle Whip
2 Granny Smith apples
1 cup packed brown sugar
½ cup chopped nuts (optional)
Fat-free margarine spray (has a pump-type spray on top)

SERVES 12

**8 GRAMS FAT
ENTIRE CAKE
(WITHOUT
NUTS)**

Prep :20
Cook :45
Stand :00
Total 1:05

Preheat the oven to 350 degrees. Lightly spray a 13 x 9-inch baking dish with vegetable oil cooking spray.

In a large mixing bowl, combine the cake mix, pudding mix, egg substitute, applesauce, mayonnaise, and ⅓ cup of water. Mix well. Pour the batter into prepared baking dish.

Peel and thinly slice the apples (up and down to make half-moon slices). Place on top of the batter, forming three lengthwise rows. Press the apple slices slightly down into the batter.

In a small bowl, combine the brown sugar and nuts if using. Mix and sprinkle over the apples. Spray the topping with margarine until it looks damp.

Bake at 350 degrees for 40 to 45 minutes, or until a toothpick inserted near the center comes out clean. Cool on a rack and serve from pan.

Variations: Serve with fat-free vanilla yogurt or ice cream. Drizzle caramel (fat-free) ice cream topping over all.

BLUEBERRY SCONE CAKE

SERVES 4

4 GRAMS FAT

Prep :10
Cook :25
Stand :00
Total :35

1 (15-ounce) package nut or banana bread mix
⅓ cup low-fat buttermilk (1 gram fat per cup)
¼ cup egg substitute
1 cup fresh or frozen blueberries (do not thaw)
2 teaspoons sugar

Preheat the oven to 400 degrees. Spray a cookie sheet with vegetable oil cooking spray.

Combine the bread mix, buttermilk, and egg substitute. Stir 50 to 75 strokes by hand, just until the dry particles are moistened. Fold in the blueberries. Turn the dough onto the cookie sheet. Using floured fingers, shape into an 8-inch circle. Sprinkle with sugar.

Bake for 20 to 25 minutes, or until golden brown and a toothpick inserted into center comes out clean. Serve warm, cut into pie-shaped wedges.

CARROT CAKE

SERVES 12

1 GRAM FAT
PER SERVING
(WITHOUT
NUTS)

Prep :15
Cook :40
Stand :00
Total :55

1¼ cups pitted prunes, halved
½ cup hot water
2 cups all-purpose flour
2 teaspoons ground cinnamon
1½ teaspoons baking soda
½ teaspoon salt
4 cups shredded carrots
2 cups sugar
½ cup pineapple juice
½ cup egg substitute
2 teaspoons vanilla extract
Cream Cheese Frosting I or II (pages 378 and 379) (optional)
½ cup chopped pecans (optional)

Preheat the oven to 350 degrees. Coat a 9 x 13-inch baking pan with vegetable oil cooking spray.

Combine the prunes and hot water in a food processor or blender container. Process or blend until finely chopped, scraping down sides occasionally. Set aside.

In a medium mixing bowl, combine the flour, cinnamon, baking soda, and salt. Set aside.

In a large bowl, mix prune purée, carrots, sugar, juice, egg substitute, and vanilla. Add the flour mixture, stirring well until blended. Pour into the prepared pan.

Bake at 350 degrees for 30 to 40 minutes or until a toothpick inserted near the center comes out clean. Cool on a wire rack, dust with powdered sugar or cover with frosting.

EASY CARROT CAKE

1 box (2-layer) yellow cake mix, light
1¼ cups fat-free salad dressing, such as Miracle Whip
1 cup egg substitute
2 teaspoons ground cinnamon
2 cups finely shredded carrots
½ cup chopped walnuts
Cream Cheese Frosting I (page 378)

SERVES 10

VERY LOW-FAT

Prep :15
Cook :35
Stand :00
Total :50

Preheat the oven to 350 degrees. Spray a 9 x 13 x 2-inch baking dish with vegetable oil cooking spray.

Put the cake mix in a large bowl and add the salad dressing, egg substitute, cinnamon, and ¼ cup of water. Beat on low speed with an electric mixer just until blended. Stir in the carrots and walnuts.

Pour the batter into the baking dish and bake for about 35 minutes, or until a wooden pick inserted near the center comes out clean.

When the cake is cool, frost with cream cheese frosting.

CHEESECAKE DELIGHT

SERVES 12

1 GRAM FAT
PER SERVING

Prep :15
Cook 1:10
Stand :00
Total 1:25

1 cup graham cracker crumbs
¾ cup plus 3 tablespoons sugar
2 tablespoons fat-free margarine, melted
3 (8-ounce) packages Healthy Choice fat-free cream cheese, at room temperature
2 tablespoons flour
3 tablespoons lemon juice
¾ cup egg substitute
1 (8-ounce) carton nonfat lemon yogurt
Light whipped topping (optional)

Preheat the oven to 350 degrees.

Combine the graham cracker crumbs, 3 tablespoons of the sugar, and the margarine; mix well. Pat into the bottom of a 9-inch springform pan. Set aside.

Mix the cream cheese, flour, and ¾ cup of sugar together with a wire whisk until fluffy and smooth. Gradually add the lemon juice and egg substitute. Beat well. Add the lemon yogurt and mix thoroughly. Pour over the prepared crust. Loosely place aluminum foil over the springform pan.

Bake for 60 to 70 minutes, or until the center of the cake is set. Gently run the tip of a knife between the cake and the edge of the pan. Cool the cake to room temperature before removing the rim of the pan. Chill. Serve with light whipped topping if desired.

CHOCOLATE CAKE

2 cups all-purpose flour
2 cups granulated sugar
⅓ cup unsweetened cocoa powder
1½ teaspoons baking soda
1½ cups skim milk
⅓ cup applesauce
1 teaspoon vanilla extract
2 egg whites
Chocolate Frosting (see page 379)

SERVES 12

**6 GRAMS FAT
ENTIRE CAKE**

Prep :20
Cook :30
Stand :45
Total 1:35

Preheat the oven to 350 degrees. Spray two 9-inch round baking pans with vegetable oil cooking spray and dust lightly with flour.

In a large mixing bowl, combine the flour, 1¾ cups of the sugar, cocoa, and baking soda. Add the milk, applesauce, and vanilla. Beat with an electric mixer on low speed until well blended. Beat on medium speed for about 2 additional minutes, scraping the sides of the bowl occasionally.

Wash the beaters thoroughly. In a small mixing bowl, beat the egg whites until soft peaks form; gradually add the remaining ¼ cup sugar, beating until stiff peaks form (tips stand straight). Fold into the batter. Pour the batter into the prepared pans.

Bake for 25 to 30 minutes or until a wooden toothpick inserted near the center of the cake comes out clean. Cool the cakes in their pans on wire racks for 10 minutes. Remove the cakes from the pans and cool them thoroughly on wire racks. Frost with chocolate frosting.

CHOCOLATE POTATO CAKE

**SERVES
8 TO 10**

**1 GRAM FAT
PER SERVING**

Prep :15
Cook :40
Stand :00
Total :55

2 cups sugar
2 cups leftover mashed potatoes (no-fat)
1 cup egg substitute
½ cup Butter Buds, liquid form
½ cup skim milk
1 tablespoon canola oil
2 cups all-purpose flour
6 tablespoons unsweetened cocoa powder
2 teaspoons baking powder
1 teaspoon ground cloves
1 teaspoon ground cinnamon
1 teaspoon grated nutmeg
1 teaspoon salt

Preheat the oven to 350 degrees. Lightly spray a 9 x 13 x 2-inch pan or two 8-inch round cake pans with vegetable oil cooking spray.

Put the sugar, mashed potatoes, egg substitute, Butter Buds, skim milk, and canola oil in a large bowl and beat with an electric mixer until smooth.

In a medium bowl, combine the flour, cocoa, baking powder, cloves, cinnamon, nutmeg, and salt. Stir with a wire whisk until thoroughly mixed.

Add the dry ingredients to the wet ingredients and mix on low speed just enough to blend. Turn the batter into the prepared pan and bake for about 30 to 40 minutes, or until the top of the cake is springy to the touch. Cool in the pan on a wire rack.

NO-FAT CHOCOLATE CAKE

:up evaporated (*not* sweetened condensed) skim milk
. cup cocoa powder
1 cup unsweetened applesauce
1 tablespoon vanilla extract
2 cups all-purpose flour
1½ cups sugar, divided
½ teaspoon baking powder
½ teaspoon baking soda
½ teaspoon salt
4 egg whites (large), at room temperature

SERVES 12

3 GRAMS FAT

Prep :15
Cook :35
Stand :03
Total :53

Preheat the oven to 350 degrees. Spray two 9-inch round cake pans or one 9 x 13 x 2-inch pan with vegetable oil cooking spray and dust with flour.

Heat the evaporated milk in a medium-size saucepan until barely simmering. Remove from the heat and whisk in the cocoa until thickened and almost smooth (some tiny lumps will remain). Let stand 2 to 3 minutes to cool slightly. Whisk in the applesauce and vanilla extract.

Mix the flour, 1¼ cups of the sugar, the baking powder, soda, and salt in a large bowl.

Beat the egg whites in a medium-size bowl with an electric mixer until thick and foamy. Gradually beat in the remaining ¼ cup of sugar and continue beating until stiff peaks form when the beaters are lifted.

Pour the cocoa mixture over the flour. Stir just until blended.

With a rubber spatula, gently stir about a quarter of the egg whites into the flour mixture. Fold in the remaining egg whites until no white streaks remain. Pour into the prepared pan or pans.

Bake for 25 to 30 minutes, or until a toothpick inserted near the center comes out clean and the edges begin to pull away from the sides.

Frost if desired with Easy Vanilla Frosting (page 381).

HERSHEY CAKE

SERVES 12

4 GRAMS FAT WITH FROST-ING; 3 GRAMS WITHOUT FROSTING

Prep :15
Cook :35
Stand :00
Total :50

1¼ cups all-purpose flour
⅓ cup unsweetened cocoa powder
1 teaspoon baking soda
6 tablespoons light margarine
1 cup sugar
1 cup skim milk
1 tablespoon white vinegar
½ teaspoon vanilla extract
Mocha Frosting (page 380)

Preheat the oven to 350 degrees. Spray 2 round 8-inch cake pans or a 9 x 13-inch jelly roll pan with vegetable oil cooking spray.

In a bowl, mix the flour, cocoa, and baking soda. In a large saucepan, melt the margarine and stir in the sugar. Remove from the heat, add the milk, vinegar, and vanilla, and stir.

Add the dry ingredients to the saucepan and whisk until well blended. Pour evenly into the prepared pans. Bake until a tooth-pick inserted near the center comes out clean (two 8-inch pans for 20 minutes; the jelly roll pan about 30 to 35 minutes). Cool and frost.

HOT FUDGE SUNDAE PUDDING CAKE

"Yum."

1 cup all-purpose flour
2 teaspoons baking powder
¼ teaspoon salt
¾ cup granulated sugar
¼ cup plus 1½ tablespoons unsweetened cocoa powder, divided
½ cup skim milk
2 tablespoons Butter Buds, liquid form
1 teaspoon vanilla extract
1 cup pecans, chopped (optional)
¾ cup firmly packed brown sugar
1¾ cups hot water

SERVES 4

3 GRAMS FAT

Prep :15
Cook :45
Stand :00
Total 1:00

Heat the oven to 350 degrees. Spray a 9-inch square baking pan with vegetable oil cooking spray.

In a large bowl, combine the flour, baking powder, salt, sugar, and 1½ tablespoons of the cocoa powder; mix well. Add the milk, Butter Buds, and vanilla; stir until blended. Stir in pecans if desired. Spread the mixture in the baking pan. Sprinkle the batter with brown sugar and the remaining ¼ cup cocoa mixed together. Pour hot water over. *Do not stir.*

Bake for 40 to 45 minutes. To serve, cut into squares while still hot and invert onto a serving dish. Top with fat-free ice cream or frozen yogurt. Spoon sauce remaining in the pan over the ice cream.

INDIVIDUAL HOT FUDGE SUNDAE CAKES

SERVES 6

1 GRAM FAT
EACH

Prep :15
Cook :25
Stand :00
Total :40

1 cup all-purpose flour
½ cup sugar
¼ cup plus 2 tablespoons unsweetened cocoa powder, divided
1½ teaspoons baking powder
⅔ cup skim milk
2 tablespoons fat-free margarine, melted
1 teaspoon vanilla extract
¾ cup firmly packed brown sugar
1½ cups hot water

Preheat the oven to 350 degrees.

Combine in a small bowl the flour, sugar, 2 tablespoons of cocoa, and the baking powder. Stir in the milk, margarine, and vanilla; mix until well blended. Spoon evenly into six 10-ounce custard cups. Place the cups in a 15 x 10 x 1-inch baking pan. Do not add water around, as is normal for baking custard dishes; this is just to make it easier to put in the oven, etc.

Combine the brown sugar and remaining ¼ cup of cocoa. Spoon 2 to 3 tablespoons of the mixture over the batter in each cup. Pour ¼ cup of hot water evenly over the sugar mixture in each cup. Do not stir!

Bake for 20 to 25 minutes, or until the centers of the cakes are set and firm to the touch. If desired, sprinkle with powdered sugar or top with fat-free ice cream or yogurt or light whipped topping.

CHOCOLATE CREAMY CUPCAKES

1 batch No-Fat Chocolate Cake batter (see recipe on page 335)
1 package (1-ounce serving size) instant French vanilla pudding
1¾ cups evaporated skim milk (*not* sweetened condensed)
Confectioners' sugar

SERVES 12

1 GRAM FAT

Prep :10
Cook :25
Stand 1:00
Total 1:35

Line 12 muffin tins with paper baking cups. Fill each with ⅓ cup batter. Bake 20 to 25 minutes at 350 degrees. Cool.

Prepare the pudding, using 1¾ cups evaporated skim milk instead of 2 cups whole milk. Refrigerate until set, about 1 hour.

With a thin sharp knife, slice off the tops of the cupcakes. Spread the bottoms with about 1½ tablespoons of pudding each. Replace tops.

Sprinkle with confectioners' sugar.

CREAM CHEESE BROWNIE CAKE

Cake Batter:
1½ cups all-purpose flour
1 cup sugar
½ teaspoon baking soda
¼ cup unsweetened cocoa powder
⅛ teaspoon salt
½ teaspoon vinegar
¼ cup fat-free mayonnaise
2 tablespoons light corn syrup
1 teaspoon vanilla extract

Cream Cheese Swirl:
⅓ cup fat-free cream cheese
1½ tablespoons sugar
¼ teaspoon vanilla extract

SERVES 6

LESS THAN 1
GRAM FAT

Prep :15
Cook :45
Stand :00
Total 1:00

(continued)

Heat the oven to 350 degrees. Spray a 9-inch square baking dish with vegetable oil cooking spray.

In a large bowl, combine the flour, sugar, baking soda, cocoa, and salt. Stir until well blended. Add the vinegar, mayonnaise, corn syrup, vanilla, and 1 cup of water and mix with an electric mixer until smooth. Pour the cake batter into the prepared dish and set aside while making the cream cheese swirl.

In a small bowl, combine the cream cheese, sugar, and vanilla. Mix with an electric mixer until smooth and creamy. Drop about 1 tablespoon of the cream cheese mixture in 4 or 5 places on top of the cake batter.

Take a table knife, place the knife blade in the center of each cream cheese drop, and drag the cream cheese to make pretty swirls on top of the cake.

Bake for 40 to 45 minutes, until the cake is springy to the touch.

FRUIT COCKTAIL CAKE

SERVES 12

0 GRAMS FAT (WITHOUT NUTS)

Prep :15
Cook :45
Stand :00
Total 1:00

2 cups all-purpose flour
1½ cups granulated sugar
1 teaspoon baking soda
1 teaspoon salt
2 cups (1 large can) fruit cocktail, light, juice and all
¼ cup egg substitute
2 egg whites
1 teaspoon vanilla extract
1 cup firmly packed brown sugar
1 cup chopped pecans (optional)
Vanilla Dessert Sauce (page 407)

Heat the oven to 325 degrees. Spray a 9 x 13 x 2-inch baking dish with vegetable oil cooking spray.

In a large bowl, combine the flour, sugar, baking soda, and salt. Mix with a whisk until thoroughly blended. Stir in the fruit cocktail (juice and all) and the egg substitute; set aside.

Beat the egg whites and vanilla until stiff. Fold into the fruit cocktail mixture until just combined. Pour into the prepared baking dish and sprinkle brown sugar and pecans over the batter. Bake for about 45 minutes, or until the center is springy to the touch. Cut into squares while still hot and serve with vanilla dessert sauce.

HONEY CAKE

1 cup honey
1 cup applesauce
1 cup egg substitute
1¼ cups sugar, divided
2½ cups all-purpose flour
1½ teaspoons baking powder
½ teaspoon baking soda
½ teaspoon instant coffee granules
½ cup hot water
½ teaspoon lemon extract
½ teaspoon almond extract
¼ cup chopped pecans (optional)
½ teaspoon ground cinnamon

SERVES 8

0 GRAMS FAT,
WITHOUT
PECANS

Prep :15
Cook 1:15
Stand :10
Total 1:40

Preheat the oven to 350 degrees. Spray two 9-inch loaf pans with vegetable oil cooking spray and dust with flour. Set aside.

In a large mixing bowl, combine the honey, applesauce, egg substitute, and 1 cup of the sugar. Beat well.

In another bowl, whisk together the flour, baking powder, and baking soda. Gradually add to the honey mixture. Mix well. Dissolve the coffee granules in hot water and add to the batter. Stir in the lemon and almond extracts. Pour into the prepared loaf pans.

Combine the remaining ¼ cup of sugar with the pecans and cinnamon. Sprinkle over the loaves. Bake for 1 to 1¼ hours, or until a toothpick inserted near the center of a loaf comes out clean. Cool in the pans 10 minutes before removing. Cool completely on wire racks.

LAZY DAZE OATMEAL CAKE

SERVES 8

4 GRAMS FAT

Prep :10
Cook :55
Stand :20
Total 1:25

1¾ cups boiling water
1 cup rolled oats
½ cup Butter Buds, liquid form
1 cup granulated sugar
1 cup firmly packed brown sugar
1 teaspoon vanilla extract
½ cup egg substitute
1½ cups all-purpose flour
1 teaspoon salt
1 teaspoon baking soda
¾ teaspoon ground cinnamon

Preheat the oven to 350 degrees. Spray a 9 x 13 x 2-inch baking dish with vegetable oil cooking spray and dust with flour.

Pour the boiling water over the oats. Let stand 20 minutes. Mix the Butter Buds with the sugars. Beat until fluffy. Blend in the vanilla and egg substitute. Stir in the oats.

Sift together the flour, salt, soda, and cinnamon. Add to the creamed mixture; mix well. Pour into the prepared baking dish. Bake for 50 to 55 minutes. Do not remove from the baking dish until serving.

LEMONLICIOUS CAKE

1 box light yellow cake mix
2 cups boiling water
1 (6-ounce) package sugar-free lemon-flavored gelatin dessert
Fluffy Lemon Pudding Frosting (page 380)

SERVES 12

5 GRAMS FAT
PER SERVING

Prep :10
Cook :35
Stand 3:00
Total 3:45

Prepare cake mix by the no-cholesterol directions on the package and bake as directed in 2 round pans. Take out of the pans and cool. Put the cakes back into the pans. Poke holes into the cakes with a fork.

Stir the boiling water into the gelatin mix in a medium bowl until dissolved. Pour half over each cake layer. Refrigerate at least 3 hours. Meantime, make the frosting.

When ready to frost, dip one cake pan in hot water for 10 seconds. Unmold onto a cake plate. Spread with about 1 cup of the frosting. Place the second layer on top of the first; frost top and sides of entire cake.

LEMON BUNDT CAKE

1 (18-ounce) package lemon cake mix
¾ cup egg substitute
⅔ cup fat-free mayonnaise (such as Miracle Whip)
⅔ cup applesauce
1 tablespoon lemon juice

SERVES 12

3.5 GRAMS FAT
ENTIRE CAKE

Prep :15
Cook :55
Stand :10
Total 1:20

Preheat the oven to 350 degrees. Spray a medium-size Bundt pan with vegetable oil cooking spray.

In a large mixing bowl, combine the cake mix, egg substitute, mayonnaise, applesauce, lemon juice, and ¼ cup of water. Mix 3 to 4 minutes with a hand-held electric mixer until well blended and smooth.

(continued)

Pour the batter into the prepared pan. Bake for 50 to 55 minutes, or until a toothpick inserted near the center of the cake comes out clean. Cool in the pan on a wire rack for 10 minutes. Remove from the pan and cool completely on the rack.

POPPY SEED BUNDT CAKE

SERVES 12

4 GRAMS FAT
PER SERVING

Prep :20
Cook :40
Stand :10
Total 1:10

1 (18-ounce) package light yellow cake mix, 97% fat-free
½ cup sugar
⅓ cup canola oil
1 cup plain nonfat yogurt
1 cup egg substitute
2 tablespoons lemon juice
2 tablespoons poppy seeds
Lemon Glaze (page 411)

Preheat the oven to 350 degrees. Coat a medium-size Bundt pan with vegetable oil cooking spray.

Combine the cake mix and sugar in a large mixing bowl. Add the oil, yogurt, egg substitute, lemon juice, and ¼ cup of water. Beat at medium speed with an electric mixer 6 minutes. Stir in the poppy seeds.

Pour the batter into the prepared pan. Bake for 40 minutes or until a toothpick comes out clean from the center area of the cake. Cool in the pan on a wire rack for 10 minutes. Remove from pan. Drizzle with lemon glaze. Cool completely on the wire rack.

PINEAPPLE CAKE

1 (18-ounce) package 97% fat-free yellow cake mix
1 (14-ounce) can crushed pineapple in light syrup, undrained
2 (3-ounce) packages fat-free vanilla instant pudding mix
4 cups skim milk
1 (8-ounce) container fat-free cream cheese
1 large container Lite Cool Whip, thawed
1 cup unsweetened shredded coconut (optional)
1 cup nuts, chopped (optional)

SERVES 10

5.4 GRAMS FAT
PER SERVING

Prep :20
Cook :45
Stand :30
Total 1:35

Prepare the cake mix according to directions on the package, substituting egg substitute for eggs and skim milk for % milk. Pour the batter into a 9 x 13-inch baking pan, sprayed lightly with vegetable oil cooking spray. Bake 35 to 40 minutes, or until done. Cool on a wire rack until completely cool. With a fork, make holes in the cake; spread pineapple, juice and all, evenly over cake.

With a wire whisk, in a mixing bowl, combine the pudding mix with 4 cups of skim milk until it thickens. Stir in cream cheese. Spread evenly over pineapple.

Stir Cool Whip; add coconut and nuts if using. Spread over the pudding mix. Sprinkle a few chopped pecans over the top for decoration, if desired.

PINEAPPLE-LEMON UPSIDE-DOWN CAKE

SERVES 4

0 GRAMS FAT

Prep :15
Cook :30
Stand :00
Total :45

This is a cake you would want to cut in half, and as my friend says, "Don't stint yourself, just you take half and give me half."
Light frozen (thawed) whipped topping may be served on top of this cake but will add a few fat grams.

1 large can crushed pineapple, drained and juice reserved
1 (3-ounce) package sugar-free lemon-flavored gelatin
½ cup egg substitute
1 egg white
¾ cup sugar
1 teaspoon vanilla extract
¾ cup all-purpose flour
1 teaspoon baking powder
¼ teaspoon salt

Heat the oven to 375 degrees. Line a round cake pan with waxed paper; spray with vegetable oil cooking spray. Spread the drained pineapple evenly in the pan. Sprinkle with the dry gelatin.

Beat the egg substitute and egg white in a medium bowl on high speed until very thick and lemon colored. Change to low speed and gradually add the sugar, ⅓ cup of the reserved pineapple juice, and the vanilla. Slowly add the flour mixed with the baking powder and salt, beating on low speed just until the batter is smooth. Pour into the cake pan.

Bake 25 to 30 minutes, or until a toothpick inserted near the center comes out clean. Immediately loosen the side of the cake and invert it onto a plate. Remove the paper.

PINEAPPLE-ZUCCHINI CAKE

2 cups shredded zucchini
1 cup (8-ounce can) crushed pineapple in juice
2 cups all-purpose flour
1½ cups sugar
2 teaspoons baking soda
2 teaspoons ground cinnamon
½ teaspoon salt
¾ teaspoon ground allspice
¾ cup egg substitute
¾ cup applesauce
⅓ cup thawed frozen pineapple juice concentrate
1 teaspoon vanilla extract
¾ cup chopped walnuts (optional)
½ cup golden raisins (optional)
Cream Cheese Frosting II (page 379)

SERVES 10

1 GRAM FAT
(IF NUTS
OMITTED)

Prep :15
Cook :55
Stand :40
Total 1:40

Place the zucchini in a sieve; let it drain 30 minutes. Drain about half the syrup off the pineapple.

Preheat the oven to 350 degrees. Coat the inside of a 10-inch tube pan with vegetable oil cooking spray.

Stir together the flour, sugar, baking soda, cinnamon, salt, and allspice in a large bowl. Mix together the egg substitute, applesauce, pineapple juice concentrate, and vanilla in a small bowl. Add to the dry ingredients. Press the zucchini to remove excess liquid. Add drained zucchini and pineapple, walnuts, and raisins to the bowl. Mix with a wooden spoon until well blended. Turn into the prepared pan.

Bake for 50 to 55 minutes, or until a wooden pick inserted near the center comes out clean. Cool the cake in the pan on a wire rack for 10 minutes. Remove from the pan and cool on the rack completely.

Frost the cake with cream cheese frosting.

PUMPKIN PATCH STORY

As you already know, my brother is a farmer. He raises many things, according to what the market is asking for. He has a big pumpkin patch almost every year alongside one of his regular crops. He has four grandchildren, and I think that the pumpkin patch is more for pleasure than profit. He should know by now that I am the biggest kid in the family and I have more enjoyment out of these types of things than anyone else on the farm.

I just love driving down the road and all of a sudden there are all these orange balls in all sizes, all shapes, and all colors. I used to think that all pumpkins were orange. Not so. He has orange, orange with green specks, orange with green streaks, yellow, white, light green, dark green, and the shapes are numerous. I was amazed the first year I got to really walk out into a pumpkin patch and choose my very own pumpkin. If you think that was an easy job, think again.

I have this most wonderful husband in the world; he has patience untold. I would say, "This one, it's the prettiest and the biggest." He would carry it to the truck. I would walk around a little longer and guess what, I found this *really* perfect one this time. "Honey, over here! Please, just this one more." The truck is starting to lean from the weight on one side. He would come get that perfect one, and meanwhile I am wandering around: "Honey." "Honey." "Honey."

I could have fed the U.S. Army pumpkin pie from that one trip. I wound up having to take some back and giving some to our children who live in the city, to decorate their yards with. But it was really fun.

In this big pumpkin patch were planted some ornamental gourds, tiny ones that looked just like miniature pumpkins, in great colors, and some really unusual shapes to say the least. Of course I had the same problem choosing as I did with the big pumpkins. This wasn't quite so hard on my poor husband, as the pumpkins might weigh as much as 30 or 40 pounds. These weigh ounces. I just needed a larger bucket to put those darling little gourds in. I had all kinds of lovely fall and holiday arrangements, all over the house, on the porch, everywhere. As you have probably guessed by now, if you have my first book and have read this book, I do like to filch off my brother's wonderful, beautiful crops. Bob and I say that you can't be much closer to God than over in the bottom in one of those large fields of swaying greens on a cool breezy morning. It is indescribably serene.

I have a granddaughter named Tracy. She has show-and-tell in school, as most children do. I also have a white car. One day I took Tracy over to the pumpkin patch to gather a couple pumpkins for Halloween. She wanted to take them to school for show-and-tell. The teacher told her mother Tracy was talking about the trip, explaining all about the goings on, when she hesitated and said, "My grandma just drove that big ol' white car right down the middle of that pumpkin patch," and giggled. That is a special memory for both of us. (We really did drive right down the middle, stopping now and then to pick just the perfect one. I also took pictures of her sitting on some of the really big ones.) I hope that every time Tracy sees a pumpkin and/or eats a pumpkin dessert she will think of her grandma.

PUMPKIN CAKE

SERVES 16

0 GRAMS FAT
(IF PECANS
OMITTED)

Prep :25
Cook 1:15
Stand :10
Total 1:50

2¾ cups all-purpose flour
1 teaspoon baking soda
½ teaspoon baking powder
¼ teaspoon salt
1 teaspoon ground nutmeg
1 teaspoon ground cloves
1 teaspoon cinnamon
¾ cup egg substitute
1¾ cups granulated sugar
1 cup applesauce
1 (16-ounce) can pumpkin
1 cup raisins, chopped (optional)
½ cup chopped pecans (optional)

Glaze:
1½ cups powdered sugar
2 to 3 teaspoons skim milk

Preheat the oven to 350 degrees. Spray a 12-cup Bundt pan or a 10-inch tube pan with vegetable oil cooking spray.

In a large mixing bowl, combine the flour, baking soda, baking powder, salt, nutmeg, cloves, and cinnamon; mix with a whisk. Make a well in the center and add the egg substitute and granulated sugar. Add the applesauce and pumpkin, stirring into the egg and sugar. Gradually start to mix into dry ingredients, stirring just until moistened. Fold in the raisins and pecans if using. Spoon into the prepared pan. Bake 1 hour and 15 minutes or until a wooden pick inserted near the center comes out clean.

Mix glaze: In a small bowl, combine the powdered sugar and gradually add the milk, stirring until smooth.

Cool the cake in the pan on a wire rack for 10 minutes. Remove from pan, place flat side down on wire rack, and position the rack and cake over a plate or piece of paper to catch drippings. Drizzle with the glaze, letting it run down the sides slightly.

Garnish: Sprinkle with a few chopped pecans, if desired. During the holidays, chopped red and green candied or maraschino cherries would be very pretty. Or use the whole cherries and make clusters of three red cherries, cut a green cherry in fourths, and use these pieces for the leaves, placing one on each side of the clusters of three red cherries. Make either 3 or 5 clusters on the top of the glaze.

FRESH RHUBARB CAKE

SERVES 12

0.5 GRAM FAT
PER SERVING

Prep :15
Cook :40
Stand :00
Total :55

½ cup fat-free margarine, at room temperature
1¼ cups sugar
¼ cup egg substitute
1 cup low-fat buttermilk (1 gram per cup)
1 teaspoon vanilla extract
2 cups all-purpose flour
1 teaspoon baking soda
½ teaspoon salt
2 cups chopped rhubarb, frozen or fresh
½ teaspoon ground cinnamon
Vanilla Dessert Sauce (page 407)

Preheat the oven to 350 degrees. Lightly spray a 13 x 9-inch baking pan with vegetable oil cooking spray.

In a medium-size mixing bowl, cream the margarine and 1 cup of the sugar. Add the egg substitute; beat well. In a small bowl, combine the buttermilk and vanilla. In another bowl, whisk together the flour, baking soda, and salt.

Add one third of the flour to the creamed mixture and beat well. Beat in half the buttermilk. Add another third of the flour, then the rest of the buttermilk, ending with the flour. Stir in the rhubarb.

Spread in the prepared baking pan. Combine the remaining ¼ cup of sugar and the cinnamon and sprinkle over the batter. Bake for 35 to 40 minutes or until the cake tests done with a toothpick. Serve with warm dessert sauce.

STRAWBERRY SUNDAE CAKE

SERVES 12

1.5 GRAMS FAT
PER SERVING

Prep :15
Cook :45
Stand :00
Total 1:00

1 (18-ounce) package strawberry cake mix
1 (3-ounce) package strawberry gelatin dessert mix (fat-free, sugar-free)
1 (10-ounce) package frozen strawberries, thawed (reserve ¼ cup juice for frosting)
½ cup applesauce
¾ cup egg substitute
¼ cup chopped pecans (optional)
Strawberry Frosting (page 381)

Preheat the oven to 350 degrees. Spray a 9 x 13-inch baking dish with vegetable oil cooking spray.

In a large mixing bowl, combine the dry cake mix, gelatin dessert mix, strawberries, applesauce, and egg substitute. With an electric mixer, mix well. Stir in pecans if desired, reserving a few for the topping.

Pour the batter into the prepared baking dish. Bake for 40 to 45 minutes, or until a toothpick inserted near the center comes out clean. Cool on a wire rack until slightly warm. Spread with strawberry frosting. Top with pecans if desired.

STRAWBERRY RHUBARB SHORTCAKE

SERVES 4

4 GRAMS FAT
PER SERVING

Prep :10
Cook :16
Stand :10
Total :36

This cake may be used as just a strawberry shortcake. Add berries and topping as desired. Yes!—Good!

Shortcake:
2¼ cups reduced-fat baking and pancake mix, such as Bisquick
⅔ cup skim milk
3 tablespoons Butter Buds, liquid form
3 tablespoons sugar, plus a little extra

Fruit:

½ pound fresh or frozen rhubarb, cut into ½-inch pieces

1 teaspoon cornstarch

½ cup sugar

1 pint strawberries, hulled and chopped, sweetened as desired (save 4 whole
    berries for garnish)

Cool Whip Lite Topping, thawed

About 1½ hours before serving or early in the day, make the shortcake:

Preheat the oven to 425 degrees. Spray an 8-inch round cake pan with vegetable oil cooking spray.

In a medium bowl with a fork, mix the baking mix, skim milk, Butter Buds, and 3 tablespoons of sugar until blended. Spoon the batter into the pan; sprinkle with extra sugar. Bake 15 minutes, or until the top is golden and a toothpick inserted in the center comes out clean. Cool the shortcake in the pan on a wire rack 10 minutes. Remove from the pan. Cool completely.

Meanwhile, prepare the fruit: In a 2-quart saucepan, over medium heat, cook the rhubarb, cornstarch, and ½ cup of sugar, stirring constantly until the mixture thickens and boils. Boil 1 minute, stir in strawberries, and remove from heat. Set aside to cool.

When the cake and strawberry mixture are both cool, they are ready to assemble. Cut the cake horizontally in half with a serrated knife. Place the bottom of the cake on a plate. Spoon the strawberry mixture over. Top with Cool Whip topping, spreading to the edge. Place the top of the cake on next.

Garnish with dollops of Cool Whip with a whole strawberry on each.

PIE PASTRY

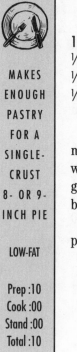

MAKES ENOUGH PASTRY FOR A SINGLE-CRUST 8- OR 9-INCH PIE

LOW-FAT

Prep :10
Cook :00
Stand :00
Total :10

1½ cups all-purpose flour
½ teaspoon salt
⅓ cup canola oil
¼ cup to ½ cup cold skim milk

Mix the flour and salt in a shallow bowl. Beat the oil and ¼ cup milk together with a fork until creamy; pour over the flour and toss with a fork until blended. If the pastry is too dry to be gathered together, add more milk, 1 tablespoon at a time, until the pastry can be gathered into a ball.

Roll out on a floured board or between two sheets of waxed paper. Fit into pie plate and crimp edges. Fill with desired filling.

GRAHAM CRACKER CRUST

1¼ cups crushed fat-free graham crackers (20 crackers)
2 tablespoons sugar
1 tablespoon egg white (½ large white)
2 tablespoons canola oil
2 tablespoons unsalted butter, melted

Preheat the oven to 350 degrees.

Combine all the ingredients with 1 tablespoon of water and stir with a fork until evenly moistened.

Pour into a 9-inch pie shell and press with the fingers evenly on the bottom and up the sides.

Bake for 8 to 10 minutes, or until lightly browned. (The crust will firm up as it cools.)

SERVES 6

VERY LOW FAT

Prep :05
Cook :10
Stand :00
Total :15

LEAN PIE CRUST

1 cup all-purpose flour
½ teaspoon salt
½ teaspoon baking powder
½ cup (1 stick) light margarine, softened
½ cup plus 2 tablespoons cold skim milk

Stir together the flour, salt, and baking powder. Cut in the margarine with pastry blender. Add milk, and continue mixing until none sticks to the side of the bowl. Shape into a ball. Wrap in waxed paper and refrigerate 1 hour. Roll out on floured board and fit into pie plate. Trim and crimp edges.

MAKES ENOUGH PASTRY FOR 1 LARGE PIE SHELL OR COBBLER CRUST

3 GRAMS FAT PER SERVING

Prep :10
Cook :00
Stand 1:00
Total 1:10

MERINGUE PIE SHELL

SERVES 6

0 GRAMS FAT

Prep :10
Cook 1:00
Stand 1:00
Total 2:10

2 egg whites, at room temperature
½ teaspoon vanilla extract
¼ teaspoon cream of tartar
½ cup sugar

Preheat the oven to 275 degrees.

In a small greasefree bowl, beat the egg whites until soft peaks form. Gradually add the vanilla, cream of tartar, and sugar. Beat at high speed until stiff and glossy. Spoon the meringue into a lightly sprayed 9-inch pie plate, building up around the sides (but not covering the rim) to form a pie shell.

Bake for 60 minutes. Turn off heat. *Do not* open oven! Allow to dry in the oven for 60 minutes longer.

Cool the shell completely before filling. Fill with fresh fruit, fat-free pudding, or whatever you desire. Fat-free ice cream is also very good.

Note: Read the Tips for Successful Meringues on page 366.

OVERNIGHT MERINGUE NESTS

6 egg whites
½ teaspoon cream of tartar
1¼ cups sugar
¼ cup chopped walnuts (optional)

SERVES 12

0 GRAMS FAT
WITHOUT
NUTS (2
GRAMS FAT
WITH NUTS)

Prep :10
Cook :00
Stand 8:00
Total 8:10

Heat the oven to 400 degrees. Line 2 cookie sheets with parchment or brown paper.

In a large bowl at high speed, beat the egg whites and cream of tartar until soft peaks form.

Gradually beat in the sugar, 1 tablespoon at a time, beating constantly until stiff and glossy.

Spoon the meringue into 12 mounds on the paper-lined cookie sheets, 4 inches apart. With the back of a spoon, shape into nests. Sprinkle with nuts if desired.

Place in the oven. *Turn the oven off. Do not open the oven door.* Let stand in the oven 8 hours or overnight.

To serve, place cooled nests on individual plates and fill with fat-free ice cream topped with favorite sauce.

BUTTERMILK PIE

SERVES 6

0.66 GRAM FAT
(FILLING
WITHOUT
CRUST)

Prep :15
Cook :45
Stand :00
Total 1:00

2 cups sugar
2 tablespoons flour
1¼ cups egg substitute, lightly beaten
⅔ cup low-fat buttermilk (1 gram fat per cup)
½ cup Butter Buds, liquid form
1 teaspoon vanilla extract
1 unbaked pie shell (page 354)

Preheat the oven to 350 degrees.

Combine the sugar and flour in a bowl, add the egg substitute and buttermilk, and stir until blended. Stir in the Butter Buds and vanilla.

Pour into the prepared pie shell and bake for 45 minutes, or until the filling is set. Cool on a wire rack.

PINEAPPLE LAYER PIE

SERVES 12

VERY LOW-FAT

Prep :15
Cook :20
Stand 6:00
Total 6:35

Crust:
1 cup all-purpose flour
1¼ cups confectioners' sugar
¼ cup almonds, finely chopped
⅓ cup (5 tablespoons plus 1 teaspoon) fat-free margarine

Filling:
1 (20-ounce) can crushed pineapple in juice
2 (8-ounce) packages Healthy Choice fat-free cream cheese, at room temperature
½ cup sugar
½ cup egg substitute

Topping:
¼ cup all-purpose flour
¼ cup sugar
½ cup light whipped topping

Combine the crust ingredients. Pat into the bottom of a 12 x 8 x 2-inch baking dish. Bake at 350 degrees for 20 minutes.

Meanwhile, make the filling: Drain the pineapple and reserve the juice. In a bowl, mix the cream cheese until smooth. Stir in sugar, egg substitute, and ⅔ cup of the reserved pineapple juice. Pour the filling over the hot crust. Bake at 350 degrees for 20 minutes. Cool.

Topping: Mix the flour and sugar in a saucepan; stir in 1 cup of reserved pineapple juice. Bring to a boil, stirring constantly with a wire whisk. Boil and stir for about 1 minute. Remove from the heat, fold in the pineapple, and cool. Fold in the whipped topping. Spread carefully over the cooled dessert. Refrigerate overnight or at least 5 to 6 hours.

PUMPKIN YUM PIE

½ cup egg substitute
1 (16-ounce) can solid-pack pumpkin
1 (12-ounce) can evaporated skim milk
¼ cup honey
½ cup packed brown sugar
⅓ cup granulated sugar
1 tablespoon pumpkin pie spice
1 unbaked pie shell

Topping:
¼ cup English walnuts, chopped
⅓ cup packed brown sugar

SERVES 6

LOW-FAT

Prep :20
Cook 1:10
Stand :00
Total 1:30

Preheat the oven to 375 degrees.

In a large mixing bowl, whisk together the egg substitute, pumpkin, milk, honey, sugars, and pie spice. Pour into the unbaked pie shell. Bake for 30 minutes.

For the topping, mix the nuts and ⅓ cup brown sugar. Carefully pull the oven rack out and sprinkle the nut mixture over the par-

(continued)

tially baked pie. Carefully move the rack back and continue baking for an additional 30 to 40 minutes, or until a knife inserted near the center comes out clean. Top with a dollop of light whipped topping. Yum!

LEAN PUMPKIN PIE

SERVES 6

0 GRAMS FAT
(FILLING
WITHOUT
CRUST)

Prep :15
Cook :55
Stand :00
Total 1:10

1¾ cups pumpkin or winter squash, cooked and mashed, well drained
1¾ cups evaporated skim milk
1 cup egg substitute
⅔ cup firmly packed brown sugar
2 tablespoons granulated sugar
1 teaspoon salt
1¼ teaspoons ground cinnamon
½ teaspoon ground ginger
½ teaspoon grated nutmeg
¼ teaspoon ground cloves
Unbaked 9-inch pie shell (page 354)

Preheat the oven to 425 degrees.

Mix the pumpkin, skim milk, egg substitute, sugars, salt, and spices. Pour into the unbaked pie shell. Bake 10 minutes at 425 degrees, then lower the heat to 350 degrees and bake until a knife inserted in the center comes out clean, about 30 to 35 minutes longer. Cool on a rack.

TOFU PUMPKIN PIE

2 (10-ounce) packages firm tofu
²⁄₃ cup honey
2 egg whites (optional, for firmer pie)
1¾ cups canned pumpkin
2 teaspoons ground cinnamon
1 teaspoon grated nutmeg
½ teaspoon ground allspice
½ teaspoon ground ginger
¼ teaspoon salt (scant) (optional)
9-inch unbaked pie shell (page 354)
Mock Whipped Cream (page 408)

SERVES 6

FILLING HAS 2
GRAMS FAT
(NO CHOLES-
TEROL)

Prep :08
Cook 1:00
Stand :00
Total 1:08

Preheat the oven to 400 degrees.

Blend the tofu in a food processor or blender until creamy smooth. Add the honey, egg whites, pumpkin, spices, and salt; blend well. Pour into the unbaked pie shell. Bake about 1 hour, or until a toothpick inserted near the center comes out almost clean. Cool and serve with mock whipped cream.

FAT-FREE FROZEN YOGURT PIE

Plan on starting this at least one day before you need it.

SERVES 8

0 GRAMS FAT
IF NUTS
OMITTED

Prep :30
Cook 1:00
Stand 1:00
Total 2:30

Meringue Crust:
2 large egg whites, at room temperature
½ teaspoon vanilla extract
¼ teaspoon salt
¼ teaspoon cream of tartar
½ cup sugar
½ cup finely chopped pecans (optional)

Filling:
2 pints frozen yogurt, fat-free of course, choice of flavor
½ cup strawberry preserves (or preserves of choice)
2 tablespoons Kahlúa (may use sherry)
¼ cup chopped pecans (optional)

Preheat the oven to 275 degrees. Lightly coat a 9-inch pie plate with vegetable oil cooking spray.

Meringue Crust: In a grease-free mixing bowl, beat the egg whites, vanilla, salt, and cream of tartar until soft peaks form. Gradually add the sugar, beating until stiff peaks form and sugar is dissolved. Fold in the ½ cup chopped pecans if using. Spread the mixture in the prepared pie plate, building up the sides to form a pie shell effect. Bake for 1 hour, turn off heat, DO NOT OPEN OVEN; let dry in the oven for an additional hour or overnight, keeping the door closed. Cool completely.

Filling: Soften the yogurt to a workable consistency. Arrange scoops of yogurt in the cooled meringue crust (about 8 scoops, 1 in center and 7 around edge). Return to the freezer and freeze for several hours until firm or overnight.

Just before serving, combine preserves and Kahlúa or sherry and drizzle over scoops of yogurt. Sprinkle with the remaining ¼ cup of chopped pecans if desired.

Serve immediately.

Cookies

LOW-FAT BROWNIES

1 cup egg substitute
½ cup canola oil
1 cup all-purpose flour
⅓ cup rolled oats
½ cup unsweetened cocoa powder
1 cup sugar
1 ripe banana, mashed
1½ teaspoons vanilla extract
⅓ cup chocolate chips

SERVES 6

1 GRAM FAT
EACH

Prep :10
Cook :30
Stand :00
Total :40

Preheat the oven to 350 degrees. Line a 9-inch square pan with aluminum foil.

Mix the egg substitute and the oil in a bowl. Beat in the flour, rolled oats, cocoa, sugar, banana, and vanilla. Fold in the chocolate chips. Pour into the prepared pan and bake for 25 to 30 minutes, until the brownies just begin to pull from the sides of the pan. Cool and cut into squares.

CARROT-DATE COOKIES

MAKES 3
DOZEN

1 GRAM FAT
PER COOKIE

Prep :10
Cook :15
Stand :15
Total :40

1½ cups chopped pitted dates
1 cup grated carrots
½ cup plain nonfat yogurt
¼ cup firmly packed brown sugar
1 tablespoon canola oil
1 teaspoon vanilla extract
1½ cups all-purpose flour
¼ cup Grape Nuts cereal
½ teaspoon baking soda
½ teaspoon salt

Preheat the oven to 350 degrees. Spray two baking sheets with vegetable oil cooking spray.

In a medium bowl stir together the dates, carrots, yogurt, sugar, oil, and vanilla. Let stand 15 minutes.

In another medium bowl mix the flour, Grape Nuts, baking soda, and salt. Using a wooden spoon, stir the dry ingredients into the date mixture until well blended. Drop by teaspoons 1½ inches apart onto the baking sheets. Bake about 15 minutes, or until the tops spring back when touched lightly. Cool on a wire rack.

CHOCOLATE CHIP COOKIES

2 cups all-purpose flour
1 teaspoon baking soda
¼ teaspoon salt
¼ cup egg substitute
3 tablespoons weak cold coffee
1 teaspoon vanilla extract
¼ cup canola oil
1 cup packed brown sugar
½ cup semisweet chocolate chips

MAKES 36

2.5 GRAMS FAT
PER COOKIE

Prep :25
Cook :08
Stand :03
Total :36

Preheat the oven to 375 degrees. Lightly spray two cookie sheets with vegetable oil cooking spray.

In a mixing bowl, combine the flour, baking soda, and salt. Set aside.

In a small bowl, combine the egg substitute, coffee, and vanilla. Set aside.

In a large mixing bowl, blend the canola oil and brown sugar with an electric mixer on low speed. Add the egg substitute mixture. Beat until smooth. Add the flour mixture in two parts at low speed. Scrape the bowl well after each addition. Stir in the chocolate chips by hand.

Drop by rounded teaspoonfuls onto the prepared baking sheets. Bake for 7 to 8 minutes or until lightly browned. Cool on baking sheets for 1 minute and remove with a spatula to a wire cooling rack for an additional 2 minutes, if you can wait that long.

Tips for Successful Meringues:

1. Beaters and bowls *must* be free and clean of any grease.
2. Separate egg whites carefully so as not to get any yellow parts.
3. Add sugar gradually.
4. Bake on paper-lined cookie sheets (either baking parchment or brown paper).
5. Wrap the meringues carefully in foil or place in a tightly covered container to store.
6. Fill *just* before serving.
7. Humid weather will adversely affect meringue performance. Hold off until a dry day if you can.

CHOCOLATE MERINGUES

**MAKES
ABOUT 30
SMALL
COOKIES**

**0.10 GRAM FAT
EACH COOKIE**

**Prep :15
Cook :45
Stand :00
Total 1:00**

3 egg whites, at room temperature
¼ teaspoon cream of tartar
6 tablespoons sugar, divided
¼ cup unsweetened cocoa powder
2 teaspoons almond extract
1 cup crumbled shredded wheat biscuits

Preheat the oven to 275 degrees. Line two cookie sheets with parchment paper or brown paper.

Combine the egg whites with the cream of tartar in a medium bowl. Beat at high speed until soft peaks form. Gradually add 3 tablespoons of the sugar and continue to beat until stiff peaks form.

Mix the remaining 3 tablespoons of sugar and the cocoa. Gently fold into the egg whites. Fold in the almond extract and shredded wheat.

Drop by teaspoons about 2 inches apart onto the cookie sheets. Bake for 45 minutes, or until dry and set. Lift the meringues on the pan lining to a rack and allow to cool. Peel from the paper, using a spatula if needed.

DEVIL'S FOOD COOKIES

Prunes are not noticeable here; they help to carry a deep chocolate flavor.

½ cup pitted prunes
½ cup hot water
1½ cups sugar
½ cup plain nonfat yogurt
¼ cup canola oil
2 egg whites, slightly beaten
1½ cups all-purpose flour
1 cup unsweetened cocoa powder
½ teaspoon salt
½ teaspoon baking soda
½ teaspoon instant coffee granules

MAKES 36

1 GRAM FAT
EACH

Prep :15
Cook :14
Stand :15
Total :44

Heat the oven to 350 degrees. Spray two baking sheets with vegetable oil cooking spray.

In a small bowl, soak prunes in the hot water for 10 to 15 minutes, until plump and soft. Place prunes and the soaking liquid in a blender; process until smooth.

In a medium bowl, whisk together the prune purée, sugar, yogurt, oil, and egg whites. In another bowl, mix the flour, cocoa, salt, soda, and coffee. Using a wooden spoon, mix the dry ingredients into the wet mixture just until blended.

Drop by tablespoons onto the prepared baking sheets 1½ inches apart. Bake for 12 to 14 minutes, or until the tops spring back when lightly touched. Cool on wire racks.

CHEWY CRANBERRY COOKIES

The leavening reacts with the cranberries, so don't be surprised by the color of the cookies— they are still delicious!

MAKES
4 DOZEN

0 GRAMS FAT
IF NUTS
.OMITTED

Prep :15
Cook :14
Stand :00
Total :29

1 cup sugar
¼ cup fat-free margarine, softened
¼ cup frozen apple juice concentrate, thawed and undiluted
2 egg whites
1½ teaspoons vanilla extract
1½ cups all-purpose flour
1 cup quick-cooking rolled oats, uncooked
1 teaspoon baking powder
1 teaspoon baking soda
½ teaspoon ground cinnamon
2 cups cranberries, coarsely chopped
½ cup walnuts, chopped (optional)

Preheat the oven to 350 degrees. Spray baking sheets lightly with vegetable oil cooking spray.

Cream the sugar and margarine, beating at medium speed until well blended. Add the apple juice concentrate, egg whites, and vanilla; beat well. Combine the flour, oats, baking powder, baking soda, and cinnamon. Gradually add to the creamed mixture, beating at low speed to form a soft dough. Stir in the cranberries and walnuts. Drop the dough by level tablespoonfuls 1 inch apart onto the baking sheets. Bake for 14 minutes, or until lightly browned. Remove from pans and cool on a rack.

CRANBERRY-PINEAPPLE BARS

1 cup cranberries
¼ cup plus 3 tablespoons firmly packed brown sugar
1½ teaspoons cornstarch
1 (8-ounce) can crushed pineapple, undrained
¾ cup all-purpose flour
¾ cup quick-cooking oats, uncooked
¼ teaspoon ground ginger
¼ teaspoon ground cinnamon
3 tablespoons margarine, cut into small pieces and chilled
1 egg white, slightly beaten
3 tablespoons chopped pecans

SERVES 16

**3 GRAMS FAT
PER SERVING**

Prep :15
Cook :50
Stand :00
Total 1:05

Preheat the oven to 350 degrees. Spray an 8-inch square baking pan with vegetable oil cooking spray.

Mix the cranberries, 3 tablespoons of the brown sugar, the cornstarch, and the pineapple in a saucepan; stir well. Bring to a boil over medium heat; cook 1 minute. Cover, reduce the heat, and simmer 12 minutes, or until the cranberry skins pop and the mixture thickens, stirring occasionally. Set aside.

Combine the flour, the oats, ¼ cup of brown sugar, and the ginger and cinnamon in a bowl. Cut in the chilled margarine with a pastry blender until the mixture resembles coarse meal.

Reserve ½ cup of the oat mixture. Combine the remaining oat mixture and egg white; stir well. Press the oat mixture into the bottom of the prepared baking pan. Bake for 10 minutes.

Spread the cranberry mixture over the hot crust. Combine the reserved oat mixture and pecans; sprinkle over the cranberry mixture. Bake for 27 minutes, or until lightly browned. Cool completely in the pan on a wire rack before cutting into squares.

LAYERED FRUIT BARS

MAKES
9 BARS

3 GRAMS FAT
EACH

Prep :15
Cook :25
Stand :30
Total 1:10

Base and Topping:
⅓ cup solid vegetable shortening
½ cup firmly packed brown sugar
¼ teaspoon vanilla extract
1 cup all-purpose flour
⅛ teaspoon salt (optional)
2 tablespoons skim milk
¼ cup quick-cooking rolled oats (not instant or old-fashioned), uncooked

Filling:
1 cup apricot preserves

Glaze:
¾ cup confectioners' sugar
1½ tablespoons skim milk
¼ teaspoon vanilla extract

Heat the oven to 375 degrees.

For base: Cream the shortening, brown sugar, and vanilla in a large bowl. Mix in the flour, salt (if used), and milk. Reserve ¼ cup of the mixture for topping. Press the remaining mixture evenly in the bottom of an ungreased 8-inch square pan. Bake for 10 minutes, or until lightly browned.

For topping: Combine reserved ¼ cup of the base mixture with the oats until crumbly.

For filling: Spread the preserves over the hot baked base; sprinkle with topping. Bake for 15 minutes, or until the top is lightly browned. Cool completely.

For glaze: Combine powdered sugar, milk, and vanilla. Drizzle over top. Allow to set before cutting into bars.

LEMON SQUARES

Crust:
1 cup all-purpose flour
¼ cup confectioners' sugar
4 tablespoons (¼ cup) fat-free cream cheese, at room temperature
3 tablespoons canola oil

Filling:
3 large egg whites
¾ cup granulated sugar
1½ tablespoons grated lemon zest
2 tablespoons flour
½ teaspoon baking powder
½ teaspoon salt
⅓ cup fresh lemon juice

Confectioners' sugar for dusting over top

MAKES
9 BARS

3 GRAMS FAT
EACH

Prep :15
Cook :45
Stand :00
Total 1:00

Heat the oven to 350 degrees. Spray an 8-inch square baking pan with vegetable oil cooking spray.

Make the crust: Stir together the flour and sugar. Using a pastry blender or your fingertips, cut the cream cheese into the flour mixture until crumbly. Gradually add the oil, stirring with a fork until evenly moistened. (This mixture will be crumbly.) Press into the bottom of the prepared pan and bake for 20 to 25 minutes, or until light golden.

Meantime make the filling: Beat the egg whites, sugar, and lemon zest together until smooth. In a separate bowl, mix the flour, baking powder, and salt. Add to the egg white mixture and beat until smooth. Beat in the lemon juice. Pour over the hot crust and bake for about 20 minutes longer, or until the top is light golden and set.

Let cool in the pan. Spray a sharp knife with cooking spray and cut into squares. Dust with confectioners' sugar.

OATMEAL COOKIES

MAKES ABOUT 3 DOZEN

0 GRAMS FAT WITHOUT NUTS

Prep :15
Cook :10
Stand :00
Total :25

1 cup all-purpose flour
½ cup sugar
1 cup quick-cooking rolled oats
¼ teaspoon salt (optional)
½ teaspoon baking powder
½ teaspoon baking soda
½ teaspoon cinnamon
¼ teaspoon ground nutmeg
2 egg whites
⅓ cup light corn syrup
1 teaspoon vanilla extract
½ cup raisins
½ cup walnuts, chopped (optional)

Preheat the oven to 375 degrees. Spray one or two baking sheets lightly with vegetable oil cooking spray.

In a large bowl, combine the flour, sugar, oats, salt if desired, baking powder, baking soda, cinnamon, and nutmeg.

Stir in the unbeaten egg whites, corn syrup, and vanilla. Mix well, then add raisins, and the walnuts if desired.

Drop teaspoonfuls of the dough 1 inch apart on the prepared baking sheets. Bake for 10 minutes. *Do not overbake.* Remove with a spatula and cool the cookies on a rack.

PEANUT BUTTER COOKIES

⅔ cup firmly packed brown sugar
½ cup smooth or chunky peanut butter
⅓ cup (5 tablespoons plus 1 teaspoon) light margarine, softened
¼ cup egg substitute
½ cup cream of wheat cereal, uncooked (regular, instant, or quick)
1 teaspoon vanilla extract
1¼ cups all-purpose flour
½ teaspoon baking soda

MAKES 36

3 GRAMS FAT
EACH

Prep :15
Cook :09
Stand :00
Total :24

Preheat the oven to 350 degrees. Spray two baking sheets with vegetable oil cooking spray.

In a medium bowl, beat the brown sugar, peanut butter, margarine, and egg substitute until fluffy. Blend in the cereal and vanilla. Stir in the flour mixed with baking soda to make a stiff dough.

Drop by rounded spoonfuls on the prepared baking sheets, spacing the cookies about 2 inches apart. Flatten the balls with the bottom of a floured glass or fork. Bake for 8 to 9 minutes. Cool on wire racks.

PINEAPPLE COOKIES

2⅔ cups all-purpose flour
1 teaspoon baking powder
½ teaspoon baking soda
⅓ cup (5 tablespoons plus 1 teaspoon) light margarine
½ cup sugar
¼ cup egg substitute
1 teaspoon vanilla extract
¼ teaspoon pineapple extract (optional)
¼ cup low-fat pineapple yogurt

MAKES 36

1 GRAM FAT
EACH

Prep :20
Cook :10
Stand :00
Total :30

Preheat the oven to 425 degrees.

Sift the flour, baking powder, and baking soda; set aside. Cream the margarine and sugar until fluffy. Add the egg substitute, va-

(continued)

nilla, and pineapple extract if using. Gradually add dry ingredients, alternating with the yogurt.

Form the dough into ball. Place on a floured surface. Roll out to ¼-inch thickness. Cut into desired shapes and place the cookies on two ungreased cookie sheets.

Bake for 8 to 10 minutes, or until lightly browned. Cool on a rack.

PUMPKIN COOKIES

MAKES 36

1 GRAM FAT
EACH

Prep :15
Cook :15
Stand :00
Total :30

¾ cup canned pumpkin purée
¾ cup firmly packed brown sugar
½ cup plain nonfat yogurt
2 tablespoons canola oil
1 teaspoon vanilla extract
1 cup raisins
2 cups sifted cake flour
1 teaspoon ground cinnamon
½ teaspoon ground ginger
½ teaspoon baking soda
½ teaspoon salt
½ teaspoon ground allspice
½ teaspoon grated nutmeg

Preheat the oven to 350 degrees. Spray two baking sheets with vegetable oil cooking spray.

Whisk together the pumpkin, sugar, yogurt, oil, and vanilla until smooth. Stir in the raisins.

In a separate bowl, mix the flour, cinnamon, ginger, soda, salt, allspice, and nutmeg. Using a wooden spoon, stir into the wet mixture until just blended.

Drop by tablespoons on baking sheets 1½ inches apart. Bake about 15 minutes, or until lightly browned. Cool on a wire rack.

S'MORES SQUARES

Brownies:
24 graham crackers (12 whole crackers)
1 package low-fat fudge brownie mix
2 egg whites

Topping:
3 cups miniature marshmallows
½ cup milk chocolate chips
½ teaspoon shortening

MAKES 15

2 GRAMS FAT
PER BAR

Prep :15
Cook :20
Stand :00
Total :35

Preheat the oven to 375 degrees. Spray a 15 x 10-inch jelly-roll pan with vegetable oil cooking spray. Line the bottom of the pan with graham crackers.

In a bowl combine the brownie mix, egg whites, and ⅓ cup water, and stir until moistened, then beat 50 strokes by hand. Spread evenly over the graham crackers. Bake for 15 to 18 minutes. Do not overbake.

Remove brownies from the oven. Immediately sprinkle with marshmallows; gently press into hot brownies. Bake an additional 2 minutes, or until marshmallows are puffed.

Meanwhile, in a small saucepan, combine the chocolate chips and shortening. Stir over low heat until melted and smooth. Drizzle the topping over the marshmallows. Cool completely. Using a knife dipped in hot water, cut into bars.

SUGAR COOKIES

MAKES
ABOUT 3
DOZEN

0 GRAMS FAT

Prep :25
Cook :10
Stand :03
Total :38

2 cups all-purpose flour
1½ teaspoons baking soda
1 cup sugar, plus additional as needed
½ cup fat-free margarine, at room temperature
1 teaspoon vanilla extract
¼ cup egg substitute

Preheat the oven to 375 degrees. Spray two baking sheets lightly with vegetable oil cooking spray.

In a small bowl combine the flour and baking soda, mix well, and set aside.

In a medium bowl, with an electric mixer at medium speed, beat 1 cup of sugar, the margarine, and vanilla until creamy. Add the egg substitute and mix well.

Stir in the flour mixture until blended. Shape the dough into balls, and roll in sugar if desired. (I desired!) Place about 2 inches apart on the prepared pans. Bake for 8 to 10 minutes, or until light brown. We like them at the geriatric stage (soft). Cool on a wire rack.

Variations:
- Add a tablespoon of cinnamon to the sugar that you roll them in.
- Add a teaspoon of cinnamon to the dough.
- Add a teaspoon of grated orange zest to the dough.
- Add a cup of chopped pecans. This gives them the snickerdoodle taste if you roll them in the cinnamon sugar. (You have added some fat grams when you add the pecans.)

ZUCCHINI COOKIES

½ cup (1 stick) light margarine
1 cup sugar
¼ cup egg substitute
1 teaspoon vanilla extract
1½ cups all-purpose flour
½ teaspoon salt
½ teaspoon baking powder
½ teaspoon baking soda
½ teaspoon ground cinnamon
¼ teaspoon ground cloves
¼ teaspoon grated nutmeg
1½ cups rolled oats
1 cup grated zucchini, drained
1 cup nuts, chopped (optional)
½ cup raisins (optional)

MAKES 36

VERY LOW-FAT

Prep :15
Cook :12
Stand :00
Total :27

Preheat the oven to 350 degrees. Spray two cookie sheets with vegetable oil cooking spray.

In a large bowl, beat the margarine, sugar, egg substitute, and vanilla together until well blended. In a separate bowl, whisk the flour, salt, baking powder, baking soda, and spices together. Beat into the margarine-sugar mixture just enough to blend. Fold in the rolled oats, zucchini, and the nuts and raisins if using.

Drop by teaspoons onto the prepared cookie sheets. Bake for 10 to 12 minutes, or until lightly browned. Remove from pans and cool on a wire rack.

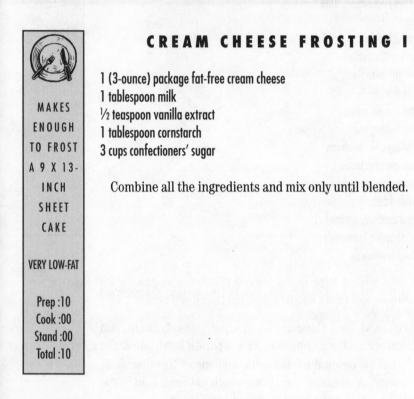

CREAM CHEESE FROSTING I

1 (3-ounce) package fat-free cream cheese
1 tablespoon milk
½ teaspoon vanilla extract
1 tablespoon cornstarch
3 cups confectioners' sugar

Combine all the ingredients and mix only until blended.

**MAKES
ENOUGH
TO FROST
A 9 X 13-
INCH
SHEET
CAKE**

VERY LOW-FAT

Prep :10
Cook :00
Stand :00
Total :10

CREAM CHEESE FROSTING II

4 ounces fat-free cream cheese, at room temperature
2 cups confectioners' sugar
1½ teaspoons thawed frozen pineapple juice concentrate

MAKES
ENOUGH
TO FROST
A 10-INCH
TUBE CAKE

VERY LOW-FAT

Prep :05
Cook :00
Stand :00
Total :05

Combine all the ingredients in a small bowl. Stir carefully until spreading consistency.

Chocolate Frosting

2 cups powdered sugar
3 tablespoons unsweetened cocoa powder
1 (8-ounce) package fat-free cream cheese, at room temperature
½ teaspoon vanilla extract

In a medium-size mixing bowl, mix the powdered sugar and 3 tablespoons cocoa; add the softened cream cheese and ½ teaspoon vanilla. Stir with a wire whisk very gently because the fat-free cream cheese will break down and be too thin if you beat it too vigorously. Spread frosting between the layers, then frost the sides and top.

MOCHA FROSTING

MAKES
ENOUGH
FROSTING
FOR 8-INCH
2-LAYER
CAKE

VERY LOW-FAT

Prep :05
Cook :00
Stand :00
Total :05

2½ cups confectioners' sugar, or more as needed
¼ cup skim milk
2 tablespoons unsweetened cocoa powder
½ teaspoon vanilla extract
¼ cup cold coffee

Mix above until smooth. Add more sugar if needed to reach spreading consistency.

FLUFFY LEMON PUDDING FROSTING

MAKES
FROSTING
AND FILLING
FOR AN
8-INCH
2-LAYER CAKE

VERY LOW-FAT

Prep :05
Cook :00
Stand :00
Total :05

1 cup cold skim milk
1 (4-serving) package instant lemon pudding mix
¼ cup confectioners' sugar
1 (8-ounce) tub Lite Cool Whip topping

Pour the skim milk into a bowl. Add the lemon pudding mix and the confectioners' sugar. Beat with a wire whisk to blend. Stir in the Cool Whip topping until thoroughly combined.

STRAWBERRY FROSTING

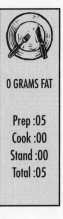

2 cups powdered sugar
2 teaspoons fat-free margarine, at room temperature
¼ teaspoon vanilla extract
3 to 4 tablespoons strawberry juice

Combine the powdered sugar, margarine, and vanilla. Add strawberry juice a tablespoon at a time until frosting is desired consistency.

0 GRAMS FAT

Prep :05
Cook :00
Stand :00
Total :05

EASY VANILLA FROSTING

2 egg whites, at room temperature
½ teaspoon cream of tartar
¼ cup honey
2 teaspoons vanilla extract
1 cup instant nonfat dry milk powder, very fine textured

In a clean, grease-free bowl, beat the egg whites until foamy. Add the cream of tartar and continue beating, adding the honey and vanilla. Gradually add the nonfat dry milk powder, beating constantly, until the frosting is a good spreading consistency.

MAKES
ENOUGH
FROSTING
FOR A
9-INCH
2-LAYER
CAKE

0 GRAMS FAT

Prep :15
Cook :00
Stand :00
Total :15

Desserts and Dessert Sauces

Desserts

**1 GRAM FAT
PER SERVING**

Prep :05
Cook :00
Stand 1:00
Total 1:05

"I WORKED ALL DAY MAKING THIS DESSERT!"

Angel food cake, cubed
Fat-free frozen yogurt or ice cream
Kahlúa
Lite whipped topping
Chopped pecans or maraschino cherries

Several hours before serving time, place a layer of cake cubes in the bottom of individual dessert dishes. On top of the cake, scoop about two scoops of frozen yogurt or ice cream of your desired flavor (chocolate is very good for this dessert, and mixing flavors such as strawberry and chocolate is also tasty as well as pretty). You may wish to add a layer of cake between the scoops of yogurt or ice cream. Pour about ¼ cup Kahlúa over each (more or less may be used; do your own thing). Place the dishes in the freezer for at least 1 hour, or until time to serve. Pour about 1 tablespoon more Kahlúa over each dessert, top with a scoop of lite whipped topping that has been thawed in the refrigerator, sprinkle chopped pecans over or top with a maraschino cherry (the one with the long stem still on is very attractive). Your guests will love this.

Use a pretty dessert dish, to complement the season or occasion. It will be frosted when served, which adds to the attractiveness. It does look like you worked all day—don't say a word! They will wonder what the Kahlúa is.

CINNAMON APPLESAUCE

This will keep in the refrigerator for several weeks. A good do-ahead recipe.

1 large jar applesauce
1 medium package red hots

SERVES 4

0 GRAMS FAT

Prep :02
Cook :12
Stand :00
Total :14

Mix the applesauce and red hots in a saucepan and stir over medium-low heat until the candy is melted. Cool before serving.

Variation: Serve over fat-free ice cream during the holidays for a quick festive dessert. Place a green maraschino cherry on top that has been cut in half, turned cut side up, and filled with brandy. Ignite the brandy for a grand finale.

APPLE BUTTER

This is worth making just to enjoy the spiced apple aroma while cooking, especially around the holidays. It's tart, because it has no sugar. You can add sweetener if desired.

1 quart apple cider
8 large Granny Smith apples
12 whole allspice berries
1 whole cinnamon stick

0 GRAMS FAT

Prep :15
Cook 2:15
Stand :00
Total 2:30

In a large heavy saucepan, boil the cider uncovered until reduced to 2 cups. Remove stems from apples but do *not* peel or core them. Cut into chunks and add to the cider. Add the allspice and cinnamon tied in a cheesecloth bag.

Bring to a boil, reduce heat to low, and simmer, uncovered, until soft, about 20 minutes. Press the apples through a strainer or food mill into a bowl. Return the pulp to the saucepan along with the

(continued)

spices. Simmer, stirring often, until the butter is very thick, about 1¾ hours. Discard the allspice and cinnamon. Let cool.

May be stored, covered, in refrigerator for up to 2 weeks.

LOW-FAT, SUGAR-FREE BREAD PUDDING

A great do-ahead dish.

SERVES 4

**7 GRAMS FAT
ENTIRE DISH**

**Prep :10
Cook :07
Stand 8:00
Total 8:17**

8 thin slices low-fat white bread, crusts removed
3 cups fresh berries, or 1 (12-ounce) package frozen dry-pack berries, such as raspberries, blackberries, or blueberries (reserve 4 for garnish)
1 (4-ounce) can crushed pineapple, drained, with ⅓ cup juice reserved

Lightly spray a deep 4-cup dish or pudding mold with vegetable oil cooking spray. Line the bottom and sides with 7 slices of the bread, overlapping them slightly.

In a medium-size heavy saucepan, bring the berries, pineapple, and reserved juice to a boil over moderately high heat for about 2 minutes. Lower the heat and simmer for 4 additional minutes.

Spoon the fruit mixture into the prepared dish and top with the remaining slice of bread. Cover with waxed paper and place a weight, such as a plate weighted down with cans of food, on top. Refrigerate overnight.

To serve: Loosen with a thin-bladed metal spatula and invert onto a serving plate. Serve plain or with nonfat frozen yogurt, ice cream, or lite whipped topping.

Place the reserved berries on the top of whatever you are serving the pudding with.

TOASTY APPLE BREAD PUDDING

This pudding is equally good served warm or cold.

SERVES 8

0.5 GRAM FAT
PER SERVING

Prep :10
Cook :45
Stand :10
Total 1:05

4 slices low-fat bread (1 gram per slice)
2 apples, peeled, cored, and chopped
½ cup egg substitute
½ cup sugar (or sugar substitute, such as Sugar Twin)
1 cup evaporated skim milk
½ cup applesauce
1 teaspoon vanilla extract
1 teaspoon ground cinnamon

Preheat the oven to 350 degrees. Lightly spray a 1½-quart baking dish with vegetable oil cooking spray.

Toast the bread slices, cut into ½-inch cubes, and place in the prepared baking dish. Add the chopped apples.

In a separate bowl, mix the egg substitute, ¼ cup of the sugar, the milk, applesauce, and the ½ cup water. Mix with a wire whisk. Pour over the bread and apples. Let stand for 8 to 10 minutes. Stir in the vanilla.

Mix the remaining ¼ cup of sugar with the cinnamon. Sprinkle over the top of the pudding mixture.

Bake for 40 to 45 minutes or until a knife inserted in the center comes out clean.

CINNAMON BREAD PUDDING

SERVES 8

**2 GRAMS FAT
PER SERVING**

**Prep :10
Cook :35
Stand :05
Total :50**

*Stir the bread and milk gently if you like
your bread pudding a little chunky. I like
mine smoother so I smash mine.*

5 cups cubed cinnamon bread, in 1-inch pieces
¼ cup raisins
1 cup egg substitute
¾ cup sugar
2½ cups hot skim milk

Heat the oven to 375 degrees. Spray a 3-quart baking dish with vegetable oil cooking spray.

Combine the bread and raisins in the baking dish. Mix the egg substitute and sugar; add the hot milk. Pour over the bread and raisins and let stand about 5 minutes. Stir.

Bake for 25 to 35 minutes, or until the liquid is absorbed and pudding is set. Serve warm.

CHOCOLATE BREAD PUDDING

SERVES 4

**2.5 GRAMS FAT
PER SERVING**

**Prep :20
Cook :45
Stand :00
Total 1:05**

*I usually serve this at room temperature,
but it is also good served hot or cold.*

1½ cups evaporated skim milk
½ cup sugar
4 teaspoons unsweetened cocoa powder
1 teaspoon vanilla extract
¾ cup egg substitute
3½ cups (½-inch) cubed French bread
2 tablespoons semisweet chocolate mini-morsels

Preheat the oven to 325 degrees. Lightly spray four 6-ounce custard cups with vegetable oil cooking spray.

In a mixing bowl, combine the milk, sugar, and cocoa. Stir with a wire whisk until blended. Add the vanilla and egg substitute; stir well. Add the bread cubes, stirring until moistened. Spoon the mixture evenly into the prepared custard cups. Top with mini-morsels.

Place the cups in a 9 x 13-inch baking pan. Add about 1 inch of hot water to the pan. Bake for 40 to 45 minutes or until a knife inserted in the center comes out clean.

Variation: The pudding may be baked in a 2-quart baking dish set in a 9 x 13-inch pan. Lightly spray the baking dish with vegetable oil cooking spray. Heat the oven to 375 degrees and add hot water to the pan to a depth of 1½ inches. Bake 40 to 45 minutes.

LEMON BREAD PUDDING

SERVES 4

2.5 GRAMS FAT
PER 1-CUP
SERVING

Prep :20
Cook :55
Stand 1:00
Total 2:15

1¾ cups buttermilk (skim or 1 gram fat per cup)
¾ cup sugar
¾ cup egg substitute
⅓ cup lemon juice
2 tablespoons Butter Buds, liquid form
2 teaspoons grated lemon rind
8 (½-inch) slices French bread, cut into 1-inch squares
Lemon Sauce (page 409)

Preheat the oven to 350 degrees. Lightly spray a 2-quart round or an 11 x 7-inch baking dish with vegetable oil cooking spray. Set aside.

Combine the buttermilk, sugar, egg substitute, lemon juice, Butter Buds, and grated lemon rind in a large mixing bowl. Add the bread cubes and toss to mix well. Let stand about 1 hour.

Spoon the mixture into the prepared baking dish and bake at 350 degrees for 50 to 55 minutes or until the pudding is set. Serve warm or at room temperature with lemon sauce.

> *Tip:* Lemon instant pudding mix is fast and easy to finish off your dessert as well as fat-free. (Read your labels!) Add about ½ cup extra liquid for a thinner consistency for ladling over pudding.
>
> Lemon regular pudding mix, cooked according to directions, is also fat-free and wonderful over the pudding. Add about ½ cup extra liquid for a thinner consistency for ladling over pudding.

COLD BREAD PUDDING

The reason this is called Cold Bread Pudding is that I also make it from leftover cold biscuits. Try it, but use the recipe in this book (page 302) for your biscuits.

SERVES 6

0 GRAMS FAT

Prep :10
Cook :60
Stand :00
Total 1:10

8 slices fat-free bread
2 tablespoons flour
1½ cups sugar
1 cup egg substitute
1 tablespoon vanilla extract
4 cups skim milk
Raisins (optional)
Lemon Sauce (page 409) or Mocha Sauce (page 410), (optional)

Preheat the oven to 350 degrees. Spray a medium casserole with vegetable oil cooking spray.

Crumble the bread in a bowl and moisten with warm water (just enough to soften—about ¼ cup).

Mix the flour with the sugar and add to the bread crumbs along with the egg substitute. Stir in the vanilla and milk. Add raisins if desired.

Bake uncovered until set in the middle, about 45 to 60 minutes.

Serve hot, topped with hot lemon sauce or mocha sauce.

ANGEL FOOD TRIFLE

Start this early in the day so you have plenty of time for chilling.

SERVES 8

0 GRAMS FAT

Prep :15
Cook :10
Stand 3:00
Total 3:25

⅓ cup sugar
¼ cup cornstarch
¼ teaspoon salt
2 cups skim milk
¼ cup egg substitute
¼ cup lemon juice
1 teaspoon grated lemon rind
2 (8-ounce) cartons nonfat vanilla yogurt
1 angel food cake, torn into bite-size pieces
½ cup sherry or Marsala wine (optional)
2 cups strawberries, hulled and sliced (reserve 3 whole berries)
3 kiwifruits, peeled and sliced

Combine the sugar, cornstarch, and salt in a saucepan. Gradually add the milk, stirring well. Cook over medium heat until the mixture begins to thicken, stirring constantly. Remove from the heat and gradually add the egg substitute, stirring constantly with a wire whisk. Cook over medium-low heat 2 minutes, while continuing to stir. Remove from the heat; cool slightly. Stir in lemon juice and rind.

Chill. Fold yogurt into the custard and refrigerate until ready to assemble the trifle.

Place ⅓ of the cake in a trifle bowl or a 2-quart serving dish. Sprinkle with ⅓ of the sherry. Spoon ⅓ of the custard over the cake; arrange half the strawberries and kiwi slices around the lower edge of the bowl and over the custard. Repeat, ending with 3 strawberries for decoration. Chill 2 hours before serving.

APPLE CRISP

Almost any fruit can be substituted for the apples—peaches, plums, etc. You can even use canned fruit, such as cherries.

3 apples, peeled, cored, and cubed
2 to 4 tablespoons granulated sugar
Dash of cinnamon or nutmeg
¼ cup quick-cooking rolled oats
2 tablespoons firmly packed brown sugar
¼ cup whole wheat flour (or you can use regular flour)
2 tablespoons Butter Buds liquid
¼ cup coarsely chopped pecans (optional)

SERVES 4

0 GRAMS FAT
(WITHOUT
NUTS)

Prep :15
Cook :45
Stand :00
Total 1:00

Preheat the oven to 350 degrees.

Put the apples in an ungreased pie pan. Sweeten with sugar and add a touch of cinnamon or nutmeg.

Combine the rolled oats, brown sugar, flour, Butter Buds, and chopped nuts. Sprinkle over the apples. Bake for 45 minutes, or until tender and golden brown. (Or you can microwave 4 to 6 minutes.)

OLD-FASHIONED BANANA PUDDING

This can be sugar-free as well as almost fat-free.

SERVES 8

LESS THAN 1
GRAM FAT PER
SERVING

Prep :30
Cook :30
Stand :00
Total 1:00

½ cup plus 1 tablespoon sugar or sugar substitute
3 tablespoons cornstarch
⅓ cup water
1 (12-ounce) can evaporated skim milk
⅓ cup egg substitute
½ cup fat-free sour cream
1 teaspoon vanilla extract
25 vanilla wafers
3 medium bananas, sliced
3 egg whites
¼ teaspoon cream of tartar

Preheat the oven to 325 degrees.

In a heavy saucepan, combine the ½ cup of sugar (or sugar substitute) with the cornstarch. Gradually stir in ⅓ cup of water, the milk, and the egg substitute. Cook over medium heat, stirring constantly, until the mixture comes to a boil. Lower the heat and boil for 1 minute, stirring constantly. Remove from the heat and fold in the sour cream and vanilla.

In an ovenproof baking dish (about a 1½-quart), arrange a layer of vanilla wafers, about ⅓ of the pudding mix, and a layer of bananas. Repeat the layers, ending with vanilla wafers. (You may end with just pudding, but I like more cookies in my banana pudding.)

In a medium-size mixing bowl, free of grease, beat the egg whites and cream of tartar until foamy. Gradually add the 1 tablespoon sugar (or sugar substitute), beating until stiff peaks form. Spread the meringue over the pudding, making sure the meringue touches all edges of the baking dish.

Bake for 25 to 30 minutes, until the meringue is golden. Let cool to room temperature or serve cold.

Your guests will think Grandma is here for sure. I don't know of a grandma in the world who doesn't make banana pudding for the little darlings.

BAKED RICE PUDDING

3 egg whites
¼ cup egg substitute
1½ cups skim milk
¼ cup sugar
1 teaspoon vanilla extract
⅔ cup cooked rice
2 tablespoons raisins (optional)
Ground cinnamon (optional)

SERVES 4

LESS THAN 1
GRAM FAT PER
SERVING

Prep :20
Cook :55
Stand :00
Total 1:15

Preheat the oven to 325 degrees. Lightly coat a 1½-quart casserole with vegetable oil cooking spray.

In a medium-size mixing bowl, combine the egg whites, egg substitute, milk, sugar, and vanilla. Beat until well combined but not foamy. Stir in the cooked rice and raisins, if desired. (I do not use raisins—I don't like them—but they are good in this recipe.) Pour egg mixture into the prepared casserole. Place the casserole in a baking pan and add boiling water to the pan to a depth of about 1 inch.

Bake uncovered for 45 to 55 minutes or until just moist, stirring after 35 minutes. Serve warm or chilled. Sprinkle with cinnamon if desired.

STOVETOP RICE PUDDING

SERVES 4

LESS THAN 1
GRAM FAT PER
½-CUP
SERVING

Prep :10
Cook :40
Stand :00
Total :50

2 cups skim milk
¼ cup long-grain rice
2 tablespoons raisins (optional)
¼ cup sugar
1 teaspoon vanilla
Cinnamon (optional)

In a heavy saucepan, bring the milk to a boil and stir in the un-cooked rice and raisins, if desired. Cover and cook over low heat, stirring occasionally, for 30 to 40 minutes or until most of the milk is absorbed. (Mixture may appear curdled.) Stir in sugar and vanilla. Spoon into dessert dishes.

Serve warm or chilled. If desired, sprinkle with ground cinnamon.

BAKED RICE CUSTARD

SERVES 6

1 GRAM FAT
PER ½ CUP
SERVING

Prep :25
Cook :55
Stand 3:00
Total 4:20

⅔ cup sugar
2 tablespoons cornstarch
¼ teaspoon salt
2¾ cups skim milk
½ cup egg substitute
1 egg white
¼ cup raisins
1 cup cooked white rice (leave out salt and butter)
½ teaspoon vanilla extract
⅛ teaspoon grated nutmeg

Heat the oven to 325 degrees. Coat a 1½-quart baking dish with vegetable oil cooking spray.

Combine sugar, cornstarch, and salt; set aside. Put the milk in a heavy saucepan; place over medium heat, stirring constantly until almost boiling. Remove from heat; gradually stir in the sugar mixture.

Beat egg mixture and egg white together until frothy. Gradually stir ¼ of the hot mixture into the egg substitute; then add to remaining hot mixture, stirring constantly. Stir in raisins, rice, and vanilla. Pour into the prepared baking dish.

Place the baking dish in a large shallow pan. Add water to a depth of about 1 inch. Bake for 30 minutes. Stir gently and bake 10 more minutes. Stir gently again, sprinkle with nutmeg, and bake 10 to 15 minutes longer, or until a knife inserted near the center comes out clean. Remove the pudding dish from the water bath; cool.

Cover and chill 3 to 4 hours before serving.

AMARETTO RICE PUDDING

¾ cup egg substitute
⅔ cup sugar
¼ teaspoon salt
2 cups skim milk
1 cup uncooked instant rice
¼ teaspoon cinnamon
¼ cup coconut amaretto or plain amaretto
1 teaspoon vanilla extract
2 tablespoons raisins (optional)
Ground nutmeg for sprinkling over top (optional)

SERVES 6

LESS THAN 1 GRAM FAT PER ¾-CUP SERVING

Prep :15
Cook :50
Stand :00
Total 1:05

Preheat the oven to 325 degrees. Lightly coat a 1½-quart baking dish with vegetable oil cooking spray.

In a large mixing bowl, combine the egg substitute, sugar, salt, milk, rice, cinnamon, amaretto, and vanilla extract. Stir in raisins, if desired.

Pour into the prepared baking dish. Place in a larger shallow baking pan; pour hot water into the pan about 1 inch deep.

Bake for 30 minutes. Stir, sprinkle with nutmeg if desired, and continue baking for 20 additional minutes. Serve the pudding warm or cool. Drizzle about 2 tablespoons of amaretto over the top before serving if desired.

CHOCOLATE PUDDING

SERVES 4

**1 GRAM FAT
PER SERVING**

Prep :05
Cook :12
Stand :00
Total :17

2 cups skim milk
2 tablespoons unsweetened cocoa powder
3 tablespoons sugar
¼ teaspoon salt
2½ tablespoons cornstarch
2 tablespoons vanilla extract
Overnight Meringue Nests (page 357) (optional)

Scald 1½ cups of the milk in medium saucepan. Combine the cocoa, sugar, salt, and cornstarch in a small bowl. Blend the remaining ½ cup of cold milk into the cocoa mixture. Mix well. Stir into scalded milk.

Cook over very low heat, stirring constantly, until the mixture is thick. Remove from the heat. Stir in vanilla. Spoon into individual dessert dishes or meringue nests.

CHERRIES JUBILEE

SERVES 6

0 GRAMS FAT

Prep :10
Cook :10
Stand :00
Total :20

1 (16-ounce) can pitted dark sweet cherries, undrained
1 tablespoon cornstarch
¼ cup brandy
Fat-free frozen yogurt or ice cream

Drain the cherries, reserving juice. In a skillet, combine the liquid from the cherries with the cornstarch. Blend well with a wire whisk. Add the cherries. Heat until the liquid boils and thickens, stirring occasionally. Transfer the cherry mixture to a heatproof serving dish.

Heat the brandy in a small saucepan; pour over the hot cherries and carefully ignite. Take flaming to the table.

Serve over frozen yogurt or ice cream.

FRUIT COBBLER

1 pound fruit (peaches, apples, cherries, or blueberries)
Sugar
Lemon juice
1 cup all-purpose flour
¼ cup egg substitute
¾ cup Butter Buds liquid

SERVES 4

LESS THAN
1 GRAM FAT

Prep :10
Cook :40
Stand :00
Total :50

Heat the oven to 350 degrees. Spray a 9-inch square baking dish with vegetable oil cooking spray.

Peel and slice the fruit (you should have about 2½ cups). Add sugar to taste, plus a few drops of lemon juice to peaches, blueberries, or apples. Dump into the baking dish.

Topping or crust: Mix the flour, 1 cup of sugar, and the egg substitute with a fork until crumbly. Pour over the fruit.

Pour Butter Buds liquid over this (stringing it around evenly) and bake for about 35 to 40 minutes, until golden brown.

FRUIT COBBLER WITH CREAM CHEESE PASTRY DOUGH

SERVES 6

1 GRAM FAT PER SERVING

Prep :15
Cook :45
Stand :30
Total 1:30

1 cup sifted cake flour
1 teaspoon sugar, plus 1 tablespoon sugar for sprinkling on top
½ teaspoon salt
¼ cup Healthy Choice fat-free cream cheese
4 teaspoons light margarine
2½ to 3 tablespoons skim milk, plus 1 tablespoon for glaze
2½ cups prepared fruit (peaches, apples, blueberries, and/or cherries, peeled, pitted, and sliced if necessary)

Heat the oven to 350 degrees. Grease a 9-inch deep-dish pie plate with cooking spray.

Mix flour, 1 teaspoon sugar, and salt. With a pastry cutter, cut the cream cheese and margarine into the flour mixture until crumbly. With a fork, stir in enough milk until clumped together. Press the dough into a circle, wrap in plastic, and refrigerate for at least ½ hour. (Can be made ahead and stored up to 2 days.)

On a lightly floured surface, roll the pastry to ⅑-inch thickness. Put the fruit into the prepared pie plate. Carefully place the dough over the fruit and tuck in the edges. Brush the top with milk and sprinkle 1 tablespoon sugar over. Cut several slashes for steam vents.

Bake about 45 minutes or until the pastry is golden and filling is bubbly.

Cool slightly and serve with fat-free ice cream or frozen yogurt.

FRUIT CRISP

You can use in-season fruit such as apples, cherries, blueberries, peaches, or pears; or use any fruit pie filling, such as cherry, apple, or peach.

SERVES 4

0 GRAMS FAT

Prep :20
Cook :40
Stand :00
Total 1:00

2 tablespoons lemon juice
2 to 3 cups peeled and chopped fruit
¾ cup packed brown sugar
2 tablespoons cornstarch
⅔ cup quick-cooking rolled oats
½ cup all-purpose flour
½ cup Butter Buds, liquid form
Fat-free frozen yogurt or ice cream (optional)

Preheat the oven to 350 degrees. Lightly spray a 1½-quart baking dish with vegetable oil cooking spray.

Add lemon juice to the fruit and stir to coat. Combine ¼ cup of the brown sugar and the cornstarch; add to fruit mixture. Spoon into the prepared baking dish. If using pie filling, pour directly into prepared baking dish.

In a separate mixing bowl, combine the remaining ½ cup of brown sugar, the oats, and flour. Mix. Stream Butter Buds over the oat mixture; stir to mix until it looks like coarse meal. Sprinkle mixture over fruit. Bake for 30 to 40 minutes. Serve with fat-free frozen yogurt or ice cream if desired. Yummy in your tummy!

FRUIT DUMPLINGS

I scream, you scream, we all scream for more.

SERVES 4

VERY LOW-FAT

Prep :20
Cook :25
Stand :00
Total :45

Dough:
1 cup all-purpose flour
3 tablespoons sugar
1 teaspoon baking powder
½ teaspoon baking soda
⅛ teaspoon salt
½ cup low-fat buttermilk (1 gram fat per cup)
1 tablespoon Butter Buds, liquid form
1 tablespoon canola oil

Fruit Mixture:
2 pints any fruit
½ cup sugar
4 teaspoons lemon juice
½ teaspoon ground cinnamon mixed with 1 tablespoon sugar

To make the dough: Mix the flour, sugar, baking powder, soda, and salt. In a small bowl mix the buttermilk, Butter Buds, and oil. Make a well in the center of the flour mixture and add the liquid mixture, mixing just until combined. Set aside.

Make the fruit mixture: In a heavy skillet combine the fruit, sugar, and lemon juice with ¼ cup water. Toss gently, cover, and bring to a boil. Reduce the heat to low; remove the cover. Drop dumpling batter by spoonfuls evenly over the simmering fruit. Sprinkle with cinnamon-sugar mixture. Cover the pan tightly with a lid or foil and cook for 15 to 17 minutes, or until dumplings are firm to the touch.

Serve hot with fat-free frozen yogurt or ice cream.

QUICK FRUIT DESSERT

1 (16-ounce) can fruit pie filling
1 tablespoon lemon juice
1 cup fat-free granola
⅓ cup all-purpose flour
2 tablespoons Butter Buds liquid

SERVES 2

0 GRAMS FAT

Prep :05
Cook :25
Stand :00
Total :30

Preheat the oven to 375 degrees.

Mix the pie filling and lemon juice and pour into an ungreased 8-inch square pan, spreading evenly.

Mix the granola, flour, and Butter Buds; sprinkle over the filling. Bake uncovered 20 to 25 minutes, or until the filling is bubbly and topping is golden brown.

Serve warm with fat-free ice cream or frozen yogurt.

PUMPKIN DELIGHT

1 (3-ounce) package sugar-free instant pudding mix
1½ cups skim milk
1 cup canned pumpkin
1 teaspoon pumpkin pie spice
1½ cups lite whipped topping, thawed, plus additional as needed
1 low-fat graham cracker crust or prebaked pie shell

SERVES 6

VERY LOW-FAT

Prep :15
Cook :00
Stand :30
Total :45

In a mixing bowl, beat the pudding mix and milk until well blended. Blend in the pumpkin and pie spice; fold in the 1½ cups of topping. Spoon into pie shell and chill. Dollop with light topping for garnish, and sprinkle a little ginger on dollops of topping.

Variations: No-Crust Pumpkin Delight: Spoon into dessert dishes, chill, and serve with a nonfat cookie.

Add pecans if desired (it will add fat grams). Chop ½ cup pecans fine and stir in just before spooning the pudding into the dish or pie shell.

STRAWBERRY DELIGHT

SERVES 12

1 GRAM FAT PER SERVING

Prep :20
Cook :20
Stand 4:30
Total 5:10

2 cups finely chopped fat-free pretzels
⅓ cup plus ¼ cup sugar
⅔ cup fat-free margarine, melted
12 ounces Healthy Choice fat-free cream cheese
2 tablespoons skim milk
1 cup Lite Cool Whip, thawed
1 (8-ounce) package sugar-free strawberry-flavored gelatin
2 cups boiling water
1½ cups cold water
2 pints strawberries, hulled and sliced
Chopped English walnuts, for garnish

Preheat the oven to 350 degrees.

Mix the crushed pretzels, ⅓ cup sugar, and the melted margarine. Press firmly into the bottom of a 9 x 13 x 2-inch baking pan. Bake for 15 to 20 minutes. Allow to cool.

Mix the cream cheese, the remaining ¼ cup of sugar, and the milk until smooth. Stir in the Cool Whip. Spread over the cooled crust and refrigerate.

Mix the gelatin and boiling water in a bowl until dissolved; add the cold water. Refrigerate 1 to 1½ hours, or until slightly thickened. Stir in the strawberries. Spoon over the cream cheese layer. Be careful not to let it get too thick.

Refrigerate for 3 hours, or until firm. Cut into squares and add a dollop of Lite Cool Whip and sprinkle a few chopped English walnuts over the Cool Whip.

SUNDAY DELIGHT

A good do-ahead recipe. Pretty for the holidays with the red cherries.

SERVES 12

4 GRAMS FAT
PER SERVING

Prep :20
Cook :25
Stand 4:20
Total 5:05

6 egg whites
¾ teaspoon cream of tartar
2 cups sugar
2 cups crushed fat-free soda crackers (about 45)
¾ cup nuts, chopped
2 teaspoons vanilla extract
2 cups Lite Cool Whip, thawed
1 (21-ounce) can cherry pie filling (see Note)

Heat the oven to 350 degrees. Spray a 9 x 13 x 2-inch baking dish thoroughly with vegetable oil cooking spray.

Beat the egg whites until frothy, add the cream of tartar, then gradually add sugar. Beat until stiff. Carefully fold in the crushed crackers, nuts, and vanilla.

Spread in the prepared dish and bake for 25 minutes. Cool on a wire rack.

Spread the Cool Whip over the cooled first layer, then spoon cherries over the Cool Whip, dotting and stringing around.

Chill several hours before serving.

Note: I use 2 cans of cherries. We like more cherries to completely cover the top of the dessert.

WINE GELATIN

SERVES 8

0 GRAMS FAT

Prep :00
Cook :05
Stand 2:00
Total 2:05

2 packets unflavored gelatin
¼ cup sugar
¼ cup cold water
3 cups red wine
1 teaspoon grated lemon rind
Mock Whipped Cream (page 406)
2 to 3 tablespoons brandy

Mix the gelatin and sugar in a heavy saucepan. Gradually add the cold water. Stir over low heat until dissolved. Remove from the heat; add the wine and lemon zest.

Divide among 8 wineglasses and allow to set. Chill until firm. Top with mock whipped cream flavored with the brandy.

CHOCOLATE FUDGE

SERVES 8

6 GRAMS FAT
ENTIRE RECIPE
IF NUTS
OMITTED

Prep :35
Cook :08
Stand :00
Total :43

1½ cups sugar
½ cup skim milk
2 heaping tablespoons Hershey's unsweetened cocoa powder
¾ teaspoon vanilla extract
½ cup chopped walnuts or pecans

In a medium saucepan, mix the sugar and milk and bring to a boil over moderate heat, stirring constantly until sugar dissolves. Continue boiling *without stirring* until a candy thermometer reaches 236 degrees, or a drop of the mixture forms a soft ball in cold water.

Remove from the heat; add cocoa and vanilla. Beat only until the mixture reaches a pudding-like consistency. Stir in the nuts and pour onto a cookie sheet sprayed with vegetable oil cooking spray. Cool completely, cut into squares, and enjoy.

Dessert Sauces

VANILLA SAUCE

1 cup sugar
2 tablespoons cornstarch
½ cup evaporated skim milk
½ cup Butter Buds (liquid form) or liquid fat-free margarine
1½ teaspoons vanilla extract

Combine the sugar, cornstarch, and milk in a saucepan. Bring to a boil over medium heat; boil for 2 minutes. Remove from heat and add Butter Buds or margarine and vanilla. Stir to blend. Serve warm.

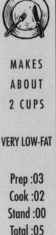

MAKES
ABOUT
2 CUPS

VERY LOW-FAT

Prep :03
Cook :02
Stand :00
Total :05

VANILLA DESSERT SAUCE

Yum yum!!

½ cup sugar
½ teaspoon vanilla extract
½ cup evaporated skim milk
¼ cup Butter Buds (liquid form) or liquid fat-free margarine

Combine all the ingredients in a medium saucepan and boil to the pudding stage, about 10 minutes. Pour over hot cake.

MAKES
ABOUT
1 CUP

VERY LOW-FAT

Prep :05
Cook :10
Stand :00
Total :15

MOCK WHIPPED CREAM

SERVES 2

0 GRAMS FAT

Prep :10
Cook :00
Stand 1:00
Total 1:10

1½ teaspoons unflavored gelatin
¼ cup boiling water
1½ teaspoons honey
1 cup ice water
½ cup nonfat dry milk powder
2 teaspoons vanilla extract

Chill a large bowl and beaters. Dissolve the gelatin in boiling water. Stir in the honey. Cool and then chill until syrupy.

In the chilled bowl, beat together the ice water, nonfat dry milk powder, and vanilla until very frothy. Gradually add the cooled gelatin mixture and continue beating until quite stiff. Chill for at least 1 hour before using.

This will keep in the refrigerator for about a day.

CHOCOLATE SAUCE I

Excellent over nonfat frozen yogurt or ice cream.

MAKES 1
CUP
SAUCE

0.6 GRAM FAT

Prep :05
Cook :10
Stand :00
Total :15

½ cup unsweetened cocoa powder
½ cup firmly packed light brown sugar
¾ cup skim milk
1 teaspoon vanilla extract

In a saucepan, mix the cocoa powder and sugar. Blend in the milk. Over medium heat, heat to boiling, stirring constantly. Lower heat and simmer, stirring constantly, for about 5 minutes or just until thickened. Cool; stir in vanilla. Serve at room temperature.

CHOCOLATE SAUCE II

1 cup sugar
6 tablespoons skim milk
2 tablespoons unsweetened cocoa powder
2 tablespoons light corn syrup
2 teaspoons vanilla extract

SERVES 2

TRACE OF FAT

Prep :05
Cook :01
Stand :00
Total :06

In a heavy saucepan, combine the sugar, milk, cocoa, and corn syrup. Bring to a boil; boil 1 minute. Remove from heat; stir in vanilla.

Serve as a fruit dip or over fat-free ice cream, frozen yogurt, your favorite dessert, such as bread pudding, or a heavy-type cake.

LEMON SAUCE

½ cup sugar
2 tablespoons cornstarch
¼ cup lemon juice
½ teaspoon grated lemon rind

SERVES 4

0 GRAMS FAT

Prep :05
Cook :05
Stand :00
Total :10

In a heavy saucepan, combine the sugar and cornstarch; stir well. Gradually whisk in lemon juice and 1¼ cups water. Set over moderate heat and bring to boil. Reduce heat to low and cook, stirring constantly, until the sauce is thickened and clear (about 2 to 3 minutes).

Remove from heat, cool, and stir in lemon rind.

Lemon Raisin Sauce: Add 2 tablespoons raisins.
Orange Sauce: Use 1½ cups orange juice instead of the lemon juice and water. Use orange rind instead of lemon rind.

MOCHA SAUCE

Serve over frozen chocolate fat-free yogurt or ice cream, fruit, cake, or bread pudding.

SERVES 4

0.9 GRAM FAT
PER TEASPOON

Prep :05
Cook :10
Stand :00
Total :15

½ cup sugar
⅓ cup unsweetened cocoa powder
⅓ cup light corn syrup
2½ tablespoons semisweet chocolate morsels
1 teaspoon instant coffee granules
½ teaspoon vanilla extract

Combine the sugar, cocoa, and corn syrup with ⅓ cup of water in a saucepan. Bring to a boil over medium heat, stirring frequently. Add the chocolate morsels and coffee granules; stir until melted. Remove from heat and cool. Stir in vanilla.

WHISKEY SAUCE

SERVES 8

0 GRAMS FAT

Prep :05
Cook :05
Stand :00
Total :10

1 cup sugar
¼ cup whiskey
¼ cup nonfat vanilla yogurt

Combine sugar with 1 cup of water; mix well. Bring to a boil and cook for 5 minutes. Remove from the heat and stir in whiskey. Cool to lukewarm. Stir in the yogurt. Serve warm over bread pudding or frozen ice cream or yogurt.

Variation: Substitute ¼ cup water and 1 teaspoon brandy extract for the whiskey. Yum.

LEMON GLAZE

1 cup powdered sugar
2 tablespoons lemon juice (you may want to add more for desired consistency)

MAKES
ABOUT 1
CUP

0 GRAMS FAT

Prep :05
Cook :00
Stand 1:00
Total 1:05

Combine these ingredients and stir until smooth.
Drizzle over Poppy Seed Bundt Cake (page 344) or any cake or bread of your preference while the cake is still warm.

Beverages

HOT APPLE CIDER

An old favorite for the holidays or entertaining; makes the house smell great.

SERVES 8

0 GRAMS FAT

Prep :05
Cook :40
Stand :00
Total :45

2 quarts apple cider
¼ cup firmly packed brown sugar
½ teaspoon grated nutmeg
2 cinnamon sticks
Peel of 1 orange

Combine all the ingredients in large pan. Bring to a boil. Reduce the heat and simmer for 30 to 40 minutes. Remove cinnamon sticks and orange peel. Keep warm in thermos pitcher or coffeepot.

MULLED CIDER

SERVES 4

0 GRAMS FAT

Prep :10
Cook :15
Stand :00
Total :25

1 quart apple cider
⅓ cup packed brown sugar
½ teaspoon whole allspice
6 to 7 (3-inch) cinnamon sticks
6 to 7 whole cloves

In a large saucepan or dutch oven, combine the apple cider with the brown sugar, allspice, cloves, and 2 or 3 cinnamon sticks. Bring to a boil, reduce the heat, cover, and simmer for 15 minutes. Remove and discard spices. Serve hot with a cinnamon stick standing up in each cup.

HOT SPICED TEA MIX

SERVES 32

0 GRAMS FAT

Prep :10
Cook :00
Stand :00
Total :10

This makes a nice gift for a special friend. Pack in a pretty glass container or a glass quart jar and decorate the top by cutting a piece of fabric, with pinking shears, in an 8-inch circle. Place a little piece of cotton or a couple of cotton balls, pulled a little to flatten out, on the lid, cover with fabric, place the ring over, and screw on. Leave the fabric hanging down like a little ruffle. Quick and easy. Choose a scrap of fabric that complements the receiver's kitchen.

2 cups instant orange-flavored breakfast drink (such as Tang)
2 cups sugar
½ cup instant tea
1 (0.31-ounce) package unsweetened lemon-flavored drink mix
1 teaspoon ground cinnamon
1 teaspoon ground cloves
Garnish: cinnamon sticks (optional)

Combine all ingredients except cinnamon sticks. Mix well.

To serve: For each serving, place 1½ to 2 tablespoons of the mix in a cup, add boiling water, and stir well. Garnish if desired with a cinnamon stick in each cup.

To store: Store in an airtight container at room temperature for up to 3 months.

RUSSIAN TEA

Remember this recipe from way back when?
It is a nice from-the-heart, for-the-heart gift.
Use the gift jar idea from the recipe for
Hot Spiced Tea Mix on page 415.

Use the gift jar idea from the recipe for Hot Spiced Tea Mix on page 415.

½ cup instant tea
2 cups instant orange drink mix
1½ cups sugar
1 teaspoon ground cinnamon
½ teaspoon ground cloves

Mix all the above ingredients; store in an airtight container.
To serve: Spoon 3½ teaspoons into each cup; fill cups with hot water.

Make a little nametag-like card with instructions for serving and attach to each gift container.

MAKES ABOUT 24 CUPS OF TEA

0 GRAMS FAT

Prep :10
Cook :00
Stand :00
Total :10

CHAMPAGNE ORANGE JUICE

1 (6-ounce) can frozen orange juice concentrate
1 cup cold water
2½ cups cold champagne
2 thin slices of orange, cut in half and split for garnish

In a glass pitcher or container, mix the orange juice concentrate and water. Stir well. Just before serving, slowly add champagne and stir gently to blend. Pour into champagne glasses and garnish with orange slices on the rim. (Chilled glasses add a nice touch.)

SERVES 4

0 GRAMS FAT

Prep :05
Cook :00
Stand :00
Total :05

BREAKFAST COCKTAIL

Place your champagne glasses in the freezer or refrigerator the night before to make this drink look prettier.

SERVES 4

0 GRAMS FAT

Prep :10
Cook :00
Stand :00
Total :10

2 cups sliced fresh peaches or thawed frozen peaches
⅔ cup peach or apricot nectar
Champagne

In the container of an electric blender, combine the peaches and nectar. Cover and process until smooth. (May be blended up to a week ahead and stored in an airtight container in the freezer. Remove 30 minutes before serving.)

To serve: Spoon about ⅔ cup of the peach mixture into a stemmed champagne glass. Add about ⅔ cup of champagne to each glass.

Variation: This may also be done with strawberries. Substitute berries for peaches, and grenadine for nectar. Very pretty during the Christmas holidays. I also save 4 fresh berries, if using fresh, and float in the top of each, especially during the summer. Cool and fresh looking. If using frozen berries, a green maraschino cherry is pretty for a seasonal touch.

LEMON-LIME PUNCH

*Very pretty, as well as good for weddings
or showers. The color is nice for
spring and summertime.*

SERVES 20

0 GRAMS FAT

Prep :05
Cook :00
Stand :00
Total :05

1 pint lemon sherbet
1 (28-ounce) can pineapple juice, chilled
1 (28-ounce) can lemon-lime-flavor carbonated beverage, chilled
1 pint lime sherbet

Blend the lemon sherbet with the pineapple juice in a punch bowl. Stir in the lemon-lime beverage and spoon the lime sherbet on top. Makes about 20 cup servings.

LEMON-LIME FROZEN DAIQUIRIS

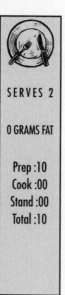

1 (14-ounce) can frozen lemonade concentrate
½ lemonade can light rum
3 drops green food coloring
5 to 6 cups ice
¼ cup lime juice (optional)
Fresh lime slices (optional)

SERVES 2

0 GRAMS FAT

Prep :10
Cook :00
Stand :00
Total :10

Put the frozen lemonade concentrate in a blender container and add the rum and green food coloring. Blend to a smooth consistency. Add ice, a cup at a time, until as thick as you like. Add lime juice if desired, and blend about 5 seconds longer.

Pour into cocktail glasses and garnish with a slice of lime on the rim if desired.

I usually make a double batch of these and store in a wide-mouth plastic container in the freezer. You can dip out as many as you want anytime you want.

SNAPPY TOMATO SIPPER

4 cups cold tomato juice
¼ cup lime or lemon juice
2 teaspoons Worcestershire sauce
2 to 4 drops hot sauce
½ cup vodka
Garnish: celery stalks with leaves

SERVES 2

0 GRAMS FAT

Prep :05
Cook :00
Stand :00
Total :05

    Combine the first three ingredients in a pitcher, blending well. Stir in a couple drops of hot sauce, taste, and add more if desired. Stir in vodka. Chill. Garnish with a celery stalk used as a stirrer in each glass.

FROZEN MARGARITAS, MIDWESTERN STYLE

1 (14-ounce) can frozen limeade concentrate (or you can use lemonade)
¾ limeade can tequila
¼ cup triple sec
4 to 6 cups ice
Fresh lime, cut into small triangle pieces
Coarse salt

SERVES 4

0 GRAMS FAT

Prep :10
Cook :00
Stand :00
Total :10

    Put the frozen limeade concentrate in a blender container. Blend long enough to liquefy. Add tequila and triple sec and start adding ice a cup at a time, blending until the desired consistency.

    Prepare cocktail glasses by rubbing the rims with a cut lime, then dipping the rims into a saucer of coarse salt.

    Fill the glasses with margaritas, squeeze a lime section over top of each glass, and add that piece of lime to the top. I make two or three batches of these ahead of time before entertaining, place them in the freezer, and am free to visit with my guests. We can dip just as many as desired when desired. Leftovers are wonderful later without any effort.

FROSTY WINE SLUSH

SERVES 4

0 GRAMS FAT

Prep :10
Cook :00
Stand :00
Total :10

1 pint frozen fat-free fruit sorbet
1 cup dry white wine
2 tablespoons lemon juice
1 cup crushed ice
Lime wedges for garnish (optional)

In a blender container, combine the first three ingredients; blend until mixed. Add the ice and blend until slushy. Pour into chilled cocktail glasses. Garnish with lime wedges if desired.

EGGNOG

Eggs I know—but what's nog? Nog, says the Oxford Dictionary, is an English word of obscure origin meaning strong ale, dating to the seventeenth century.

SERVES 12

1 GRAM FAT

Prep :10
Cook :15
Stand 2:00
Total 2:25

1½ cups sugar
¼ cup flour
Pinch of salt
4 large eggs
2 egg whites
8 cups skim milk, scalded
2 teaspoons vanilla extract
½ to 1 cup brandy, rum, or whiskey (optional)
Freshly grated nutmeg

Whisk the sugar, flour, and salt in a large heavy nonaluminum saucepan. Add the eggs and whites; whisk until smooth. Gradually whisk in the milk. Cook over low heat, stirring with a wooden spoon, for 15 minutes, or until thick enough to coat spoon. Remove immediately from the heat and strain into a bowl. Cover and refrigerate until chilled, at least 2 hours or overnight.

Before serving, stir in the vanilla and liquor. Pour 2 cups of custard into a blender. Add 2 ice cubes and blend until frothy. Repeat with remaining custard. Serve immediately, topped with a dusting of nutmeg.

LEGAL EGGNOG

Who said we can't have any eggnog!

1 (12-ounce) can evaporated skim milk, chilled
1 teaspoon rum or brandy extract (2 tablespoons rum or brandy)
4 teaspoons sugar
2 large egg whites
Freshly grated nutmeg

SERVES 4

0 GRAMS FAT

Prep :15
Cook :00
Stand :00
Total :15

Combine the milk, rum, and sugar in a medium-size bowl. Stir until the sugar is dissolved.

In another medium bowl, free of any grease and chilled, beat the egg whites until they hold soft peaks, then fold into the milk mixture.

Ladle into chilled punch cups or wine glasses and sprinkle with nutmeg.

LOW-FAT EGGNOG

SERVES 6

1 GRAM FAT
PER CUP

Prep :05
Cook :12
Stand 24:00
Total 24:17

4 cups skim milk
1 (12-ounce) can evaporated skim milk
1 (8-ounce) carton egg substitute
½ cup sugar
⅓ cup light rum
1 teaspoon vanilla extract
Grated nutmeg

Over medium heat stir the skim milk, evaporated milk, egg substitute, and sugar for about 10 minutes, or until slightly thickened. *Do not boil.* Stir over bowl of ice for about 2 minutes. Cover. Chill for 4 to 24 hours.

Stir in the rum and vanilla. Add more skim milk if needed for desired thickness. Sprinkle with nutmeg.

YE OLD WASSAIL

SERVES 12

0 GRAMS FAT

Prep :10
Cook 2:00
Stand :00
Total 2:10

Christmas memories are added to with the aroma of this drink brewing. When your guests walk in they will be sure they are going to see chestnuts roasting over an open fire.

2 oranges
40 whole cloves
1 gallon apple cider
⅔ of 1 (46-ounce) can pineapple juice
⅔ of 1 (6-ounce) can frozen orange juice concentrate
Juice of 2 lemons
¾ box or jar of cinnamon sticks

Stud the oranges with cloves. In a large kettle, combine the cider with the pineapple, orange, and lemon juices. Add the cinnamon sticks and clove-studded oranges. Bring to a boil and simmer for 1½ to 2 hours before time to serve.

CHRISTMAS WASSAIL

The fragrance in the house during the holidays makes this worth making whether you drink it or not.

½ gallon apple cider
4 cups orange juice (fresh is nice and in season at Christmas)
⅓ cup lemon juice (about 2 lemons and also in season)
½ cup honey
4 to 5 (3-inch) cinnamon sticks
¼ teaspoon ground nutmeg

In a large saucepan or dutch oven, combine all ingredients. Bring to a boil over medium heat. Remove and discard the cinnamon sticks; serve hot. Makes about 14 cups.

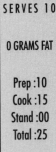

SERVES 10

0 GRAMS FAT

Prep :10
Cook :15
Stand :00
Total :25

HOT CHOCOLATE MIX

Makes a great gift. Follow the instructions for decorating the container in the Hot Spiced Tea Mix recipe on page 415.

2¼ cups powdered sugar
2 cups nonfat dry milk powder
2 cups powdered fat-free nondairy coffee creamer
2 cups chocolate milk mix
¾ cup instant coffee granules
3 tablespoons ground cinnamon
Garnish: cinnamon sticks

Combine all ingredients except the cinnamon sticks. Stir well.

To serve: For each serving, spoon ¼ cup mix into a cup, fill the cup with boiling water, and stir well. Garnish if desired with a cinnamon stick.

To store: Store in an airtight container at room temperature for up to 3 months.

MAKES 32
SERVINGS

TRACE OF FAT
IN EACH
SERVING

Prep :10
Cook :00
Stand :00
Total :10

HOT CHOCOLATE COFFEE

SERVES 1

0 GRAMS FAT

Prep :01
Cook :00
Stand :00
Total :01

1 teaspoon instant coffee
1 (0.53-ounce) package Swiss Miss sugar-free fat-free cocoa mix
1 cup hot water
1 cinnamon stick (optional)

   Place the coffee and cocoa mix in a cup; add hot water; stir well
to blend. Add a stick of cinnamon if desired.

Index

Metric Equivalencies

LIQUID AND DRY MEASURE EQUIVALENCIES

CUSTOMARY	METRIC
1/4 teaspoon	1.25 milliliters
1/2 teaspoon	2.5 milliliters
1 teaspoon	5 milliliters
1 tablespoon	15 milliliters
1 fluid ounce	30 milliliters
1/4 cup	60 milliliters
1/3 cup	80 milliliters
1/2 cup	120 milliliters
1 cup	240 milliliters
1 pint (2 cups)	480 milliliters
1 quart (4 cups, 32 ounces)	960 milliliters (.96 liters)
1 gallon (4 quarts)	3.84 liters
1 ounce (by weight)	28 grams
1/4 pound (4 ounces)	114 grams
1 pound (16 ounces)	454 grams
2.2 pounds	1 kilogram (1000 grams)

OVEN TEMPERATURE EQUIVALENCIES

DESCRIPTION	°FAHRENHEIT	°CELSIUS
Cool	200	90
Very slow	250	120
Slow	300–325	150–160
Moderately slow	325–350	160–180
Moderate	350–375	180–190
Moderately hot	375–400	190–200
Hot	400–450	200–230
Very Hot	450–500	230–260

For more information or if you have questions or comments, please write to:

Betty Rohde
P. O. Box 37
Gore, OK 74435